W9-CLB-661

CARNEGIE LIBRARY
LIVINGSTONE COLLEGE
SALISBURY, NC 28144

WELFARE DEPENDENCE
AND
WELFARE POLICY

Recent Titles in
Studies in Social Welfare Policies and Programs

Social Planning and Human Service Delivery in the Voluntary Sector
Gary A. Tobin, editor

Using Computers to Combat Welfare Fraud:
The Operation and Effectiveness of Wage Matching
David Greenberg and Douglas Wolf

Poverty and Public Policy:
An Analysis of Federal Intervention Efforts
Michael Morris and John B. Williamson

Social Work: Search for Identity
Leslie Leighninger

Social Security after Fifty: Successes and Failures
Edward D. Berkowitz, editor

Legal Services for the Poor:
A Comparative and Contemporary Analysis of Interorganizational Politics
Mark Kessler

No Longer Disabled:
The Federal Courts and the Politics of Social Security Disability
Susan Gluck Mezey

129838

Welfare Dependence and Welfare Policy

A STATISTICAL STUDY

Vicky N. Albert

Foreword by Michael Wiseman

STUDIES IN SOCIAL WELFARE POLICIES AND
PROGRAMS, NUMBER 8

GREENWOOD PRESS
New York • Westport, Connecticut • London

Library of Congress Cataloging-in-Publication Data

Albert, Vicky N., 1954–
    Welfare dependence and welfare policy : a statistical study /
Vicky N. Albert.
        p. cm. — (Studies in social welfare policies and programs,
ISSN 8755-5360 ; no. 8)
    Bibliography: p.
    Includes index.
    ISBN 0-313-26175-X (lib. bdg. : alk. paper)
    1. Public welfare—California.   2. Family allowances—California.
3. Welfare recipients—California.   4. Income maintenance programs—
California.   I. Title.   II. Series.
HV98.C3A46   1988
362.5′09794—dc 19   88-15495

British Library Cataloging in Publication Data is available.

Copyright © 1988 by Vicky N. Albert

All rights reserved. No portion of this book may be
reproduced, by any process or technique, without the
express written consent of the publisher.

Library of Congress Catalog Card Number: 88-15495
ISBN: 0-313-26175-X
ISSN: 8755-5360

First published in 1988

Greenwood Press, Inc.
88 Post Road West, Westport, Connecticut 06881

Printed in the United States of America

The paper used in this book complies with the
Permanent Paper Standard issued by the National
Information Standards Organization (Z39.48-1984).

10 9 8 7 6 5 4 3 2 1

To my husband,
William Charles King

Contents

Figures

Tables

Foreword

When Ronald Reagan left the presidency, the number of families and the total number of people receiving assistance through the Aid to Families with Dependent Children program—what most people term "welfare"—were virtually the same as was recorded on his inauguration day. Despite much talk, major changes in federal AFDC policy initiated with the Omnibus Budget Reconciliation Act (OBRA) of 1981, and widely touted state workfare initiatives, the level of welfare dependence in the country was unchanged. Indeed, the average number of people receiving benefits in January 1989 was almost identical, at approximately 11 million, to the count 16 years earlier, when Richard Nixon began his ill-fated second term as chief executive. Given this information alone, one might conclude that nothing changed on the welfare front during the Reagan years.

In fact, major shifts in the emphasis of both empirical research on welfare and welfare policy were witnessed in the 1980s. On the research side, a change first became apparent in 1983, when policy analysts released three important studies of the dynamics of welfare dependence over time. Mary Jo Bane and David Ellwood reported estimates of the duration of dependence for AFDC families which implied that, although many families who came on to welfare soon left, a substantial proportion of cases stayed open for a very long time. SRI International issued a final report on the results of the Seattle–Denver income-maintenance experiment, which confirmed the substantial labor-supply effects of negative tax–type income-support systems and suggested that income support, when combined with certain types of training programs, actually operated to destabilize two-parent families. And Janet D. Griffith and Charles L. Usher of the Research Triangle Institute reported results of research which seemed to indicate that the adverse consequences for case turnover predicted for OBRA by many authorities had failed to materialize. Taken together, the message of this work was that (*a*) long-term welfare dependency is a problem, (*b*) the effects of welfare systems on behaviors are complex and not well understood, and (*c*) much more research was needed.

The Bane-Ellwood, SRI, and Griffith-Usher studies were all based on data on the experience of individual families over time. This dynamic, microanalytic orientation reflects a general shift in policy concern toward asking questions about the consequence of welfare systems not only for family well-being at any instant, but also for the outlook on improvements in family status over time. Welfare policy is no longer a matter of income maintenance; the system is now supposed to be directed to achieve income improvement. As President Reagan stated in his 1986 State of the Union address, "the success of welfare should be judged by how many of its recipients become independent of welfare." Although the microanalytic emphasis has permitted the application of very sophisticated theories of household behavior to welfare studies, it is difficult to translate such research into implications for the big picture—aggregate welfare dependence. Nevertheless, the president and others ask questions in aggregate terms. Of all recipients, they ask, how many become independent, and what is the consequence of such improvement for the system?

Welfare Dependence and Welfare Policy retains the emphasis on welfare dynamics that characterizes the best of recent research, but also breaks new ground by studying aggregate movements in dependency. It is the first such study for California, a state that now accounts for 15 percent of the country's welfare recipients. The state provides an excellent laboratory for studying the effects of both dynamic economic growth and generous welfare benefits on the extent and character of welfare dependence. Dr. Albert's study focuses on trends in the aggregate number of families receiving assistance in California; she thus moves immediately to the "big picture." However, she decomposes changes in the caseload over time into the components of month-to-month changes in dependence: additions, as new families come on to welfare, and terminations, as old ones leave. Her work allows for the calculation of the numerical consequences of policy changes, such as those brought about by the Reagan administration, and provides insight into the way in which such consequences unfold. Throughout the work she exhibits a command of theory as well as careful attention to empirical detail. The result is interesting not only for what she tells us about California, but also as a template for similar research in other states. It is an excellent example of what can be done when the opportunities provided by the agency data for policy-related research are intelligently exploited. It is a useful complement to approaches based on analysis of case and survey data. Hopefully, Dr. Albert's research will contribute in a significant way to laying the foundation for policies that will ultimately lead to improvement in the circumstances and outlook of those people now counted among the country's 11 million welfare dependent, and of those who, without policy change, sooner or later will be.

MICHAEL WISEMAN, Professor of Public Policy, LaFollette Institute of Public Affairs, University of Wisconsin-Madison

Preface

This book is about a controversial income-maintenance program, Aid to Families with Dependent Children, which has undergone important changes within the past two decades. Changes in policies are sometimes made in the absence of good evidence of their impact on the behaviors of recipients or on their economic well-being. This book was motivated by a desire to further the understanding of this program, its policies, and especially its impact on families. The perspective taken is longitudinal, allowing for careful analysis of changes in welfare policies, labor-market conditions, and demographic shifts. Close attention is paid to recent welfare policy shifts brought about by the Reagan administration. The impact of major policy changes is analyzed by forecasting what would have occurred in their absence.

This longitudinal perspective on dynamics of welfare receipt somewhat resembles recent research using Panel Study of Income Dynamics (PSID) data from the University of Michigan in Ann Arbor. Research using these data partially motivated this work. Unlike studies that investigate the dynamics of poverty or welfare receipt using household data, this study uses aggregate data. By developing a model that uses aggregate data, it was possible to understand the consequences for the Aid to Families with Dependent Children caseload under alternative assumptions about external developments.

This book was written over a period of three years. The work has benefited from the assistance of many people, of whom only a few I will be able to thank here. I am particularly grateful to Michael Wiseman of the University of Wisconsin, Madison, who provided me with much feedback. His deep interest in this work was inspiring. The critical suggestions he offered were always useful, and for this I am especially grateful. I would also like to thank several other faculty members of the University of California, Berkeley. For their helpful comments and support I would like to thank Harry Specht, Neil Gilbert, and John Quigley.

I am especially indebted to my husband, William Charles King, who was also a great inspiration in my work. His critical comments and continuous support made the writing of this book possible. I would also like to thank Nora Harlow, whose comments were very helpful. Special thanks are directed to my sister, Lori Alpert, for her assistance with artwork associated with this book, and to my parents, who supported me throughout this endeavor.

I thank several of the staff members at the California Department of Social Services, Employment Development Department, and numerous other members of other departments across the nation. Special thanks are owed to staff members from Department of Health and Human Services, Social Security Administration, Office of Family Assistance, Washington, D.C.

Introduction

At both national and state levels, Aid to Families with Dependent Children (AFDC) is one of the most controversial and debated income-maintenance programs. Among other issues, the controversy reflects the fiscal importance of welfare as well as traditional American misgivings about caring for the able-bodied poor. In addition to political interest, AFDC attracts academic attention because of its relationship to more general problems of poverty and income maintenance. Both the program's operations and its clients have been the objects of investigation.

This country supports welfare systems that provide diverse experiences for poor families. The large state-to-state variation in welfare benefits, economic conditions, and overall commitment to helping poor families creates a situation in which an in-depth analysis of welfare dependence needs to consider one state at a time. This book examines welfare dependence in California, one of the states most committed to providing welfare to the poor. California is also the most populous state in the country, and it supports a large portion of the nation's total AFDC caseload. Many lessons can be learned from the California experience.

This study specifically examines welfare dependence among families eligible for assistance under the Family Group (AFDC-Basic) segment of California's Aid to Families with Dependent Children program for the period 1972 to 1985. Knowledge about welfare dependence is gained by studying caseload dynamics, that is, the movement of families to and from the AFDC-Basic program. Movements to and from welfare are termed welfare accessions and terminations, respectively. Accessions and terminations are two components of the caseload.

The book consists of three major parts: description, modeling, and forecasting. The descriptive part of the book provides in-depth analyses of several important welfare system characteristics that affect welfare accessions and terminations. In particular, trends in AFDC need standards, benefit standards, and breakeven levels are analyzed. Close attention is paid to recent welfare policy shifts brought about by the Reagan administration and their effects on AFDC program characteristics and the economic well-being of recipients. Included in this part is a comparison between California's AFDC program and the AFDC programs of other states. Much is learned about recent welfare policy shifts by comparing the effects of the Omnibus Budget Reconciliation Act (OBRA) of 1981 on recipients' income in three states that are markedly different in their commitment to providing aid to poor families.

The descriptive part of the book proceeds by investigating the dynamics of California's AFDC caseload in the context of economic developments and demographic shifts. Here the scope of analysis is expanded to include the rest of the country. Striking differences between economic and demographic trends in California and the rest of the nation are used to explain differences in rates of growth in welfare caseloads.

The modeling aspect of the research develops an analytic structure for investigating determinants of changes in the welfare caseload. It concentrates on specification and estimation of parameters of a linear simultaneous equation model of the caseload and its components.

In the forecasting part of the book, the model is used to forecast the caseload, given the results from estimation of the model's parameters. Forecasting is also used to clarify the separate impacts of changes in aggregate unemployment and welfare benefits on the caseload and to evaluate the effects of OBRA.

The section below discusses what can be learned from studying the movement of families to and from the AFDC program. The organization of the book is outlined in the final section of this chapter.

SIGNIFICANCE OF WELFARE CASELOAD DYNAMICS

Changes in welfare accessions and terminations reflect social and economic changes. Increases in welfare accession rates, with more low-income people entering the rolls, suggest that more people at risk of welfare receipt are experiencing pregnancies, job losses, or marital separations and perhaps also that employment opportunities for this population are declining.

Lower termination rates mean that welfare recipients tend to stay on welfare for a longer period of time. This may suggest a greater need for welfare due to labor-market conditions or the existence of more recipients who lack marketable skills. Another possible explanation is that welfare is becoming more attractive as an income alternative in relation to the economic benefits available in the marketplace. Welfare may offer more disposable income to recipients than the wages available to them in the marketplace.

Clearly, changes in movements to and from welfare have fiscal and administrative consequences. High accession rates, with other factors remaining constant, mean that welfare costs are increasing because the caseload is growing. Everything else constant, higher accession and termination rates mean greater administrative costs; each application must be processed, and this takes time and money.

There is a need for both theoretical and empirical understanding of factors that influence the movement of families to and from welfare. Welfare accessions and terminations are, in a sense, outcomes of the interaction of three classes of variables: labor-market conditions, program characteristics, and characteristics of households. Some of the variables in these classes are the number of unemployed and the employment levels in certain low-skill industries; the welfare system's need standard, breakeven, and benefits; and the number of children and the size of the at-risk population.

Prior to incorporating the three classes of variables into a model of caseload dynamics, we must understand the dynamics of change in the variables themselves and in external factors that affect them. This requires analyses of economic and demographic trends as well as of policy changes in other income transfer programs or in federal or state taxes. A thorough understanding of the factors that influence welfare accessions and terminations is necessary for specification of a valid model.

Once changes in predictor variables are well understood, it is possible to construct an empirically estimable model of AFDC caseload dynamics. This model can be used to test hypotheses about the nature of welfare dependence by measuring the extent to which external factors affect the movement of families to and from welfare. This could lead to more informed and effective policy making designed to reduce welfare dependence. For example, if it is found that the demand for low-wage, low-skill employment is highly associated with welfare dependence, this may call for strategies that stimulate this demand.

With a model of AFDC caseload dynamics in hand, it should be possible to forecast consequences for the caseload under alternative assumptions about external developments. A particularly interesting application of this exercise is in estimating the impact of major policy changes by forecasting what would have occurred in their absence and comparing these results with what actually occurred with the policy changes in effect. In this study such forecasting is done for policy changes generated by the Omnibus Budget Reconciliation Act of 1981. Understanding the consequences of past policies for the caseload and its components may foster better design of future policies.

It should be recognized that the approach used here to analyze welfare caseload dynamics differs from most such research. Most studies of welfare accessions and terminations employ data gathered for each household in the selected sample. The present study uses aggregate data, which can provide considerable information on the nature of dependence and the effects of past policies on dependence. Substantial knowledge also can be gained about demographic or economic developments and about changes in the characteristics of the transfer system. In addition, costs and workloads associated with future caseload growth can be forecasted, thus allowing for better planning.

ORGANIZATION OF THE BOOK

This book is divided into ten chapters, covering description, modeling, and forecasting. Chapters 2 and 3 describe California's welfare system and policies and put California's system in a national context. Chapter 2 provides historical information about the nature of California's welfare system and the effects of major national welfare policies on its characteristics and on recipients' economic well-being. Chapter 3 compares California's welfare program with other AFDC programs.

Chapter 4 describes California's AFDC caseload in the context of its economic and demographic environment. Chapter 5 analyzes economic and demographic trends in California and in the rest of the nation, highlighting those that may explain difference in caseload growth rates.

In Chapter 6 a monthly time-series model is developed for the purpose of analyzing the effects of labor-market conditions, AFDC program characteristics, and characteristics of households on two component equations of the AFDC-Basic caseload in California. The dependent variables in these equations are cases added and cases closed. The equations are used for predicting the entire caseload from 1972 to 1984.

Chapter 7 reviews the literature on the dynamics of welfare receipt. Chapter 8 analyzes the extent to which the three classes of variables affect accessions and terminations. The effects of these variables are examined in relation to their theoretical reasonableness and findings from past research.

Chapter 9 discusses simulation findings and policy implications. The first set of simulation results presented in this chapter concerns the ability of the model to replicate historical data of the caseload. The second set of simulation results reflects the consequences for welfare dependence of varying welfare payments and number of unemployed by a fixed percentage. The last set of simulation results allows for an examination of the consequences of OBRA for the caseload. The effects of OBRA are analyzed separately for caseload accessions, terminations, and the entire caseload, with special attention given to changes in effects over the years. These latter findings are compared to those found on a national scale. The final chapter discusses important policy objectives.

2

The AFDC System in California

Welfare benefits and other welfare system characteristics undergo changes. Some of these happen in response to changes in the inflation rate or in federal and state taxes, while others are due to changes in welfare policies. Changes in welfare system characteristics can alter recipients' economic well-being and caseload accessions or terminations. Consequently, this chapter analyzes trends in several AFDC program characteristics. Close attention is paid to recent welfare policy shifts brought about by the Reagan administration.

CHARACTERISTICS OF THE AFDC PROGRAM

The AFDC program is part of the general state welfare system that includes the Supplemental Security Income (SSI) program for the elderly and disabled, medical assistance provided through California's Medicaid (called Medi-CAL) program, general assistance for people in need who are not eligible for other programs, and the Food Stamp program for the non-elderly poor.[1] The AFDC program is California's principal income-transfer system. As its name implies, the program provides financial assistance to needy households with children. While part of the federal Social Security system, AFDC is jointly funded by federal and state monies and operated by counties.

The AFDC program has two major components.[2] AFDC Family Group, titled AFDC-Basic by the federal government, includes all households with either a single parent or a disabled parent. AFDC Unemployed Parent (UP) includes households with two non-disabled parents. Two-parent families are eligible for AFDC-UP assistance only if the principal earner in the household has been employed in the past and currently is involuntarily working less than 100 hours per month. The state provides a short-duration program for poor two-parent families in which neither adult has a work history, but this program is very small.

Determination of Eligibility and Payments

The discussion that follows describes eligibility and payment procedures for families applying for AFDC-Basic assistance in July 1985. The first step in going onto welfare is for a family member to fill out an application form at the county welfare office or one of its branches. State law requires that applicants provide birth certificates for children and information on income and assets. The application process includes an interview with an eligibility technician who assists in completion of the application form.

If categorical eligibility is established, the family qualifies for income payments under AFDC by demonstrating financial need. Financial need is determined by application of a fixed sequence of criteria. First, the family's assets must not exceed a maximum amount under rules in force in July 1985. Second, the family's gross income must not exceed 185 percent of a specified standard of need (*SN*), often called the minimum basic standard of adequate care (MBSAC). MBSAC, the income eligibility level for AFDC, represents an estimate of the minimum monthly income requirements for subsistence and varies with family size. Finally, the household's income less certain allowed deductions is compared to the state's need standard for families of the same size. If net income (*NI*) calculated in this way is less than this standard, eligibility is achieved.[3]

In considering a family's net income, the family's gross income, which is the sum of the family's gross earned income (E) and its income from other sources (I), is taken into account. Allowable deductions for calculating net income include federal and state tax withholdings, Social Security taxes, child care costs, and other costs associated with retaining employment. Program rules establish a standardized work deduction of $75 and a ceiling on child care deductions of $160.[4] It is useful to view involuntary work expenses (X) as the sum of those deductions (x_o) that do not vary with gross earnings, such as child care or transportation expenses, and those that vary with gross earnings (x_eE), such as taxes. Involuntary work expenses can be written as:

$$X = x_o + x_eE. \qquad (2.1)$$

A simple formula for a family's net income is

$$NI = E + I - X. \qquad (2.2)$$

Once net income is calculated for the family, it must fall below the MBSAC in order to establish eligibility. To be eligible for welfare, a household's gross earnings cannot exceed a maximum amount. Thus, if E^e is the maximum amount of gross earnings for a household to be eligible for welfare entry, then the above discussion implies that:

$$E^e = SN - I + X \qquad (2.3)$$

which is found by setting $NI = SN$ and $E = E^e$ in the above formula for net income.

Once a family meets both categorical and income eligibility requirements, AFDC payments are calculated. If the family has no outside income, then it receives the AFDC maximum aid (M) or guarantee. As does the standard of need, the maximum monthly benefits a dependent family without any other resources can receive varies with family size.

If the family has earned income, then payments are calculated by a more complicated procedure.[5] During the first four months of employment, the first $30 of gross earnings is completely disregarded and an additional one-third of the family's gross earnings, net of the $30 and the deductible work expenses, is also disregarded. Thus arises the concept of countable income (CI), which is the portion of income that reduces welfare payments dollar for dollar. That is, for every dollar of countable income, a dollar of benefits is lost. Countable income is defined by:

$$CI = \max [0, E - X - 30 - 1/3 (E - X - 30)] + I. \qquad (2.4)$$

Due to the income disregards, a recipient's initial gross earnings cause no reduction in benefits. Thus also arises the concept of the taxpoint (E^*), which is the amount of gross earnings at which benefits start to be reduced. The countable income formula is used to derive a formula for the taxpoint by finding the maximum gross earnings for which $CI = I$. Thus, we find that:

$$E^* = (30 + x_o) / (1 - x_e). \qquad (2.5)$$

Welfare payments (P) equal the difference between maximum aid and countable income, provided all other eligibility criteria as defined above are met and countable income is less than maximum aid.[6] Thus we have the following:

$$P = \max (0, M - CI). \qquad (2.6)$$

Once payments are initiated, continued eligibility requires monthly filing of a status form reporting earnings and other income. Under welfare regulations, as much as six weeks can elapse between the filing of a welfare application and receipt of assistance; in some cases emergency assistance is provided through a separate program.[7]

A family becomes ineligible for welfare when its payments are reduced to zero or when its total income exceeds 185 percent of the standard of need. The gross earnings level at which eligibility is lost is the breakeven point (E^{**}). Thus, by setting $P = 0$ and using the countable income formula, we have:

$$E^{**} = \min \left[(M + 2/3x_o + 20 - I) / (2/3 - 2/3x_e), 1.85SN \right]. \quad (2.7)$$

For a family with a gross earned income between the taxpoint (E^*) and the breakeven (E^{**}), a change in income will cause benefits to be lost. This loss of benefits can be thought of as an implicit tax. For analyzing this effect it is useful to define two measures. One measure is the marginal benefit reduction rate, which is the additional loss of benefits for each dollar increase in gross earnings. Another measure is an average benefit reduction rate (BRR), which is the negative of the change in benefits over the change in gross earnings.[8] Thus, for the latter measurement we have the following for earnings changing from E^* to E^{**}:

$$BRR = M / (E^{**} - E^*). \quad (2.8)$$

Families leave welfare by reporting a change in status that eliminates eligibility or by failing to return the monthly status form. When eligibility for AFDC is lost, categorically eligible families are entitled to Medi-CAL benefits for 4 to 12 months, depending on income.[9]

The above discussions apply to earners in AFDC-Basic and to earnings received by AFDC-UP families up to the point that the principal earner is working 100 hours per month. At that level AFDC-UP eligibility is lost and, for AFDC-UP families, so is eligibility for Medi-CAL. There is no one-year grace period of Medi-CAL eligibility for AFDC-UP families, because by definition two-parent families are categorically eligible for AFDC-UP only if the principal earner is unemployed. In contrast, single-parent families are always categorically eligible; they may lose eligibility for payments while retaining Medi-CAL for the grace period. Poor two-parent families in which the principal earner is employed more than 100 hours may still qualify for medical assistance from county hospitals, but standards for this tend to be more stringent and access is more difficult.

Figure 2.1 presents the traditional plot of net income against earnings. It depicts maximum aid or guarantee for a family of three, the taxpoint, and the breakeven level. In this case, net income equals welfare benefits plus gross earnings net of taxes. This net income concept differs from the one used to determine welfare eligibility.

The non-diagonal curve in Figure 2.1 represents a welfare recipient's benefits plus her income net of taxes versus her gross earnings in the case where the $30 and one-third income disregards apply. The diagonal line represents points where AFDC benefits plus earnings net of taxes equal gross earnings.

Figure 2.1
Welfare System Features:
Guarantee, Taxpoint, and Breakeven

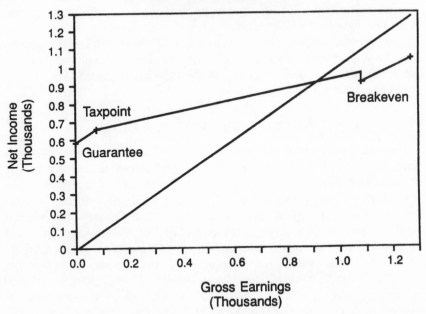

At the point where the other curve intercepts this diagonal line, the amount of benefits a recipient receives is equal to the amount of federal or state taxes she pays. At levels lower than the gross earning levels of the intercept point, the recipient receives more in AFDC benefits than she pays in taxes; at higher gross earning levels she receives less than she pays.

Several facts stand out in Figure 2.1. First, if the welfare recipient has no gross earnings, her net income equals the guarantee or maximum aid (M). Second, as gross earnings increase up to the taxpoint, welfare benefits are not reduced and net income increases one dollar for every dollar earned. Here the AFDC system completely compensates for any work expense and taxes the recipient pays. Since no benefits are lost up to the taxpoint, her marginal benefit reduction rate is zero. Third, at the taxpoint (E^*) the slope of the curve abruptly changes since benefits start to be reduced. The recipient's marginal benefit reduction rate has increased. Furthermore, with increasing earnings her net income increases up to the breakeven (E^{**}), where net income falls abruptly due to the stipulation that gross earned income must not exceed 185 percent of the state's standard of need. For gross earnings at least as large as E^{**} the recipient is off welfare and her net income is derived solely from her own resources.

The discussion above applies to earners in the AFDC-Basic program after October 1984 and earnings received by AFDC-UP families up to the point that principal earners are working 100 hours per month. Moreover, this discussion applies to the first four months of employment, since after this period countable income does not include all of the disregards described earlier. Payment procedures and eligibility criteria, which have changed for families over the years, are described in detail in later sections of this chapter. Appendix A outlines historical variations in the calculation procedures for both countable income and the breakeven.

AFDC AND ITS COMPLEMENTARY PROGRAMS

The AFDC program in California interacts with other income-maintenance programs. An AFDC recipient's purchasing power reflects not only her AFDC payment and other outside income but also the amount of benefits received from other programs. Families qualifying for AFDC automatically become eligible for food stamps and Medi-CAL. In-kind benefits are not considered for the purpose of determining the amount of AFDC payments; the amount of food stamp benefits received is dependent upon the size of the family's AFDC grant and any other outside income. Medi-CAL coverage does not vary with a family's income once AFDC eligibility is established.

The purchasing power of AFDC recipients has changed over the years because of changes in food stamp and AFDC benefits relative to the rate of inflation. Over time, Medi-CAL coverage has stayed constant for California's AFDC recipients. The amount of combined benefits, excluding Medi-CAL, provided to households of various sizes on AFDC in July 1985 is reported in the next section.

Table 2.1
Combined Benefits, California AFDC, July 1, 1985

Household Size	AFDC Maximum Aid	Food Stamp Allotment Min-Max Deductions	Total Benefits
Two	$474	$31- 71	$505-545
Three	587	60-101	647-688
Four	698	83-123	781-821

Source: See Appendix B.

Combined Benefits

AFDC and food stamp benefits are summarized in Table 2.1. For reference, the monthly poverty standard for a family of three was $738 in 1985.[10] Since the figures in Table 2.1 do not include a valuation for Medi-CAL, and the poverty standard does include medical payments, it is reasonable to say that California's welfare benefit is roughly the equivalent of the poverty standard. California's welfare payment is among the highest in the nation.[11]

CHANGES IN AFDC PROGRAM CHARACTERISTICS

The following three sections examine changes in the AFDC standard of need, combined benefit levels, and the gap between the AFDC standard of need and maximum aid. As are all other variables valued in dollars in this study, the need standard and combined benefits are brought to real terms (for deflation sources see Appendix F). Changes in the real level of benefits reflect the economic well-being of recipients. Importantly, changes in real levels of the standard of need and benefit levels may affect AFDC accessions and terminations and thus the size of the caseload. In the empirical portion of this investigation, the standard of need is used to determine caseload accessions and combined benefits to determine both accessions and terminations.

Trends in the AFDC Standard of Need

In California, the AFDC standard of need is based on a market basket survey conducted in the 1950s.[12] In 1967, for the first and last time, Congress required all states to update their need standard for inflationary effects.[13] This one-time mandatory adjustment has had a long-term effect on the need standard in California.

Figure 2.2 presents the eligibility standard in California for a family of three in both nominal and real terms.[14] The nominal curve shows a steady step increase because the standard of need has been adjusted routinely by the state legislature to reflect general price changes and, overall, the 1970s and 1980s have been inflationary periods. The constant dollar curve has a trough and peak structure, appearing as an uneven jagged saw. The peaks are due to abrupt increases in the eligibility standard. These are followed by gradual monthly declines due to inflation until the raising of the standard produces the end of a trough and the beginning of the next peak.

Prior to July 1981 California's minimum basic standard of adequate care was set at a higher monetary value than maximum aid for a given family size. Since July 1981 the eligibility standard for welfare has equaled maximum aid. In Figure 2.2 all peaks and troughs are lower after July 1981 than they were in previous years, suggesting that the need standard was lowered to the level of maximum aid rather than vice versa. As shown on the graph, the standard of

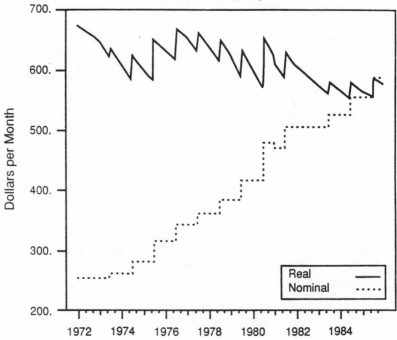

Figure 2.2
AFDC Standard of Need:
Family of Three Headed by Single Adult

need was not raised in July 1982. This precipitated the decline that is evident toward the end of the graph. In real terms, the standard of need is on average about 8 percent lower after 1981 than it was in previous years.[15]

The overall decline in the standard of need implies that some standard-of-living levels that would have allowed AFDC eligibility a decade ago now are considered too high for welfare eligibility. It is likely that in recent years the system has served fewer families in need or, perhaps, during these years more families may have lowered their standard of living in order to receive assistance.

Trends in Combined Benefits

The state legislature created the California Welfare Reform Act (CWRA) of 1971 while Ronald Reagan was governor of California. The CWRA included a provision for adjusting the state's basic AFDC benefit in response to inflation.[16] While inflationary adjustments have been rejected by the legislature on occasion (for example, following passage by popular referendum of Proposition 13, a tax-cutting initiative, in 1978), in general benefits have kept up with inflation. Evaluated in terms of the products and services that low-income households buy, the mean yearly AFDC benefits in California were 5 to 6 percent lower in 1985 than they were in 1978.[17] This is the exception when viewed in comparison with policies pursued by other states, where in general AFDC benefits have fallen much more.[18] As a result of these provisions—somewhat ironically the product of the Reagan reforms—California moved from being the state with median benefits in 1970 to a position of being the state with the most.

Food stamp benefits, like AFDC benefits, have been routinely adjusted for inflation. Since the Food Stamp program is a nationwide federal income-maintenance program, its benefits have been subjected to adjustment rates and periods different from those of California's AFDC program. Under the jurisdiction of the Department of Agriculture, food stamp benefits are adjusted for inflation in a uniform fashion across the country.[19]

The food stamp allotment, or the total value of coupons an eligible household is authorized to receive each month, varies by household size and income. From 1964 through 1975 the allotment was based on the Economy Food Plan. This plan was devised using daily allowances of nutrients recommended by the National Academy of Sciences for various sex-age categories and using food consumption patterns of persons in the lowest food-cost quartile identified in a 1955 survey. To eliminate nutritional deficiencies found in food consumption patterns, these were adjusted by the Department of Agriculture. By substituting lower-priced foods for higher-priced ones, the total costs of the plan were held to a minimum. This Economy Food Plan was used by the Department of Agriculture to determine the dollar cost of a nutritionally adequate diet. The Economy Food Plan relied heavily on groups of very inexpensive foods purchased at the best possible prices.[20]

Subsequently, the National Academy of Sciences increased the recommended daily allowances of nutrients, and the Economy Food Plan was deemed insufficient to support a nutritionally adequate diet. In 1976 the Thrifty Food Plan (TFP) replaced the Economy Food Plan. The TFP includes more nutrients for adequate nutrition, but both plans were developed in essentially the same manner. Since 1976 the cost of the TFP for a family of given size has served as the maximum food stamp allotment for a household with zero income.

Legislation passed in 1973 (Public Law No. 93–86) provided that food stamp allotments were to be adjusted semi-annually, rather than annually, to better reflect changes in food prices. The monthly food stamp allotment increased semi-annually from July 1973 to July 1976. Contrary to the law, the TFP was not adjusted to reflect price changes from January 1976 to June 1977. Thereafter, until 1980, the TFP was adjusted semi-annually. Since 1980 the TFP has been adjusted at least on an annual basis.

Figure 2.3 presents trends in AFDC and food stamp benefits for a family of three in both nominal and real terms.[21] The nominal curve shows a steady step

Figure 2.3
Maximum Aid and Food Stamps:
Family of Three Headed by Single Adult

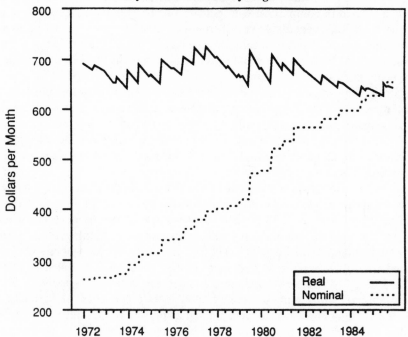

increase due to inflationary price adjustments. The constant dollar curve has a sawtooth structure. The peaks are due to an abrupt increase in either AFDC or food stamp benefits.[22]

Following California's popular tax-cutting initiative in 1978, welfare benefits were not increased by the state legislature. As seen in Figure 2.3, total benefits fell from July 1977 to June 1979. Here maximum aid is not adjusted for inflation; increasing food stamp allotments account for all the peaks. These increases slightly alleviate, but do not halt, the overall decline in benefits. This phenomenon illustrates how a decline in maximum aid is somewhat offset by an increase in total food stamp benefits. With the onset of a politically conservative atmosphere in the 1980s, California's AFDC recipients have received less in welfare payments. Taken together, AFDC and food stamp benefits show a real average monthly decline of about 1 percent per year from 1980 to 1985. Although historically California has been a generous state, the decline in real benefits should not be taken lightly.

Figure 2.4
MBSAC and Maximum Aid

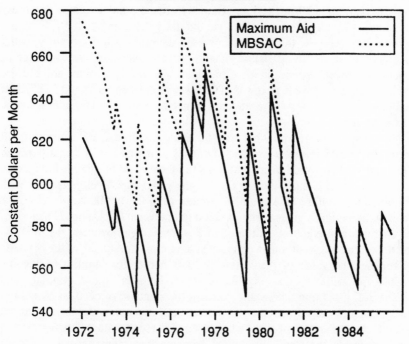

Note: Both amounts are deflated by the CNI for June 1985 = 100.

AFDC Benefits and the Standard of Need

Figure 2.4 presents both the Minimum Basic Standard of Adequate Care and the AFDC guarantee for a family of three.[23] Since July 1981 California's MBSAC has been the same as maximum aid. Consequently, it is now true that any adjustment for price changes in maximum aid adjusts the level of the eligibility standard as well. Scaling of this graph exaggerates the impression of the amount of fluctuation for both of these parameters.

During the entire period under consideration, if an AFDC applicant's net income falls below the standard of need, welfare eligibility is established; however, if gross earnings increase so that the net income rises above this level, eligibility is not always lost once it is established. This is because once a person is found eligible for welfare, countable rather than net income is considered for further eligibility. As discussed earlier, countable income, unlike net income, includes additional disregards for earnings that allow the family to maintain eligibility above the standard of need.[24] If found eligible, the amount of benefits paid equals the difference between maximum aid and the family's countable income.

During the years in which the standard of need exceeded maximum aid, applicants' net income could fall below the eligibility standard but remain above maximum aid. For two interrelated reasons this did not mean that these applicants were eligible for welfare yet did not receive any benefits. First, net income falling below the standard of need determines welfare entry, while countable income falling below maximum aid determines the amount of benefits received. Second, if the differential between maximum aid and the standard of need is small, as it was in California between 1972 and 1985, then when net income is below the standard of need, countable income falls below maximum aid.[25]

What does the differential between the standard of need and maximum aid mean? If the differential were much larger than it was in California between 1972 and 1985, it would mean that some families would be eligible but receive no benefits. In this case, the maximum gross earnings level consistent with eligibility for welfare (E^e) could be greater than the breakeven level (E^{**}). Thus, an individual's gross earnings could fall between (E^{**}) and (E^e), producing a situation of eligibility with no aid. For a small gap between the MBSAC and maximum aid, assuming a constant value for maximum aid, as the MBSAC approaches the value of maximum aid it is harder for families to become eligible for welfare; once eligible, however, families almost certainly will receive aid. Assuming a constant value for the standard of need, as maximum aid approaches the value of the standard of need it is not harder for families to become eligible and all of those who are eligible receive more benefits.

In California the small differential between maximum aid and the need standard between 1972 and 1985 was meaningless. But a lower real level of the need standard creates a situation in which certain families are denied welfare entry who otherwise would be found eligible.

Figure 2.4 suggests that there has not been a gradual closure of the gap over time. When maximum aid stayed the same between July 1977 and July 1979 the standard of need was raised. Both maximum aid and the need standard show similar fluctuation. Both have been adjusted for price changes above and below inflation. When benefits and need were made equal in July 1981, maximum aid was adjusted for price changes more than the standard of need; yet neither was adjusted quite as much as called for by the inflation rate. In a sense, California let inflation play a role in making the standard of need equal to maximum aid. This is further demonstrated by the fact that the standard of need decreased by 7 to 8 percent from its average monthly value for January 1972 to July 1981 to its average monthly value for July 1981 to December 1985. An identical calculation for maximum aid shows a decrease of only 2 to 3 percent.

CHANGES IN TREATMENT OF EARNINGS

The economic well-being of recipients can be measured not only by the amount of benefits received, but also by the way in which benefits are reduced in relation to recipients' other income. As discussed in Chapters 7 and 8, the way in which recipients' earnings are treated has been shown to affect the likelihood that recipients will move to employment or from the welfare system. The following sections provide a historical account of how earnings in the AFDC system have been treated and the effects that changes in the treatment of earnings have had on recipients' disposable income.

Welfare Benefits and Income

A great deal of attention has been paid to the treatment of earnings in welfare benefit computation. Traditionally, it has been argued that a dollar-for-dollar reduction in benefits as earnings increase will lead to withdrawal of welfare recipients from the labor force and thus that it is necessary to discount some portion of earnings in benefit computation in order to make employment attractive. Critics of this position, while acknowledging that financial incentives may be important, point out that payments systems that do not reduce benefits dollar for dollar with earnings make it possible for families with incomes in excess of eligibility standards to receive benefits. This leads to special advantage for welfare recipients compared to similarly situated families that have not been eligible for welfare because, in the past, their incomes were too high to allow entry.[26] It also means that some share of welfare expenditure goes to families not in need.

The Social Security Act amendments of 1967 modified AFDC payments procedures to allow "disregards" of a portion of earnings in benefit computations. The disregards amounted to $30 plus one-third of the excess of gross earnings over $30 per month and were applied as long as the recipient, given the disregards, retained eligibility. Welfare payments were no longer based on the difference between maximum aid and income beyond taxes and certain deductible expenses. Rather, in 1967, when the $30 and one-third disregards were implemented, payments essentially equaled the difference between maximum aid and a recipient's countable income. That is, in addition to taxes and deductible expenses, $30 and one-third of gross earnings in excess of the $30 were not counted as income for the purpose of reducing welfare payments. Only income in excess of these deductions counted for a dollar-for-dollar reduction in AFDC benefits; this income was considered countable income. The effect of the disregard of one-third of earnings beyond $30 was that, as gross earnings rose high enough, the recipient retained about 33 cents for every dollar's worth of earnings until gross earnings raised countable income to equal maximum aid, at which time welfare eligibility was lost. The intent was to provide recipients with a work incentive, motivating them to achieve ever-higher levels of income and gradually to work themselves off welfare.

The Omnibus Budget Reconciliation Act of 1981 severely curtailed the disregards, mandating their computation on earnings net of other expenses and allowing full application for only four months. OBRA added an overall restriction: regardless of expenses, if a family's gross earnings reach a level greater than 150 percent of the standard of need, eligibility is lost.

With passage of the Deficit Reduction Act (DRA) of 1984, the 150 percent gross income cutoff was raised to 185 percent of the standard of need. At the same time the $30 disregard, but not the one-third, was extended to the first 12 months of employment.

Overall, treatment of earnings while receiving aid changed from 1972 to 1984, the period under consideration in the empirical portion of this study. The changes are reflected in the way in which countable income, the taxpoint, and the breakeven are calculated (see Appendixes A and B). Nonetheless, the payments procedure during this period stayed the same, with payments equal to the difference between maximum aid and countable income provided the difference is positive.

The 1967 system and OBRA-induced changes are illustrated in Table 2.2, in which benefits are calculated for a single-parent family of three with and without a working mother. Three cases are considered. One, the reference family, covers payments in the absence of outside income. As already shown in Table 2.1, in July 1985 welfare and food stamps total $688 in this case when the mother receives the Food Stamp program's maximum "excess shelter" allowance.

In the other two cases it is assumed that the woman can make $5 per hour as the starting wage in a low-skill job. The second case assumes part-time employment working 80 hours per month; the third assumes full-time employment at 173 hours per month. Both cases assume child care expenses for one child, $160 per month for full-time employment, and one-half that for part-time work. In addition, $75 of deductible work expenses other than withholdings are assumed in both cases. The woman employed part time has take-home pay of $369. She would have gained $227 in disposable income from this effort under welfare calculation procedures in effect before OBRA. Under OBRA rules, for the first four months of employment, her net income increase will be on the order of $184; from 5 to 12 months of employment, with elimination of the one-third disregard, the gain will be $141; thereafter the gain amounts to just $120. Even working full time produces a gain of only $173 after 12 months.

With either full- or part-time employment the loss of the $30 disregard after 12 months produces a drop in total income of only $21. This illustrates the apparent fact that losing $30 will not have much impact on one's income. Thus, in discussing the elimination of the disregards it usually is not necessary to present both of them separately. In this chapter it is usually assumed that both disregards have been eliminated.

The results of these calculations are sensitive to what is assumed about work expenses, child care deductions, and other factors. But the basic conclusion will survive any variant: if welfare recipients decide to work on the basis of costs and benefits accrued immediately, they are less likely to take a job now than they were prior to OBRA.

Table 2.2
Treatment of Earnings, California AFDC-Basic,
for Family of Three Headed by Single Adult

Benefits and Income	Benefits Calculation Procedure	Assumed Earnings (per Month)		
		None	$400	$865
AFDC Net Grant	Pre–OBRA	$587	$526.17	$391.98
	Post–OBRA (1)	587	464.23	271.43
	Post–OBRA (2)	587	402.84	113.65
	Post–OBRA (3)	587	372.84	83.65
Food Stamp Allotment	Pre–OBRA	101	20.00	0.00
	Post–OBRA (1)	101	39.00	0.00
	Post–OBRA (2)	101	57.00	30.00
	Post–OBRA (3)	101	66.00	39.00
Total Income after Withholding	Pre–OBRA	688	915.33	1130.33
	Post–OBRA (1)	688	872.39	1009.78
	Post–OBRA (2)	688	829.00	882.00
	Post–OBRA (3)	688	808.00	861.00
Net Income Gain from Employment	Pre–OBRA	—	227.33	442.33
	Post–OBRA (1)	—	184.39	321.78
	Post–OBRA (2)	—	141.00	194.00
	Post–OBRA (3)	—	120.00	173.00

Source: See Appendix B.

Notes: "Post–OBRA (1)" refers to first four months following beginning of employment; "Post–OBRA (2)" refers to period from 5 to 12 months of employment; "Post–OBRA (3)" refers to period after 12 months of employment.

From the perspective of some, the positive aspect of this is that people whose eligibility while working was secured only by the $30 and one-third disregards were eliminated from welfare four months after OBRA was implemented in November 1981. Despite dire warnings from critics, few of these families returned to welfare and, indeed, initial research indicated that the incidence of welfare termination among families with no earning members did not seem to decline after OBRA when compared to the behavior of dependent families before OBRA.[27]

Trends in the AFDC Breakeven

For gross earnings levels above the breakeven AFDC, eligibility is lost. In general, the breakeven changes with changing tax rates, unearned and earned income, work deductions, maximum aid, and welfare benefit calculations.

Increasing benefit levels increase the range of earnings protected by the earnings disregards. The greater maximum aid for a particular family, everything else constant, the more gross earnings are needed in order to reduce benefits to zero. Using Equation 2.7, it is seen that in one case, if an individual's breakeven is less than 185 percent of the standard of need, and her tax withholdings (x_eE), work deductions (x_o), and unearned income (I) are constant, an increase in maximum aid (M) increases her breakeven (E^{**}). In fact, in this case and given these assumptions, each \$1 increase in maximum aid increases the breakeven by more than \$1.50 since $2/3 - 2/3x_e < 2/3$. For example, in July 1985, increasing M by \$1 from \$587 produces a \$2.12 increase in the breakeven. In the other case, when an individual's breakeven is at 185 percent of the standard of need, a \$1 increase in maximum aid will produce a \$1.85 increase in the breakeven. In either case, high benefit levels are associated with a large range of gross earnings protected by the earnings disregard computation procedure. This allows a larger number of recipients to retain welfare eligibility, assuming that gross earnings for the pool of recipients are constant.

Since taxes are disregarded in the welfare benefit computation, when Social Security or federal or state taxes increase or decrease, the breakeven increases or decreases as well. The same is true when changes in work deductions occur. On the other hand, when unearned income increases, the breakeven point decreases.

Two breakevens are presented in Figure 2.5. Both include the \$30 and one-third disregards.[28] The solid line represents the breakeven over time while using the actual welfare payment formula present in any month. Henceforth, this will be referred to as the actual breakeven (E_r^{**}). The dashed line leaving the actual breakeven in October 1981 represents what the breakeven would have been had OBRA not been implemented, but includes the actual variations in maximum aid and tax rates received or paid at the time. Henceforth, this will be called the pre-OBRA breakeven (E_o^{**}). Both versions of the breakeven are deflated by the Consumer Price Index (CPI).

Both actual and pre-OBRA breakevens are simplified since they do not capture the variations in work deductions or unearned income of the average wage-earning welfare recipient. Rather, these two variables capture variations in maximum aid, federal and state withholding rates, and Social Security tax rates at their precise month of implementation. The actual breakeven also

Figure 2.5
AFDC Breakeven

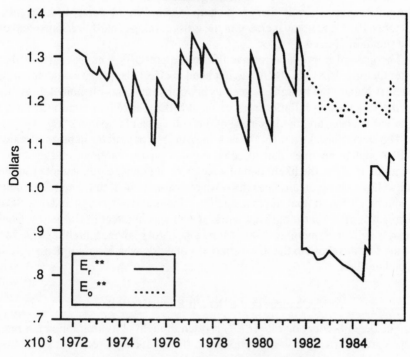

Note: Both variables are calculated with $30 and one-third
disregards. Dollars are deflated by the CPI.

reflects the OBRA changes in welfare benefit computation. It is also assumed
that work expenses, child care deductions, and unearned income equal zero.
With these assumptions, it is correct to say that the actual breakeven represents the minimum breakeven faced by a recipient with no outside income and
the pre-OBRA breakeven is the same concept assuming that OBRA had not
taken effect.

Both curves in Figure 2.5 show the uneven sawtooth shape of a government-
controlled variable deflated by a price index. Here the rapid ascent to a high
point usually occurs because maximum aid increased that month.The very
steep downward trends prior to 1981 usually are caused by falling federal or
state withholding rates. The gradual falls once again are due to inflation.

Looking first at the actual breakeven (E_r**), three periods deserve special
attention. The first is the long inflationary decline from July 1977 to June
1979, during which California did not raise its maximum aid. Next, there is a
steep fall (more than 32 percent) in November 1981, exaggerated by scaling,
that represents the 150 percent gross income eligibility restriction of OBRA.

Many families made ineligible by this OBRA regulation would not have become ineligible under pre-OBRA regulations, as seen on the corresponding pre-OBRA curve. Lastly there is a sharp increase in the actual breakeven in October 1984 due to the increase in the gross earnings cutoff to 185 percent of the standard of need.

The general impression received from the pre-OBRA curve (E_o**) is that after October 1981, if OBRA had not been in effect, the peaks would not have been as high or the troughs as deep as in prior years. This phenomenon is due to the diminishing inflation rate of the 1980s, the Reagan administration's gradual tax cuts, and the lessening of the real value of maximum aid.

The actual breakeven (E_r**) is a measurable parameter capturing major OBRA policy changes that affected earners on the caseload and probably continue to affect the likelihood of a recipient obtaining employment or going off welfare. By no means does this variable capture all of the changes brought about by OBRA. It does not measure the elimination of the $30 and one-third disregards after four months of work, which was in effect in California from March 1982 to September 1984. Moreover, it does not measure the extension of the $30 disregard to the first 12 months of work, which was implemented in October 1984.

Changes in the Benefit Reduction Rate

The benefit reduction rate (*BRR*) is often thought of as an implicit tax rate. Once gross earnings rise high enough to start reducing a recipient's benefits,

Table 2.3
Benefit Reduction Rates, July 1985,
for Family of Three Headed by Single Adult

Calculation Procedure	AFDC Taxpoint	AFDC Breakeven	AFDC BRR	Combined AFDC & FS BRR
Pre-OBRA	$159.35	$1,457.71	0.45	0.50
Post-OBRA (1)	112.96	1,085.96	0.60	0.68
Post-OBRA (2)	80.69	767.05	0.86	0.85

Source: See Appendix B.

Notes: "Post–OBRA (1)" refers to first 4 months following beginning of employment; "Post–OBRA (2)" refers to period after 12 months of employment.

she feels this loss as a tax on her welfare check. Table 2.3 presents the AFDC and the combined AFDC and food stamp benefit reduction rates. It is assumed that in July 1985 an earner in a family of three received $75 in work deductions and the maximum food stamp deductions.

Three possible systems are compared: pre-OBRA, or the system had OBRA not been adopted; post-OBRA (1), or the system during the first four months of employment; and post-OBRA (2), or the system after 12 months of employment. For each system the benefit reduction rate is calculated for gross earnings from the taxpoint to the breakeven point.[29] Consider what the benefit reduction rate means. For example, a benefit reduction rate between a taxpoint of $159.35 and a breakeven of $1,457.71 means that for each dollar earned in this range, the recipient loses an average of 45 cents of her AFDC benefits. As expected, the benefit reduction rates in either post-OBRA system are much higher than those in the pre-OBRA system due to both the gross income cutoff and the elimination of the $30 and one-third disregards. The effect of any gross income cutoff will increase the benefit reduction rate since there is a sudden loss of benefits.

As expected, benefit reduction rates for the AFDC and Food Stamp programs combined, except when the $30 and one-third disregards are eliminated, are larger than benefit reduction rates when only AFDC is considered. On the surface an increase of eight cents on the dollar seems minimal, but it represents a $73 monthly loss in food stamps. The tax rate for recipients after 12 months of employment with or without food stamps is almost the same. This is because food stamps compensate for the nearly dollar-for-dollar reduction (86 cents per dollar) in AFDC benefits.

Pre-OBRA benefit reduction rates are moderate and would be expected to motivate recipients to either gain or continue employment when compared to post-OBRA benefit reduction rates. Most observers would view an 85 to 86 percent tax rate as a strong work disincentive. However, this large tax rate is experienced only after 12 months of employment. By the end of 12 months some recipients may have already left welfare. Furthermore, there are sanctions against those who voluntarily withdraw from the labor force. This substantial increase in benefit reduction rates due to OBRA has an ambiguous effect on work incentives.

Net Income and Earnings

Figure 2.1 presented a plot of net income against earnings in order to demonstrate several AFDC program characteristics. Figure 2.6 compares pre-OBRA and post-OBRA provisions across all gross earnings levels. Curves are presented for each of the three welfare systems considered in the last section, plus a diagonal line in which net income equals gross earnings.

This income-earnings graph is only for the AFDC system. Food stamp benefits are not taken into account. It is assumed that in July 1985 an earner

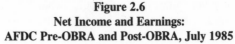

Figure 2.6
Net Income and Earnings:
AFDC Pre-OBRA and Post-OBRA, July 1985

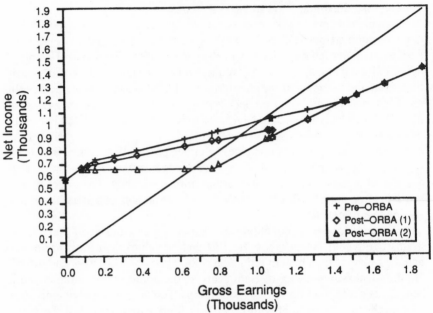

in a family of three received the maximum allowed work deductions of $75. Net income equals gross earnings minus federal and state withholding taxes plus AFDC benefits.

The marked points on the three curves represent AFDC taxpoints, the gross earning levels where federal and state tax rates change, and the AFDC break-evens. At each point the slope of the curve and the marginal benefit reduction rate change. One of OBRA's perverse regulations is apparent in the second curve. A notch appears just before the two post-OBRA curves merge. This comes about because, regardless of expenses, if a family's gross earnings reach a level greater than 185 percent of the standard of need, eligibility is lost. This notch was more significant when the gross income cutoff was set at 150 percent of the standard of need in 1981 and would be larger for greater amounts of work deductions. With the elimination of the $30 and one-third disregards, there is no notch because the breakeven here is far lower than 185 percent of the standard of need.

The graph shows that only for certain gross earnings do the three systems affect net income differently. If welfare recipients decide to go to work on the basis of how much net income is gained, then the effect of OBRA on this decision depends on their expected gross earnings. For gross earnings near any of the tax points, the effect of OBRA is minimal. With increasing gross earnings, the difference between the pre-OBRA system and the post-OBRA system during the first four months of employment is never very great, except possibly around the gross income cutoff. It is after elimination of the $30 and one-third disregards that OBRA substantially lowers net incomes as gross earnings start to increase from the taxpoint. For gross earnings near the after-12-month breakeven point, net incomes are substantially less. After each of the breakeven points shown in Figure 2.6, as earnings increase the difference in net income between the systems decreases toward zero.

ISSUES

Three important social welfare issues stem from the discussions in this chapter. These issues concern horizontal equity, target efficiency, and work incentives.

Changes in the welfare guarantee or benefit reduction rate result in changes in the breakeven level. These changes in welfare system features produce changes in horizontal inequities between some groups of the working poor and welfare recipients.

One kind of horizontal inequity occurs between those on welfare and those who are categorically ineligible for welfare. As demonstrated earlier, high benefit levels create high breakeven levels. California's relatively high benefit levels thus allow some working or non-working welfare recipients to have greater net incomes than some non-participants, as is evident in Figure 2.6. When a recipient and a non-recipient have equal gross earnings below any of the three systems' breakevens, the recipient's net income exceeds that of the non-recipient. This horizontal inequity generally is reduced as gross earnings increase. Moreover, a low breakeven due to elimination of the $30 and one-third disregards reduces the gross earnings range over which horizontal inequity occurs.

To further minimize the inequity between categorically eligible and ineligible populations, California could lower its benefit levels, which would lower its breakeven levels. However, the essential issue is whether welfare recipients should be made economically worse off in order to reduce horizontal inequity or whether some other means should be found to improve the economic well-being of the working poor. Since California's history suggests that benefits are not likely to be substantially reduced, the state needs to find some method of extending benefits to those who are not adequately supported.

Within the categorically eligible population the issue of horizontal inequity, which was significant before OBRA, has been minimized by the OBRA reforms. Most people in the conditional eligibility range (that is, for their gross earnings, if they had not been on welfare, they would not be eligible) can stay there for at most a few months. At present the $30 and one-third disregards serve only as a launching pad to the world of work. The OBRA reforms seem to have embellished this launching pad idea and thereby minimized this type of horizontal inequity.

An interrelated issue concerns target efficiency. A high benefit reduction rate, which occurs with elimination of the $30 and one-third disregards, creates a system that provides benefits to those who are "truly needy" by not allowing employable recipients with more substantial earnings to stay in the system. The issue is whether work incentives associated with low benefit reduction rates should be sacrificed for the goal of target efficiency. The welfare reforms implemented during the Reagan administration provide an answer: Work incentives should not be sacrificed for the first four months of employment, although they may be sacrificed after this period.

The issues addressed above are relevant to the study of AFDC caseload dynamics. Large horizontal inequities may motivate some ineligible families to change their economic status so that they become eligible for welfare or may impede those on welfare from leaving. But caseload dynamics also are affected by developments in the economy and population, which are discussed in Chapter 4. Before proceeding with the discussion of these developments in California, it will be helpful to examine the extent to which the California welfare system is different from AFDC systems elsewhere in the nation.

NOTES

1. For details about the components of the California welfare system see Michael Wiseman, "The Welfare System," in *California Policy Choices*, vol. 2, ed. J.J. Kirlin and D.R. Winkler (Sacramento: Sacramento Public Affairs Center, 1985), p. 139.

2. A third sub-program, AFDC Foster Care (FC), not considered here, covers state payments on behalf of children in boarding homes and institutions.

3. The discussion in this section concerns welfare system's eligibility requirements for July 1985. From November 1981 to October 1984 the eligibility ceiling was set at 150 percent of the state's standard of need. Prior to November 1981 only two financial eligibility requirements existed: the assets test and the net income test. The section in this chapter titled "Changes in Treatment of Earnings" further describes changes in eligibility and payment procedures. A historical account of California's procedures for calculating countable income is found in Appendix A.

4. These caps on work and child care expenses were set by provisions under the Omnibus Budget Reconciliation Act of 1981. Prior to this time these deductions were not standardized.

5. The procedure described here is in effect during the first four months of work. For disregards after the first four months, see the section in this chapter titled "Changes in Treatment and Earnings" and Appendix A.

6. Two different concepts of income are used in the AFDC program. Net income is used for determining AFDC eligibility only in the month in which eligibility is gained. Countable income is used to determine the amount of AFDC payments.

7. This information was provided by the California Department of Social Services, Sacramento.

8. All information about AFDC program characteristics and benefit calculation

procedures are from Michael Wiseman, *Work Incentives and Welfare Turnover*, Working Paper 84–01 (Berkeley: University of California, Department of Economics Welfare and Employment Studies Project, 1984).

9. If eligibility is lost during the first four months of employment despite the application of the $30 and one-third income disregards (described in this chapter in the section titled "Changes in Treatment of Earnings"), then Medi-CAL benefits extend for four months. If after the first four months eligibility would be retained were the $30 and one-third disregards still to be applied, Medi-CAL benefits are continued for nine months.

10. The federal poverty guidelines were provided by the U.S. Department of Agriculture, Food and Nutrition Service, Washington, D.C.

11. A discussion of California benefits in a comparative perspective is provided in Chapter 3.

12. For greater detail on measuring the MBSAC see H. I. Halsey and P. E. Vincent, *Analysis of Alternative Cost-of-Living Indices for Adjusting California AFDC and SSI/SSP Benefit Standards* (Sacramento: California Commission on State Finance, 1981), Section II, pp. 19–23.

13. Urban Systems Research and Engineering, *AFDC Standards of Need: An Evaluation of Current Practices, Alternative Approaches and Policy Options*, Contract No. SSA 600-79-0029 (Washington, D.C.: U.S. Social Security Administration, Office of Research and Statistics, 1981).

14. For the purpose of this graph the MBSAC is deflated using the California Necessities Index (CNI). See note 16 and Appendix D for a description of the CNI.

15. To find the percentage decrease, the average monthly MBSAC for January 1972 through June 1981 was compared to the average monthly MBSAC from July 1981 through December 1985.

16. Deflation is done on the basis of the California Necessities Index, the price index used for escalation of welfare benefits. The CNI differs from the Consumer Price Index in that costs of medical care, mortgage interest, and certain other items were excluded. The procedures followed in CNI construction are difficult to defend. The index was created by a committee of the California Legislature in 1980 (see AB 2982, chapter 4511) and was first used in fiscal year 1981–82. Analysis of the CNI shows that it serves principally to eliminate from price trends the jump created by the upsurge in mortgage interest rates in the late 1970s and the influence of the exceptional rise in health care costs. The adjustments are appropriate for evaluations of real purchasing power of welfare recipients since none buy homes and Medi-CAL benefits are not subject to erosion through inflation.

17. The average AFDC maximum aid for a family of three for the years 1978 and 1985 was used to find the percentage decrease.

18. For details on California's benefits in a comparative perspective see Chapter 3.

19. For a history of the Food Stamp program see U.S. House of Representatives, Committee on Agriculture, *Food Stamp Act of 1977*, Report No. 95–464, 95th Congress (Washington, D.C.: U.S. Government Printing Office, 1977).

20. For a discussion of the Economy Food Plan see M. McDonald, *Food Stamps and Income Maintenance*, Institute for Research on Poverty monograph series (New York: Academic Press, 1977), pp. 27–31.

21. Deflation of the AFDC and food stamp benefits is done by using the CNI. See note 16 and Appendix D for more information about the CNI.

22. Thrifty Food Plan amounts were provided by the U.S. Department of Agriculture, Food and Nutrition Service, Washington, D.C.

23. Both benefits and the standard of need are deflated by the CNI.

24. Countable income is less than or equal to net income when the $30 or one-third disregards are in effect. When both disregards are eliminated, countable income equals net income.

25. It is conceivable to have a system wherein the gap between the standard of need and maximum aid is very large, causing all categorically eligible to be income eligible, but providing payments only to those whose countable income falls below maximum aid. In this case there would be income-eligible families receiving no aid. This did not occur in California between 1972 and 1985 since the standard of need exceeded maximum aid by at most $28. This forces E^e to be less than E^{**}.

26. The system does not have to work this way. The "duck down" feature of the system means that a household head may have to lower her income in order to attain eligibility, but once eligible she is allowed to raise her income and still remain eligible. This feature would be absent from a true negative income tax system in which everyone applying for welfare receives the allowed disregards.

27. See C. L. Usher and J. D. Griffith, *The 1981 AFDC Amendments and Caseload Dynamics* (Research Triangle Park, N.C.: Research Triangle Institute, 1983).

28. For an explanation of the construction of the breakeven variables see Appendix B.

29. For a recipient who is considering increasing her work efforts, it is the marginal benefit reduction associated with an increase in gross earnings that serves as a work incentive or disincentive. Since marginal benefit reduction rates vary with earnings, the benefit reduction rate between the taxpoint and the breakeven does not capture all the variations that occur with changing earning levels. Rather, it serves as an average benefit reduction for the particular AFDC system. Since three different AFDC systems are compared, their average benefit reduction rates can be used to determine which system has built into it more work incentives and, on the average, how much more.

3

Welfare Systems across the Nation

In part this book is about the consequences of the Reagan administration's policy for caseload dynamics of the Aid to Families with Dependent Children program. The focus is on California, but the value of the conclusions for the rest of the nation depends to a degree on how closely California, or at least California's welfare system, resembles other states. This chapter compares the AFDC program in California with AFDC elsewhere. The following questions are addressed: In what respect is California unusual? Have differences between California and other states changed over time? What are the implications of these differences for the likely effects of OBRA and other welfare innovations? Why is California's welfare system different?

DIMENSIONS OF VARIATION IN AFDC

Under Title IV-A of the Social Security Act, federal funds are available to all states and the District of Columbia for the purpose of aiding dependent children. To receive federal funds, each state must submit a statewide plan for approval by the secretary of Health and Human Services. For the states' plans to be approved, they must comply with broad federal guidelines regarding the administration of AFDC programs and eligibility requirements. In 1985, for example, all states were required to have a single agency to administer or supervise administration of the program by local agencies, to provide a fair hearing to those denied assistance, and to consider an AFDC applicant's income and resources when determining both eligibility and payments.[1]

AFDC federal guidelines allow states considerable discretion in setting rules and regulations. States have some latitude with regard to whom they may choose to offer assistance and the amount of assistance they provide. These two factors determine whether states vary along the dimensions of breadth and depth of AFDC programs.

Federal financial participation (FFP), that is, federal reimbursement for part of the benefit payment, is available to states electing to provide aid to families with children where the principal earner is involuntarily unemployed (AFDC-UP). FFP is also available to states electing to extend emergency assistance to needy families where both parents are present and working. Emergency assistance also can be provided to AFDC recipients who need it. In other instances FFP is available to states that elect to cover women with no children during their third trimester of pregnancy, or to those states that elect to extend eligibility to teenagers age 18 to 19 who are attending school.[2] States may also extend aid to certain individuals without any FFP. States may choose to support 20-year-old students, or anyone else for that matter, solely with their own funds.

While states can vary in breadth, or scope of coverage, as described above, they can also differ in depth, or maximum AFDC payments. Each state defines the amount of income essential for basic consumption (need standard) and the portion of this standard paid to families (benefit standard).[3] These two factors can affect welfare caseload dynamics.

An additional dimension of variation is federal financing. AFDC programs across the nation are financed and administered under federal-state partnerships. Federal matching for AFDC benefit payments, by using a Medicaid cost-sharing formula specified in Title XIX of the Social Security Act, considers the state's per capita income. Federal matching for AFDC benefit payments based on each state's per capita income reflects a widespread feeling that not all states can equally well afford welfare. Irrespective of a state's wealth, the federal government pays 50 percent of administrative costs.[4]

Although AFDC programs can vary in ways other than those mentioned here, variations along the dimensions of federal financial participation, scope of coverage, and maximum amount of AFDC payments are important. Before these differences are analyzed for 1985, the interaction between AFDC and other complementary programs is examined.

AFDC and Related Programs in 1985

All AFDC recipients are categorically eligible for Medicaid benefits. Except under certain circumstances, this ends with the elimination of AFDC receipt. The Child Support Enforcement Amendments of 1984 require all states to extend Medicaid coverage for four months to families that lose AFDC eligibility because of the receipt of child support payments. The Deficit Reduction Act of 1984 requires all states to extend Medicaid coverage for nine months to families who lose AFDC eligibility solely because of the elimination of the one-third disregard. At regular federal matching, states also may elect to extend these benefits for an additional six months to families ineligible for AFDC because of the elimination of the $30 and one-third disregards. In 1985, through their medically needy programs, 33 states and the District of

Columbia also offered medical assistance to some non-AFDC poor families who were not otherwise eligible under the above criteria. Medically needy programs are not as comprehensive as the Medicaid program.[5]

Almost all AFDC families across the nation participate in the Food Stamp program. In all states food stamp benefits are disregarded in calculating AFDC payments, and in almost all states AFDC benefits are counted as income for the purpose of calculating food stamp benefits.[6] As discussed in Chapter 2, the effect of food stamps is partially compensatory. The compensatory nature of food stamps for lower AFDC benefits is further illustrated in later discussions.

DIFFERENCES AMONG STATE WELFARE PROGRAMS

The extent to which states vary along the dimensions discussed above is addressed here, with special emphasis on the need and benefit standards. These two are given special consideration because they can affect the economic well-being of individuals and the dynamics of welfare caseloads.

Federal Financial Participation

Since FFP is based on the state's per capita income, major variation exists along this dimension. In 1985 the federal government's share of benefit payments exceeded 70 percent or more in 11 states. The federal share ranged from as low as 50 percent in California to as high as 77.6 percent in Mississippi. California's high per capita income was responsible for its small federal share.[7]

Scope of Coverage

Since FFP is available to states electing to extend aid to certain categories of people under AFDC programs, variation in scope of the programs is found. In 1985, while all U.S. jurisdictions elected to have the AFDC-Basic component of the AFDC program, only 27 jurisdictions offered cash assistance to intact poor families under the AFDC-UP component.[8] The number of states providing AFDC-UP assistance fluctuates from year to year. Since its inception in 1961, the unemployed-parent component of the program has been eliminated and sometimes restored by several states. Elimination of this program, or failure to adopt it, is often due to funding problems but also reflects the lack of nationwide political support for providing this type of aid. This segment is much more controversial than the AFDC-Basic component, which provides income support mostly to single-parent families. As expected, most high-benefit states participate in the AFDC-UP program.[9]

Further variation among states is found in the scope of coverage. In 1985, 28 states provided emergency assistance to poor families, 34 states provided aid to pregnant women during the third trimester of pregnancy, and 42 states opted to aid 18- to 19-year-old students. As do some other states, California chooses to extend aid to individuals whose coverage is optional.[10]

Need and Payment Standards

Since states are allowed to set their own need standards, variations exist in the number and type of items included in the need standard and in turn in the adequacy of the standard. All jurisdictions consider items such as food, clothing, shelter, and utilities to be basic needs items. In 1985, 34 jurisdictions included special needs items, which, as the name implies, are provided to recipients only under special circumstances. Special needs items are considered to be recurring or non-recurring and suited for some individuals but not for all.[11]

Special needs items vary from state to state. For example, in 1985, in California recurring special needs items included special diets, laundry, transportation related to medical treatment, and household cleaning. Arkansas paid $25 for children or adult relatives in nursing homes, and Iowa paid for some of the costs of school items.[12] Since recipients receive monetary compensation for these items, the practical consequence is that, at least for a short while, these recipients may be better off than recipients in states that offer similar benefit levels but address no special needs. However, it is safe to assume that, on the average, recipients in high-benefit states that do not address special needs are better off than their counterparts in low-benefit states that do.

Since standards of need vary widely from state to state, families in similar economic situations may be found eligible for welfare in some but not in others that provide comparable benefit levels. This occurs because to be eligible for welfare a family's total income must be less than 185 percent of the need standard, including special needs, before income disregards apply, and net income must fall below the standard.

States pay either a portion or the full amount of their need standards. When a state's payment standard is less than its needs standard, the reduction is usually justified on the basis of budgetary constraints. In July 1985, 30 states paid less than their full need standards. Ten states paid 50 percent or less.

Marked differences exist across the nation with regard to payment standards. These differences are amplified by the fact that many states pay only a reduced standard and, in many cases, the full standard is less than adequate. Some of the differences in assistance payments may reflect differences in cost of living or in the ability or willingness of states to support poor families. Irrespective of the reasons for variation in assistance payments, such variation creates horizontal inequity problems: Similarly situated families across the nation are not elevated to the same economic condition.

The sizeable differences in both need and payment standards across the country are illustrated in Table 3.1. In July 1985 California ranked second in

Table 3.1
Need Standard and Benefits by State,
Ranked by AFDC Maximum Aid, July 1985

	Standard of Need	AFDC Maximum Aid	FS Benefits w/ Max Deductions	Combined Benefits	Percent of Poverty Threshold	Change in Maximum Aid 1970–85
Alaska	$719	$719	$197	$916	99%	-22%
California	**587**	**587**	**101**	**688**	**93**	**10**
Vermont	841	550	112	662	90	-25
Wisconsin	628	534	116	650	88	7
Minnesota	528	528	118	646	88	-25
Connecticut	487	487	131	618	84	-29
New York	474	474	150	624	85	-38
Hawaii	468	468	276	744	88	-24
Washington	728	462	152	614	83	-32
Massachusetts	439	432	147	579	78	-46
Rhode Island	409	409	192	601	81	-39
New Jersey	404	404	155	559	76	-53
Michigan	467	394	158	552	75	-29
New Hampshire	389	389	160	549	74	-47
Oregon	386	386	196	582	79	-24
Utah	693	376	164	540	73	-27
North Carolina	371	371	165	536	73	-43
Maine	510	370	166	536	73	-2
Kansas	365	365	167	532	72	-36
Iowa	497	360	169	529	72	-37
Wyoming	360	360	169	529	72	-50
Nebraska	350	350	172	522	71	-23
Pennsylvania	587	348	172	520	70	-48
Colorado	421	346	173	519	70	-35
Montana	401	332	177	509	69	-32
Maryland	455	329	191	520	70	-30
South Dakota	329	329	178	507	69	-55
Dist. of Col.	654	327	179	506	69	-39
Idaho	554	304	185	489	66	-48
Illinois	632	302	186	488	66	-52
Virginia	322	291	189	480	65	-47
Ohio	652	290	190	480	65	-34
Delaware	287	287	191	478	65	-34

(continued)

Table 3.1 (continued)

	Standard of Need	AFDC Maximum Aid	FS Benefits w/ Max Deductions	Combined Benefits	Percent of Poverty Threshold	Change in Maximum Aid 1970–85
Nevada	$285	$285	$191	$476	64%	-29%
Oklahoma	471	282	192	474	64	-31
Missouri	312	273	195	468	63	-13
New Mexico	258	258	199	457	62	-37
Indiana	307	256	200	456	62	-23
West Virginia	497	249	202	451	61	-34
North Dakota	492	246	203	449	61	-36
Florida	400	240	205	445	60	-22
Arizona	233	233	207	440	60	-38
Georgia	366	223	208	431	58	-33
Kentucky	197	197	208	405	55	-52
Arkansas	234	192	208	400	54	-30
Louisiana	579	190	208	398	54	-21
South Carolina	187	187	208	395	54	-19
Texas	494	167	208	375	51	-59
Tennessee	339	153	208	361	49	-52
Mississippi	286	120	208	328	44	-37
Alabama	384	118	208	326	44	-33

Source and Calculation Procedure: See Appendix B.

Notes: Thrifty Food Plan amounts for Alaska and Hawaii are higher than for other jurisdictions. For information on calculation of the food stamp benefits for all jurisdictions consult Appendix B.

In calculating combined benefit amounts for each state it was necessary to consider the amount of the AFDC grant designated as an energy payment and disregarded in calculating food stamp benefits. For information see Appendix B.

The poverty standard in the 49 contiguous jurisdictions in July 1985 was $738. In Alaska and Hawaii it was 25% and 15% higher, respectively.

Maximum aid changes are for a family of four.

AFDC maximum benefit levels for a family of three. The higher benefit levels in this state partially compensate for a higher cost of living. Calculations show that in this time period a moderate correlation (−0.56) existed between adequacy of AFDC payments and federal share of benefits payments. Here adequacy is measured by the AFDC payment for a family of three expressed as a percentage of the poverty standard. The negative correlation coefficient suggests that the larger the federal share of a state's benefit payments, the less benefits are paid by the state. This suggests that if states set benefits low due to their inability to pay, then the federal criterion for determining the amount of its matching share is not generous enough.

Some states with low per capita incomes do provide high benefits, mainly Vermont, Utah, and Maine. There is no doubt that the high federal share of their benefits helps to keep benefits high. Nonetheless, most states with low benefits are also less wealthy. Of course, a state's ability to pay is not the only criterion state legislatures use to set benefit levels. Some affluent states offer low benefits. In Texas, for example, benefits are only 23 percent of the poverty standard (the fourth lowest benefit level), while per capita income is relatively high (in the top 40 percent of all states). Clearly, the other factors besides ability to pay play a major role in Texas.

Table 3.1 further illustrates that in July 1985 the need standards in a few low-benefit states exceeded the need standards in some high-benefit states. As elaborated later on, this is due partially to the fact that some low-benefit states substantially raised their need standards after passage of OBRA. On one end of the spectrum, a dozen states have set their need standards at more than 75 percent of the poverty threshold. The median standard of need is $421, which is 57 percent of the poverty threshold.

At the other extreme, figures suggest that in many states the need standard is not taken seriously. Eight states have a need standard below $300, a level not consistent with an adequate standard of living. This is less than 40 percent of the poverty standard. These states are not following federal guidelines, which suggest that the need standard should reflect cost of living within the states. In addition, most states do not pay their full need standards and some pay only a small portion. For example, in July 1985 in Alabama, Louisiana, and Texas AFDC benefits were 31, 32, and 34 percent of their respective AFDC standards of need.

The Effect of Food Stamps

Most AFDC recipients across the country participate in the Food Stamp program. Food stamp benefits supplement the AFDC cash grant and help to minimize the horizontal inequity caused by acute variations in AFDC payments across the nation. As seen in Table 3.1, the food stamp benefit varies from $101 in California to $276 in Hawaii.[13]

As expected, food stamp benefits generally are largest in states that pay the least amount of AFDC payments, in turn disproportionately increasing the combined benefit level. Under the assumption that maximum food stamp deductions apply, nine states have AFDC benefits so low that recipients receive the maximum food stamp allowance. In essence, these states are maximizing the federal share of total welfare support for their recipients. However, for these states combined benefits range from $326 to $431 per month. These payments are so low (less than 60 percent of the poverty standard) that they can be considered inadequate to support a minimally sufficient standard of living.

Interestingly, for several reasons families may not be better off in states with higher AFDC benefits. Differences among states in cost of living may not be compensated by higher benefits. Furthermore, some states apportion their benefits in such a way that a recipient gets more food stamp deductions than she otherwise would with the same benefit level in most other states. For example, in Oregon, $118 of a recipient's AFDC cash payment is designated as energy aid and is disregarded in calculating food stamp benefits. For a family of three, this designation serves to increase the food stamp benefit from $161 to $196. In effect, if a state defines part of the AFDC grant as an energy aid, then the federal government contributes more than it otherwise would.[14]

The interaction of food stamps and AFDC has another repercussion. For states wishing to increase the total package of benefits available to recipients by one dollar, it is necessary to increase maximum aid by more than one dollar. This is because food stamp benefits are reduced by 30 cents for each dollar of countable cash income. For a median-benefit state such as Montana, to increase its total combined benefits by one dollar from $509 would necessitate raising maximum aid by $1.43. Of this amount Montana would pay only 51 cents because of federal contributions to AFDC cash benefits. The federal government would pay the rest of the increase. The interaction of food stamp and AFDC benefits, however, actually provides a marginal disincentive for states to raise maximum aid. If the amount of food stamp aid were not increased as maximum aid increased, then Montana's share of setting its total benefit package $1 higher would only be 36 cents. Thus, Montana must pay a higher percentage than its federal matching percentage in order to increase total benefits.

Table 3.1 also shows that combined benefits as a portion of the poverty standard are very high in California and nine other states. These states have combined benefits at least 80 percent of the poverty standard. While these states do not lift recipients to the poverty threshold on the basis of AFDC cash grant and food stamp benefits alone, if Medicaid benefits are included they almost do (medical benefits account for 7 to 8 percent of low-income budgets). If a recipient receives public housing, then in these states benefits exceed the poverty threshold.

Trends in Benefits

For the most part, state-to-state trends in AFDC benefits portray a gloomy picture. Table 3.1 shows that from 1970 to 1985 most states let their benefits erode with inflation. During this period, in real terms and on the average, AFDC benefits fell by about 33 percent.[15] Change in real AFDC benefits ranges from +10 percent to −59 percent with 13 states decreasing their benefit levels by more than 40 percent. Interestingly, in 1985 the median benefits for these 13 states was $329, a figure almost equal to the median benefits of the remaining states, which was $332. This means that the states in which benefits fell the most still had relatively high benefits. These states simply let inflation move them toward median benefit levels. On one end of the spectrum, Wisconsin and California showed an increase in real AFDC benefit levels. At the other extreme, benefits in Texas decreased by 59 percent from 1970 to 1985. This dramatic decrease is important since the economic well-being of many families worsened in one of the nation's most populous states with one of the largest AFDC caseloads.[16]

Most states are reducing their commitment to AFDC by letting their benefit levels erode with inflation. Most of this erosion in benefits occurred in the high-inflation years of the 1970s. During the 1980s, a period in which a conservative administration aimed to change the scope of the AFDC program, inflation lessened and benefits, while still falling, somewhat stabilized. Yet in the 1980s the economic well-being of some working recipients changed nationwide, especially in high-benefit states. These issues and the magnitude of these changes are discussed in later sections of this chapter.

WELFARE POLICIES: THEIR NATIONAL CONSEQUENCES

Federal welfare policies often are set to change the economic well-being of those receiving welfare and to affect their behaviors. By influencing recipients' behaviors, federal policy makers hope to control the size of the national AFDC caseload and, in turn, welfare costs. As expected, the responses of state officials to federal policies and the consequences of these policies for recipients vary across the country.

Changes Accompanying OBRA

The most important income eligibility restrictions accompanying OBRA were discussed in Chapter 2. Another restriction, not mentioned in that chapter, concerns the requirement that states count a stepparent's income in determining AFDC eligibility and payments. Prior to OBRA, a stepfather's income was counted only if state law required all stepfathers, whether they were on AFDC or not, to support their children. OBRA also changed the assets requirement. Since passage of OBRA a family is no longer eligible if it owns more than $1,000 worth of personal property besides an automobile and a home. To be eligible an automobile can be worth no more than $1,500. OBRA's only liberalization was to prevent states from denying eligibility because of the value of an applicant's home.[17]

Also embodied in this national legislation were changes in categorical eligibility for AFDC. The age limit for children eligible for AFDC was lowered from 21 to 19, and states were given the option of providing aid to students between age 18 and 19. No longer were pregnant women with no other children eligible for AFDC prior to their third trimester of pregnancy. From the inception of the AFDC-UP program until 1979, categorical eligibility for AFDC-UP was determined when the father was unemployed. In 1979, due to a court ruling, either parent could be categorically eligible for AFDC-UP. OBRA required that states restrict eligibility of this program to families where the "principal earner" was unemployed.[18]

The Reagan administration narrowed the scope of the AFDC program by denying assistance to some families who were categorically eligible for welfare prior to 1981 by imposing new income and assets restrictions and by changing the way in which recipients' earnings are treated.

States' Responses to OBRA's Changes

As mentioned earlier, by 1985 the majority of states had elected to extend categorical eligibility to women in their third trimester of pregnancy and students between age 18 and 19. Some states chose to continue to provide support to people previously considered categorically eligible, even in the absence of federal matching funds. For example, in 1982 California and Massachusetts elected to provide aid to pregnant women before their third trimester.[19] In the case of California, in 1985 pregnant women could receive support for themselves and $70 in special needs for the unborn as soon as their pregnancy was verified. New York State changed its general assistance requirements so that older students and pregnant women during their second trimester would receive aid. These types of cases are rare.[20] In an extensive analysis of states' responses to OBRA, Schram found that, while most OBRA reforms were not counteracted by the states, increasing the need standard was one method some states used to thwart the Reagan reforms.[21]

Increasing the need standard may counteract some of OBRA's eligibility restrictions. In Chapter 2 it was noted that, in order to receive payments in any month, a recipient's gross income must be less than 185 percent of the standard of need and countable income must be less than maximum aid (see Equation 2.4). If a recipient satisfies the countable income test (because her work deductions or income disregards are large relative to maximum aid) but does not pass the gross income test (because her gross income without all the deductions is larger than 185 percent of the need standard), she will be found ineligible. This situation is more apt to happen when maximum aid and the standard of need are equal or almost equal. For standards of need much larger than maximum aid, many fewer recipients will be in the situation of satisfying the countable income restriction but not the gross income restriction. Increasing the need standard increases the range of income for which both countable income and gross income tests will be satisfied. In essence, making the need standard much larger than maximum aid nullifies the restriction on the latter.

Increasing the standard of need has a side effect of relaxing another income eligibility restriction. Recall that net income must be less than the standard of need in order to gain welfare entry (see Equation 2.2). It is possible for applicants to satisfy both gross and countable income tests but fail to meet the net income test. Those states that increase their standard of need make it easier for applicants to pass the net income test. A state that raises its need standard thus makes it possible for more applicants in this situation to meet all three income tests and consequently gain entry, provided, of course, other eligibility criteria are met.

From July 1981 to July 1982 seven states raised their need standards by 43 percent or more, at least somewhat circumventing the income cutoff rules. Some low-benefit states, for example, Georgia, increased their need standards by a large amount. These states, however, did not increase their benefits by an equal amount. Large increases in the need standard most likely helped some working recipients to stay on welfare and others to gain entry, but most of them for only an additional four months because once the one-third disregard no longer applies, satisfying the countable income test becomes much less likely.

From the author's analyses it is not known whether states raised their need standards by a large amount in order to counteract the OBRA reforms. However, Schram maintains that some states raised their standards to do just that. Some policy makers, he suggests, were afraid that any immediate savings due to OBRA eligibility restrictions eventually would turn into long-term costs.[22] Those recipients made ineligible by the OBRA reforms would return to the rolls having discontinued working. With no earnings to offset their welfare benefits and being less likely to work due to the previous loss of eligibility, these recipients would be more dependent and an even larger financial burden to the state.

A major effect of OBRA is on working recipients' income after four months of work. Even if state policy makers intend to undermine this consequence, there is no way this could be done. The impact of OBRA's provisions on recipients' income varies from state to state and some of this variation is illustrated next.

Consequences of OBRA: A Comparison

Table 2.2 illustrates the effects of both the 1967 and OBRA systems of recipients' income in California. The following discussion compares the consequences of OBRA for recipients in the states of Texas and Pennsylvania with those in California.

In fiscal year 1984–85 both Texas and Pennsylvania were among the most populous states in the country with AFDC caseloads of about 3.3 percent and 5 percent, respectively, of the total national AFDC caseload. Taken together, these two states' AFDC caseloads were much smaller than California's, which constituted about 15 percent of the total caseload.[23] Federal shares of benefit payments in Texas and Pennsylvania also were more than in California, accounting for about 56 percent and 55 percent, respectively, of total benefit payments. Although these two states are slightly less wealthy than California, they are by no means poor.[24]

Resembling one another with respect to caseload size and federal matching share, Texas and Pennsylvania differ significantly in AFDC benefit levels. In 1985, and similarly in previous years, Texas' combined benefits constituted only 51 percent of the poverty line, whereas Pennsylvania's were 70 percent (see Table 3.1). After passage of OBRA, Texas raised its need standard by a substantial amount, creating a large gap between its benefit level and need standard. Overall, Texas and Pennsylvania can be characterized as low- and median-benefit states. This, along with their large populations, is the primary reason for comparing them with a high-benefit state such as California.

Table 3.2 compares the consequences of the 1967 system and OBRA-induced changes for AFDC families in Pennsylvania and Texas. The working assumptions used for Table 2.2 apply here as well.[25] Comparing Table 2.2 and Table 3.2, several observations may be made about the similar impact of OBRA across the three states. These observations are made for recipients with earned income and only when eligibility is retained.

First, an important effect of OBRA is on welfare payments. Under any of the three OBRA systems, payments are reduced by about the same amounts across the three states as long as eligibility is maintained. This statement applies to other states as well when the same assumptions are maintained. During the first four months of work, OBRA rules lower payments from pre-OBRA levels by one-third of total deductions, including income taxes, child care expenses, and the standard work deduction. During the next nine months, the loss of the one-third disregard lowers payments by one-third of gross earnings, less $10. Losing the $30 disregard after 12 months of work results in an additional $30 reduction in payments.[26]

What is important about this is that OBRA lowers payments by amount that do not depend on parameters that vary from state to state, except for state income taxes, and then only during the first four months of work. These parameters include the states' need and maximum aid standards. Thus, for a given level of gross earnings, the only variation across the states in the decrease in payments is due to a variation in state income taxes during the first four months of work. Clearly this difference is small. Furthermore, provided eligibility is retained, there is no variation among the three states in the amount

Table 3.2
Treatment of Earnings, Pennsylvania and Texas,
Family of Three Headed by Single Adult

Benefits and Income	Benefits Calculation Procedure	Pennsylvania Assumed Earnings (per Month)			Texas Assumed Earnings (per Month)		
		None	$400	$865	None	$400	$865
AFDC Net Grant	Pre–OBRA	$348	$296.57	$173.31	$167	$106.17	$0.00
	Post–OBRA(1)	348	231.49	45.99	167	44.23	0.00
	Post–OBRA(2)	348	173.24	0.00	167	0.00	0.00
	Post–OBRA(3)	348	143.24	0.00	167	0.00	0.00
Food Stamp Allotment	Pre–OBRA	172	89.00	12.00	227	146.00	64.00
	Post–OBRA(1)	172	109.00	50.00	227	165.00	64.00
	Post–OBRA(2)	172	126.00	64.00	227	178.00	64.00
	Post–OBRA(3)	172	135.00	64.00	227	178.00	64.00
Total Income	Pre–OBRA	520	745.33	903.33	394	621.33	808.73*
	Post–OBRA(1)	520	700.25	814.01	394	578.39	808.73*
	Post–OBRA(2)	520	659.00	788.40*	394	591.16*	808.73*
	Post–OBRA(3)	520	638.00	788.40*	394	591.16*	808.73*
Net Income Gain from Employment	Pre–OBRA	—	225.33	383.33	—	227.33	414.73*
	Post–OBRA(1)	—	180.25	294.01	—	184.39	414.73*
	Post–OBRA(2)	—	139.00	268.40*	—	197.16*	414.73*
	Post–OBRA(3)	—	118.00	268.40*	—	197.16*	414.73*

Source: See Appendix B.

Notes: "Post–OBRA (1)" refers to first four months following beginning of employment; "Post–OBRA (2)" refers to period from 5 to 12 months of employment; "Post–OBRA (3)" refers to period after 12 months of employment.

* Includes Earned Income Tax Credit.

of payments lost due to OBRA after four months of work. Everyone loses one-third of their gross earnings minus $10 or plus $20, depending on their eligibility for the $30 disregard.

The second similar effect of OBRA across the states is on net income as long as the working recipient maintains AFDC and food stamp eligibility. The effect of OBRA on the decrease in net income gained from employment is virtually the same for all three states. The possible variation is due to different state taxes or because of rounding procedures used in computing food stamp benefits.

By further observing Tables 2.2 and 3.2, it is apparent that some significant variations do exist. These differences arise when comparing states in which eligibility is retained with states in which eligibility is lost. Working recipients become ineligible for welfare sooner in lower-benefit states than their counterparts in higher-benefit states whether or not OBRA rules apply. Such effects on recipients' eligibility and income are due largely to variation in AFDC maximum aid. Widely varying amounts of maximum aid cause large differences in the states' breakevens. To some extent OBRA exaggerates this effect of maximum aid by making some recipients ineligible even sooner.

As seen from Table 3.2, in Texas, where welfare benefits are very low, under OBRA rules recipients working part time are eligible for AFDC benefits only for the first four months of work. For the part-time worker in this case, OBRA's provisions lower total income by about 7 percent. Working full time for $5 per hour makes recipients ineligible for welfare even when pre-OBRA rules are applied. In Texas, under any of the welfare systems, it is unlikely that full-time workers with families of three receive AFDC; their full-time wage almost inevitably makes them ineligible. Most likely only full-time workers with very large families could be eligible. With full-time employment, even at minimum wage, a family of three would be ineligible for welfare in the state of Texas.

In Pennsylvania, during the first four months of work, our part-time worker's total income declines by the same amount as it does in Texas. With elimination of the $30 and one-third disregards, the situation is more grim. During this time our part-time and full-time workers' incomes decline from their pre-OBRA levels by about 12 percent and 13 percent, respectively. More importantly, the full-time worker is no longer eligible and after nine months loses Medicaid.

Referring to Table 2.2, under the present assumptions, full-time workers receive welfare in California irrespective of how long their employment lasts. However, the consequences of OBRA's provisions for recipients employed full-time in California appear more drastic. With elimination of the one-third disregard, the full-time worker suffers a substantial decline in income of about 22 percent. This is more than any other percentage decline, because at this level of income and under these rules, recipients in the other two states are ineligible. The large decline is a result of OBRA's high benefit reduction rates once the one-third disregard is eliminated.

Overall, it appears that OBRA's provisions have their greatest effect in high-benefit states where the standard of living of welfare families fell the most. This effect is due to variations in maximum aid and OBRA's provisions affecting the breakevens. Living in a high-benefit state, however, has combined advantages of retaining welfare eligibility and categorical eligibility for Medicaid at higher gross earnings levels. Although former recipients can receive Medicaid for an extended period of time if they are found ineligible because of the elimination of the $30 or one-third disregards, in low-benefit states they may not be eligible for this benefit. Recall that in Texas working full-time makes one ineligible not because of OBRA but because of low aid levels. Consequently, the former recipient does not have the added advantage of receiving Medicaid for an extended period of time because of eligibility for AFDC.

The Reagan administration intended to narrow the welfare "safety net." From the present analysis it seems that prior to OBRA low-benefit states already had narrow safety nets. In these states recipients are suffering from losses of income even more than in the past. In high-benefit states such as California, OBRA successfully narrows the breadth of the safety net. However, there can be tradeoffs associated with narrower breadth, including work disincentives or incentives to stay on welfare. The extent to which OBRA affected welfare terminations in a high-benefit state is addressed in chapters pertaining specifically to California.

CALIFORNIA'S WELFARE SYSTEM
IN A NATIONAL CONTEXT

California is committed to providing aid to poor families, as is evident in the fact that when states are given the option of providing aid to certain categories of poor families, California policy makers usually elect to support those families. Yet the range of variation across states in eligibility criteria actually is limited. The major distinction involves AFDC-UP. Only half the states, including California, elect to offer this program. Overall, however, the scope of coverage under AFDC does not make California an unusual state.

California's commitment to poor families is especially evident in its high benefit levels. AFDC payments have virtually kept up with price changes in California as a result of periodic adjustments. Compared to almost all states, California is the exception in adjusting welfare payments. In the long run, families with earners and non-earners enjoy a higher standard of living in this state than in many others because of the Reagan reforms in early 1970s.

As demonstrated in this chapter and in Chapter 2, the role that benefit levels play for both earners and non-earners is of paramount importance. Everything else constant, California's welfare recipients and applicants are economically better off than their counterparts in most other states, even in the face of welfare policies that are set to undermine the role of generous benefit levels.

Two facts about California's welfare system might be expected to attract a larger number of welfare recipients: Some of those deemed ineligible for AFDC in other states are found eligible in California, and benefit levels in absolute terms are higher in California than in other states. These facts have two important implications. First, categorically eligible individuals in California may have more incentives to apply for welfare and fewer incentives to leave it than those in lower-benefit states. Although this is not directly tested in the present study, the regression model presented in Chapter 6 provides a gauge for measuring the effect of benefit levels on welfare accessions and terminations. Second, because California's welfare system is more generous, it may be expected that some categorically eligibles would migrate to California from other states. There is, however, not much evidence supporting the notion that high benefit levels promote interstate migration.[27]

In recent years many refugees have migrated to California, more than to any other state, and many of these refugees are on public assistance. In 1983 about one-third of the refugees on public assistance in California were originally assigned to other states. However, most welfare recipients in California are residents of California.[28] Refugees are likely to come to California for reasons other than the state's high benefit levels. Some are in this state simply because California is part of the Pacific Basin, a convenient landing place. Others are there because of the presence of large ethnic communities or of relatives already in the state.

Why Is California so Generous?

According to available literature, generosity of AFDC payments in any state will increase with a larger or more "attractive" recipient population, higher per capita personal income, and an increase in federal financial participation.[29] California is a rich state with the third highest personal per capita personal income in the nation in 1980. In 1982 it ranked fourth in the nation with respect to the number of AFDC recipients per 1,000 population, and it has the largest number of recipients.[30] Yet on the other hand, the federal government pays the smallest share of AFDC benefits.

Attractiveness of the recipient population is related to racial composition and perceived legitimacy of need for aid. Attractiveness thus may depend on the percentage of minorities and median age of the recipient population. There is more popular support for programs that aid the elderly than for programs that aid the able-bodied poor and more support for providing aid to people who closely resemble the general population. The recipient population in California probably is less attractive now than it was in the late 1960s when the AFDC caseload more closely resembled the general population. At that time 50 percent of the recipient population and 90 percent of the general population was white. In 1982 the AFDC caseload consisted of 36 percent whites, while 76 percent of California's population was white. The larger racial difference between recipients and the general population may help to explain recent pressures to reduce benefits in California to levels more closely resembling the rest of the nation's.[31]

The AFDC recipient population apparently is perceived by California taxpayers as less deserving of aid than the population receiving Supplemental Security Income. In recent years there has been no pressure to reduce aid to SSI recipients. Most likely this is because the AFDC population consists of able-bodied poor and a disproportionate number are members of minority groups, while the population receiving SSI consists of indigent elderly and disabled individuals who are not expected to work.

Irrespective of recent pressures to lower benefit levels in California, the state's benefit levels remain relatively high. As we shall see, the greater level of commitment to AFDC in California may indeed affect welfare accessions and terminations. Nevertheless, welfare system features alone do not determine the level of accessions and terminations. Economic and demographic developments play major roles. These factors are discussed in Chapter 4.

NOTES

1. See U.S. Health and Human Services Department, Social Security Administration, Office of Family Assistance, *Characteristics of State Plans for AFDC under the Social Security Act Title IV-A: Administrative Eligibility Assistance Payments* (Washington, D.C.: U.S. Government Printing Office, 1986).

2. Ibid.

3. Ibid.

4. This information was taken from U.S. House of Representatives, Committee on Ways and Means, *Background Material and Data on Programs within the Jurisdiction of the Committee on Ways and Means* (Washington, D.C.: U.S. Government Printing Office, 1986).

5. Ibid.

6. Ibid.

7. Ibid.

8. See U.S. Health and Human Services Department, Family Support Administration, Office of Family Assistance, *Research Tables Based on Characteristics of State Plans for AFDC: Administration Eligibility Assistance Payments, in Effect October 1, 1985* (Washington, D.C.: U.S. Government Printing Office, 1986).

9. U.S. House of Representatives, *Background Material and Data on Programs.*

10. U.S. Health and Human Services Department, *Research Tables Based on Characteristics of State Plans.*

11. Ibid.

12. Ibid.

13. In July 1985, as in previous years, the food stamp maximums for Hawaii and Alaska were higher than in the rest of the jurisdictions. See Appendix B for source.

14. This information was provided by the U.S. Department of Agriculture, Food and Nutrition Service, Washington, D.C.

15. Only two points are considered in this calculation. This may somewhat over-

estimate or underestimate the change in real AFDC benefits. For California, this figure is an underestimate since welfare benefits were changed to reflect price changes in 1972. It was not possible to obtain figures for all states in the 1970s for a family of three from the Office of Family Assistance. Consequently, the percentage changes are for a family of four. See U.S. House of Representatives, *Background Material and Data on Programs.*

16. Texas population and AFDC caseload as a percentage of the nation's population and AFDC caseload is discussed later.

17. OBRA's revisions are described in Sanford F. Schram, "State Discretion in AFDC Eligibility: Response to Reagan Welfare Revisions," Unpublished manuscript, University of Wisconsin, Madison, 1987. Also see U.S. House of Representatives, *Effects of the Omnibus Budget Reconciliation Act of 1981 (OBRA) Welfare Changes and the Recession on Poverty* (Washington, D.C.: U.S. Government Printing Office, 1984).

18. Ibid.

19. Ibid.

20. Ibid.

21. Schram, "State Discretion in AFDC Eligibility."

22. Ibid.

23. Monthly national AFDC caseload data were provided by the U.S. Health and Human Services Department, Social Security Administration, Office of Family Assistance, Washington, D.C.

24. Federal matching share for AFDC benefits were provided by U.S. House of Representatives, *Background Material and Data on Programs.*

25. Calculation procedures used to construct Table 3.2 are described in Appendix B.

26. Relevant derivations regarding amounts that OBRA lowered payments are provided in Appendix A.

27. For more discussion see E.M. Gramlich and D.S. Laren, "Migration and Income Redistribution Responsibilities," *Journal of Human Resources* 4 (1984): 489–511.

28. For more information see Michael Wiseman, "The Welfare System," in *California Policy Choices*, vol. 2, ed. J.J. Kirlin and D.R. Winkler (Sacramento: Sacramento Public Affairs Center, 1985), pp. 133–202.

29. For more information see L.L. Orr, "Income Transfers as a Public Good: An Application to AFDC," *American Economic Review* 5 (1976): 359–371. Also see Wiseman, "The Welfare System."

30. Wiseman, "The Welfare System."

31. Ibid.

4

California's AFDC Caseload
and Its Environment

Changes in the AFDC caseload and its components are likely to be associated with demographic shifts and changing economic conditions. This chapter examines both the AFDC-Basic and AFDC-UP caseloads in the context of California's population and economy. Both caseloads are examined since families move between the two and an understanding of both allows for a broad picture of the AFDC caseload.

CALIFORNIA'S POPULATION AND ECONOMY

The following sections examine the growth rates of several sub-populations in California likely to contribute to overall growth of the AFDC caseload. Also of interest are trends in California's economy and the effects of economic conditions on AFDC caseload dynamics.

The Sub-populations

As of July 1972, California's population was slightly less than 21 million. Over the next 13 years it increased by 26 percent to 27 million. Over the same interval the number of children in the population grew only about 3.5 percent. Children currently account for about one-quarter of the state's population. In 1972 they accounted for almost one-third.[1]

The total number of females age 15 to 44 in California grew by 40 percent from 4.5 million in July 1972 to 6.3 million in July 1985.[2] This sub-population is of child-bearing age and includes female household heads on welfare and females in the population at risk of becoming welfare recipients. The size and growth rate of this sub-population are expected to affect the size and growth rate of the caseload.

Table 4.1
Poverty Rate by Household Type, 1976 to 1985,
and Percentage of Female Household Heads with Children

| Year | Poverty Rate | | Percentage of Female Household Heads with Children |
	Married Couples with Children	Female Household Heads with Children	
1976	4.0%	30.5%	7.7%
1977	2.9	26.0	7.6
1978	2.9	26.3	8.3
1979	3.0	23.1	7.6
1980	2.9	22.6	7.7
1981	4.0	21.2	7.4
1982	4.7	28.8	8.3
1983	5.5	28.4	7.7
1984	5.6	29.3	7.6
1985	5.3	26.3	7.0

Source: Calculations derived from data provided by California Department of Finance, Population Research Unit.

Note: All estimates were developed from the Current Population Survey conducted by the U.S. Census Bureau.

Changes in number of female household heads with children are important in assessing changes in the AFDC caseload since the economic vulnerability of these families often results in welfare use. It is well known that households headed by females are, in general, economically more vulnerable than other families. In California, as in other states, a significantly greater percentage of female household heads with children, compared with all other types of families, fall below the official poverty line.

Table 4.1 compares poverty rates of two household types: female household heads with children and married couples with children.[3] As expected, throughout the decade 1976-85 female household heads were economically more vulnerable than married couples; their chance of falling under the poverty line was five to nine times greater. Over time, however, a greater percentage of married couples with children seem to be falling below the poverty line. Females with children show a less definite trend: in California it appears that the percentage of female-headed families under the poverty line is not increasing.[4]

Table 4.1 also shows the percentage of female household heads with children out of all householders. The portion of categorically eligibles has stayed about constant over the interval considered. A female-headed household with children is formed because of illegitimacy, separation, divorce, or death of a spouse and obviously cannot be formed if a woman chooses not to have children. The figures suggest either that, over the interval considered, the illegitimacy rate or the percentage of marriages dissolving has not changed much or that an increase in either of these factors is balanced by a decrease in the percentage of women having children.

The fact that females of child-bearing age have increased at a much faster rate (25 percent) than children in the population (5.2 percent) suggests that fewer females are giving birth. However, this is not the case. Since the percentage of female household heads with children has stayed about constant, the large increase in the number of females of child-bearing age is not producing a corresponding increase in the population categorically eligible for welfare. Stabilization of the categorically eligible population is expected to help control growth of the AFDC caseload.

An important demographic development affecting both the AFDC-Basic and AFDC-UP caseloads has been the influx of refugees, especially in 1981-82. Refugees come to California from all over the world, but over 90 percent of refugees on welfare are from Vietnam, Laos, and Cambodia.[5] By July 1, 1985, there were approximately 335,000 Southeast Asian refugees in the state. Slightly more than half of all the state's Southeast Asian refugees were on AFDC at that time. Southeast Asian refugees get to California through both direct placement and secondary migration from other states. When categorically eligible for AFDC, these refugees are counted in the caseload even in the three-year interval in which the cost of their assistance is wholly covered by the federal government. During this interval they are considered time-eligible refugees. Thereafter the states pay a portion of refugee welfare costs. As of fiscal year 1984-85, the portion of refugees in the California caseload whose full federal support had expired was more than 70 percent.[6]

California has experienced a sizeable inflow of illegal immigrants in addition to the sanctioned refugee flows. At least initially, illegal immigrants are much less likely to raise welfare costs, since only citizens or legally resident aliens are eligible for AFDC.

Economic Conditions in California

Certain features of the economy are relevant to the analysis of welfare dependence, including employment and unemployment conditions and alternative wage levels available to those receiving aid or at risk of receiving it. The following sections examine some changes in these features in California.

Employment. Economic growth is often measured by growth in overall employment. As of July 1972, almost 8.2 million people in California were employed. Over the next 13 years this figure increased by 42 percent to 11.6 million.[7] As indicated earlier, during the same interval California's population grew by 26 percent. Over the years there also has been an increase in the number of jobs per person. While in 1972 there were 0.39 jobs per person, 13 years later this figure had increased by 10 percent to 0.43. These two facts indicate that California's economy has been doing quite well.

On the other hand, the situation for California's sub-population of females of child-bearing age shows no improvement during this interval. The number of jobs in California and the number of individuals in this sub-population grew at virtually identical rates. The finding that females of child-bearing age are holding their ground can be misleading if a large part of the job growth is in jobs for which poor female household heads are unlikely to be qualified.

The Unemployment Rate. The state has experienced two major recessions in the past 15 years. The first occurred during 1974–75; the second began in 1979 and produced maximum joblessness in 1982. Figure 4.1 presents the unemployment rate since 1972 to help fix the timing of recessions; as we shall see, recessions are associated with caseload growth. For later use, two 12-

Figure 4.1
California Unemployment Rate

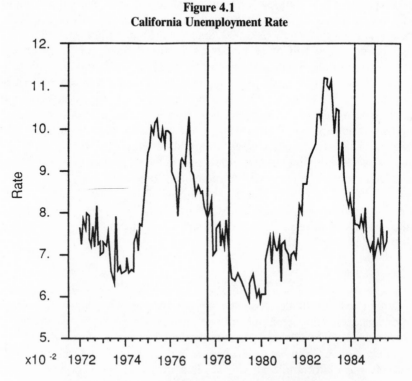

Note: Vertical lines show comparable unemployment periods.

month periods for which unemployment rates were low and average unemployment rates were about the same are marked on the graph.[8]

Employment in Selected Industries. Change in the welfare caseload is in part a result of aggregate unemployment conditions in California. Moreover, past research has shown that selected industries characterized as low-wage, high-turnover, and seasonal support those who are likely to move into and out of welfare.[9]

Table 4.2 presents the number of workers in all non-agricultural industries and in two low-wage, low-skill nondurable goods manufacturing industries. The concentration index in Table 4.2 is the percentage of women in a particular type of industry divided by the percentage of women in all non-agricultural industries. An employment concentration index larger than one means that the percentage of women in the particular industry is larger than the percentage of women in all non-agricultural industries.

Table 4.2
Wage and Salary Workers in Selected Nondurable Goods Industries,
1975 and 1985 (in Thousands)

Industry	Total Workers (9/1975)	Total Women Workers (9/1975)	Employment Concentration Index (9/1975)
Total Non-agricultural	7832.0	3155.0	1.00
Food & Kindred	209.8	73.4	.87
Apparel & Other Textile	86.8	64.7	1.85

Industry	Total Workers (9/1985)	Total Women Workers (9/1985)	Employment Concentration Index (9/1985)
Total Non-agricultural	10821.3	4726.8	1.00
Food & Kindred	207.7	76.9	.85
Apparel & Other Textile	103.4	72.9	1.61

Source: California Employment Development Department, **Interim Series of Wage and Salary Workers in Non-agricultural Establishments, by Industry.**

Note: Calculation procedures for employment concentration index are discussed in text.

The food and kindred products industry is selected because it has a strong seasonal component with high demand for work in summer and sharp declines thereafter. The concentration index for this industry is less than one, showing a slight underrepresentation of women workers, yet it employs a fairly high number of women workers in 1975 and a decade later.

The apparel and other textile products industry employs more than the average share of women workers in non-agricultural industries. Demand for workers in the apparel industry is not seasonal. Demand for workers in the two types of industries together does not show a decline from 1975 to 1985. This implies that the availability of low-wage, high turnover, and seasonal jobs has persisted over time to support those likely to move to and from welfare.

The figures in Table 4.2 provide additional interesting information. First, from 1975 to 1985 the share of jobs held by women workers in total non-agricultural industries has increased from 40 percent to 44 percent. Second, both the total number of workers and the total number of female workers in all non-agricultural industries increased from 1975 to 1985 by 38 percent and 50 percent, respectively. However, the increase in both low-skill industries together is only 4.9 percent for all workers and 8.5 percent for women workers. During the same period the sub-population of females of child-bearing age grew by slightly more than 28 percent. Thus, while there has been an increase in the number of low-skill jobs, the supply of these jobs, at least in the two types of industries analyzed here, seems not to have kept up with the growing number of females of child-bearing age.

Wages. Wage levels associated with low-skill jobs, in part, are expected to influence the decision of individuals to enter or exit welfare. Over time, in real terms, changes in the levels of these wages in relation to the level of welfare benefits can affect AFDC caseload growth. Consequently, when studying welfare dependence it is important to select wages that appropriately characterize the wages welfare recipients and those at risk of welfare can expect to receive in the marketplace in addition to analyzing the gain, if any, these wages pose relative to welfare benefits.

Figure 4.2 presents California's minimum wage and wages of receptionists in real terms. Receptionists' wages are selected because this occupation is representative of low-skill, low-wage jobs that have not undergone technological changes from the 1970s to the 1980s. Furthermore, receptionist jobs are thought to be widespread throughout California.[10] The occupation of receptionist is representative of the type of job for which a typical AFDC recipient might be qualified. Minimum wage is selected since it reflects the lowest legal wage that a recipient could earn and therefore represents the minimal standard of living provided by the private economy.[11]

When comparing AFDC payments to wages of standard jobs in the private sector, in real terms, minimum wage has declined by about 25 percent since 1978. An index of wages of receptionists in the three largest metropolitan statistical areas of California shows a decline of about 4 percent over the

Figure 4.2
Wages

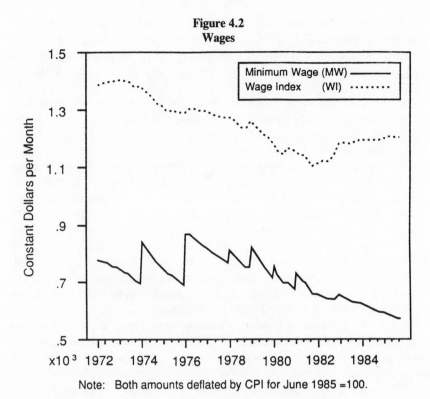

Note: Both amounts deflated by CPI for June 1985 =100.

same period.[12] On balance it appears that from 1978 through 1985 California's welfare benefits posted a significant gain relative to minimum-wage occupations but did not gain relative to common wages for low-skill work in the private economy.[13]

As expected, Figure 4.2 shows that receptionists' wages are higher and have a smoother and more constant variation than the sawtooth nature of the minimum wage. This is because, as do other wages in the private sector, receptionists' wages continuously respond to changing economic events, while then minimum wage is raised periodically by governmental fiat, as are AFDC and food stamp benefits. Receptionists' jobs are more attractive than minimum-wage jobs since they offer higher levels of income that vary less with inflation.

California's Economy and AFDC-Basic Dynamics

General economic trends in California have important implications for AFDC caseload dynamics. First, since over the years the total number of jobs in California has grown at about the same rate as the number of females of child-bearing age, growth in California's total employment would be expected to have at most a neutral effect on caseload dynamics. Second, during non-recessionary periods California's unemployment rate stayed between 6 and 8 percent, and fluctuations within this range may affect caseload movement and size. The recessionary periods California has experienced also would be expected to impact caseload growth. Third, although jobs have been available in the low-skill, low-wage industries examined here, employment growth in these industries has lagged behind the growth of California's sub-population of females of child-bearing age. Employment trends in these industries suggest that women with few skills now may be more likely to enter welfare and find it more difficult to leave via the route of employment. This conclusion is tentative, however, because employment growth in other low-skill industries may have kept up with growth in the number of females of child-bearing age. Fourth, since in recent years welfare benefits have posted a significant gain relative to the minimum wage, welfare may have become a more attractive income alternative to those at risk of welfare receipt who can expect only minimum-wage employment. For those who qualify for better-paying jobs, such as receptionist, the relative attractiveness of welfare has not changed in recent years—welfare and employment for this group post about the same percentage decline in the standard of living offered.

On the whole, trends in California's economy probably are unfavorable to households at risk of welfare receipt. While California's economy is robust and growing, some parts of the labor market in which welfare recipients are likely to participate do not seem to be. Women are working more in California but probably not at jobs for which the typical welfare recipient is qualified.

TRENDS IN AFDC-BASIC AND AFDC-UP CASELOADS

Earlier discussions provided background information about the state's population and economy. Some of the state's sub-populations and economic conditions will be accounted for in Chapter 6 in modeling AFDC-Basic caseload accessions and terminations. The following sections examine three sets of trends. The first deals with patterns of change in the flow of families to and from welfare and movements between AFDC-Basic and AFDC-UP caseloads. The second deals with changes in two caseloads. The third deals with changes in the characteristics of welfare recipients. After these trends are considered, the incidence of welfare dependence over the years is examined.

Patterns of Change

Changes in the caseload from one period to the next are the result of adding new cases (accessions to welfare), closing cases (terminations), and, if one is considering each sub-program separately, adjusting for movement of families from one program component to another. In studying these dynamics it is important, if possible, to normalize by looking at rates instead of total numbers because some caseload changes since 1972 simply reflect general population growth.

Structural changes in welfare will show up as changes in these rates over time. Concern should center on increases in accessions because this means that people are more frequently experiencing the kinds of life events— pregnancy, job loss, separation, and so on—that precipitate going onto welfare. We should be concerned about termination rates because lower termination rates mean that the average duration of welfare spells is increasing. That is one facet of welfare dependence. Movement from one sub-program to another is interesting because these shifts identify changes in the status of parents in the household. A move from AFDC-UP to AFDC-Basic, for example, occurs as the result of a separation or when the unemployed principal earner becomes disabled by illness or accident.

The following are considered in order: accessions, terminations, movement between sub-programs, and changing caseload dynamics.

Accessions. Figure 4.3 shows rates of accession. This figure is the most difficult to normalize. The number of women age 15 to 44 in the state minus an estimate of the number of all open AFDC-Basic and AFDC-UP cases whose head is from that age group was used for the denominator. This calculation produces roughly the total number of all non-dependent women of child-bearing age in the state. The estimate is rough because some AFDC house-

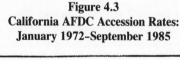

Figure 4.3
California AFDC Accession Rates:
January 1972–September 1985

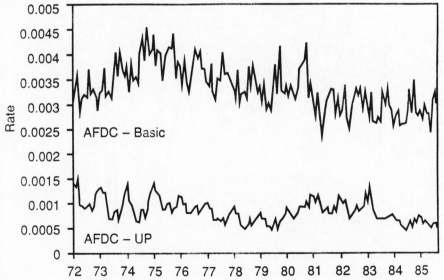

holds do not include adult women, and the correction data are spotty for the approximately 8 percent of women in AFDC who are over 44.[14]

The general impression from Figure 4.3 is that accession rates have not changed much, especially since about 1975. Every month about .4 percent of women not on welfare go onto welfare as either AFDC-Basic (.33 percent) or AFDC-UP (.08 percent) cases. Both programs saw substantial increases during the period 1979–81; this probably is a result of the recession and the inflow of refugees. Since that time, accession rates in AFDC-Basic have been very slightly lower than they were between 1975 and 1980. For AFDC-UP the period of expansion stretched out to 1983; more recently, accessions have slowed for this sub-program as well.

Terminations. Figure 4.4 shows rates of termination. For each month this is the total number of cases in the program leaving AFDC (either Basic or UP) divided by the beginning-of-month caseload. Obviously, there is much more movement in AFDC-UP than in AFDC-Basic. Looking first at AFDC-Basic, termination rates appear remarkably constant over the long run. The only significant event is the spike in November 1981 created by OBRA closures.[15] Tabulation of the data suggests that termination rates for the period 1978–81 were slightly higher than for 1982–84, but this could be associated with recession.

Figure 4.4
California AFDC Termination Rates:
January 1972–September 1985

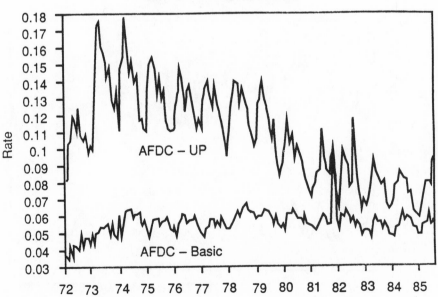

Looking at AFDC-UP one is struck by at least three things. The first is the seasonality of the series: obviously, many of the cases that open in winter close in spring. The second is the pronounced downward trend in termination rates. The AFDC-UP caseload is up because accession rates are up, at least until recently (see Figure 4.3), and termination rates are down. This trend is evident in the data accumulated before refugees began to arrive in large numbers, but it was clearly accelerated by that influx. The third observation is that there is a lot more turnover in AFDC-UP than in AFDC-Basic.

Overall, termination rates always have been higher in AFDC-UP than in AFDC-Basic, in part because the AFDC-UP program provides aid to individuals with work histories. Individuals in AFDC-UP are more likely to find employment and terminate than those in AFDC-Basic. Moreover, for individuals in AFDC-UP, once employment is obtained, the 100-hour rule makes terminations likely.

Intraprogram Movement. The intraprogram movement rate is the portion of AFDC-Basic cases that switch to AFDC-UP and vice versa. Rates of program transfer appear in Figure 4.5. These changes are not included as terminations in the data used to make Figure 4.4. Movement from AFDC-UP to AFDC-Basic far outstrips movement in the opposite direction. Such adjustments occur either when an unemployed parent, usually the father, leaves or when the

Figure 4.5
California AFDC Intraprogram Transfers:
January 1972–September 1985

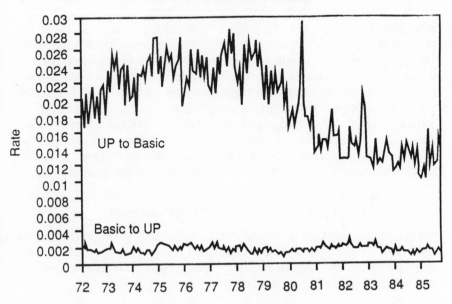

Table 4.3
Changes in Caseload Dynamics, 1978–84

		Average Monthly Rate of							
Time Period	Unem- ployment Rate (%)	Termi- nations(%)		Acces- sions(%)		Program Change(%)		Caseload Change(%)	
		UP	Basic	UP	Basic	UP to Basic	Basic to UP	UP	Basic
9/77-8/78	7.5	12.1	5.7	.08	.34	2.5	.19	-.01	-.79
3/84-2/85	7.6	7.1	5.2	.06	.28	1.3	.17	.07	-.52

Source: Calculations derived from data provided by California Department of Social Services.

unemployed principal earner becomes disabled. For reasons that are unclear, it appears that AFDC-UP families are more stable now than they were prior to 1979. This may be attributable in part to the influx of refugee families into the AFDC-UP program; at least for the time being these families may be more stable than historically has been the case for dependent two-adult households.

Changing Caseload Dynamics. In Figure 4.1 two periods were delineated, one in the late 1970s and the other more recent, during which unemployment rates were falling and, over the entire interval, virtually identical. Table 4.3 presents the results of calculation of mean termination, accession, program change, and caseload growth rates for these intervals. Despite similarity of economic conditions and roughly equivalent rates of caseload accession, caseloads fell less rapidly during the more recent period (AFDC-Basic actually grew). There is less turnover in the more recent period in both the AFDC-Basic and AFDC-UP caseloads, principally because of reduced rates of termination. The lower termination rate in AFDC-UP is associated in part with the increase in the number of refugees in the caseload, but the downward trend in termination rates (see Figure 4.4) predates the arrival of the refugees.

The AFDC-Basic and AFDC-UP Caseloads

Figures 4.6 and 4.7 present the AFDC-Basic and AFDC-UP caseloads since 1970. Caseload trends are considered from 1970 in order to place caseload growth over the last 14 years in perspective. The caseload numbers are cases open at the beginning of each month.[16]

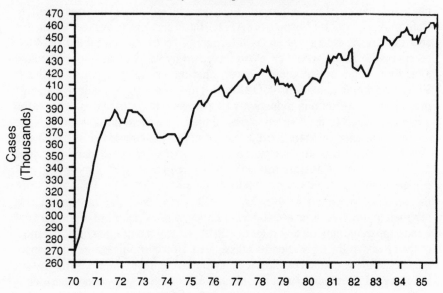

Figure 4.6
California AFDC-Basic Caseload:
January 1970–September 1985

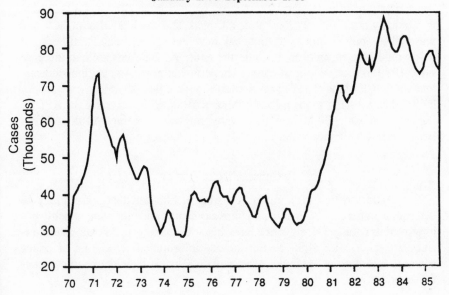

Figure 4.7
California AFDC-UP Caseload:
January 1970–September 1985

Looking first at AFDC-Basic, four observations will figure in the discussion that follows. First, between January 1970 and summer 1971 the caseload grew by a tremendous amount and at an extraordinarily rapid rate. This is the last phase of the caseload explosion that precipitated the California Welfare Reform Act of 1971.[17] Second, the AFDC-Basic caseload is cyclically sensitive and appears to respond with a lag to economic recovery. During the 1974–75 recession the AFDC-Basic caseload increased by 9.5 percent, and it was only after three years of economic recovery that the caseload began to decline.[18] Third, the implementation of OBRA in November 1981 produced an immediate and precipitous reduction (3.3 percent) in the caseload. This came about as a result of the restriction placed upon household gross income.[19] The second reduction, in March 1982, occurred with elimination of the $30 and one-third disregards for all households that had reported earnings since November 1981. This time the effect was a reduction of slightly less than 2 percent of the caseload. Fourth, following full imposition of the OBRA reforms, the caseload began to recover rapidly. By early 1983 the case count had returned to pre-OBRA levels, and it continued to grow. Simple extrapolation of trends apparent immediately prior to OBRA implementation suggests that most of the effects of the legislation had dissipated. However, this ignores the consequences of the continued expansion in unemployment rates after 1981 apparent in Figure 4.1. Without control for this and other factors, one cannot be sure.

The first thing to note about AFDC-UP, in Figure 4.7, is that the scale is much different from AFDC-Basic. In July 1985 there were approximately 580,000 AFDC-Basic cases and 77,000 AFDC-UP cases, with a ratio of over 7:1. As would be anticipated, the AFDC-UP caseload shows considerable cyclical sensitivity: Between July 1974 and July 1975 the caseload increased by one-third.[20] But as bad as the 1974–75 recession was, the more recent recession was much worse: The caseload almost tripled. The caseload also has a strong seasonal component that leads to a peak in winter and a trough in fall.

It would be a mistake to attribute the entire AFDC-UP caseload increase since 1979 to recession or any other single factor. Some calculations indicate that about half of the change is attributable to the influx of refugees, in particular Southeast Asians, to the rolls. By October 1984, 37.8 percent of the AFDC-UP caseload, some 28,500 families, were refugees; 4.3 percent of the AFDC-Basic caseload, another 19,862 families, were refugees.[21]

Recipient Characteristics

The characteristics of families receiving public assistance are likely to determine, in part, the size of the welfare caseload. While the state recently has improved its data-gathering procedures, historical data on recipients' characteristics are spotty and often do not include information on factors of policy concern. Information has been assembled on selected recipient characteristics for several years.

Table 4.4
General Case Characteristics, 1977–84,
Group Percentage of Total Caseload

Program and Group	1977 (Oct.)	1980 (July)	1982 (Oct.)	1984 (Oct.)
AFDC-Basic				
Children < 6	35.8 %	42.0 %	43.6 %	47.3 %
Mothers < 21	13.7	14.7	15.1	11.8
Mothers > 29	41.2	42.5	41.8	39.8
AFDC-UP				
Children < 6	45.6	49.5	51.8	51.0
Mothers < 21	13.9	16.4	10.9	8.8
Mothers > 29	45.0	41.4	46.9	46.2

Source: State of California, Department of Social Services, **Aid to Families with Dependent Children: Recipient Characteristics Survey,** various issues.

Table 4.4 presents the percentage of children under six years of age out of all children in the caseload, the percentage of young mothers (under age 21), and the percentage of older mothers (over age 29) on the caseload in various years. These age groups are selected because past research has shown that the likelihood of closure varies with the age of recipients.

Table 4.4 shows that the percentages of mothers under 21 and those over 29 have gone down in both AFDC-Basic and AFDC-UP caseloads. The reasons for these declines are unclear. There is a consistently increasing percentage of young non-school-age children in both AFDC-Basic and AFDC-UP case-loads. If non-school-age children impede mothers from leaving welfare via work or marriage, then this would contribute to the slight decrease in case closures.

Table 4.5 presents information on family size and the share of families reporting earnings. The data indicate that family size in AFDC-Basic has declined by 16 percent since 1972. In part, this is due to the decrease in the number of children per family in the general population. Family size in AFDC-UP varies, but since the AFDC-Basic caseload is much larger, the former trend dominates. As would be expected from the discussion of OBRA in Chapter 2, the incidence of reported earnings among recipient families in AFDC-Basic is down. This need not mean, of course, that job taking is down;

Table 4.5
General Case Characteristics, 1972–84,
Size and Earnings

Program and Group	1972 (July)	1977 (Oct.)	1980 (July)	1982 (Oct.)	1984 (Oct.)
AFDC–Basic					
FBU size	3.2	2.9	2.8	2.7	2.7
Reported Earnings (%)	n.a.	13.1	11.4	4.9	6.5
Average Earnings*	n.a.	$691.81	$462.42	$245.82	$310.47
AFDC–UP					
FBU size	4.5	4.4	4.5	4.3	4.6
Reported Earnings (%)	n.a.	12.2	10.2	6.4	12.0
Average Earnings*	n.a.	$402.22	$501.61	$306.72	$261.29

Source: State of California, Department of Social Services, **Aid to Families with Dependent Children: Recipient Characteristics Survey**, various issues.

* Average earnings of those who work and receive welfare deflated by the CPI (6/1985).

it may be that people who take jobs while receiving welfare are less likely now to continue receiving benefits. The employment rate in AFDC-UP has returned to pre-recession levels. This is consistent with the contention that it is the 100-hours rule, not work incentive disregards, that dominates behavior in AFDC-UP.[22]

Table 4.5 shows average gross earnings of recipients with reported earnings. For October 1982, after passage of OBRA, the average AFDC-Basic earner's gross earnings fell by over 60 percent, while the average for AFDC-UP fell by about 24 percent. It may be that the sharp decrease in gross earnings among AFDC-Basic earners is due to a decrease in their work efforts, perhaps associated with the work disincentives accompanying OBRA. Interestingly, AFDC-UP earnings have continued to fall since 1980, whereas among AFDC-Basic cases average earnings have recovered somewhat. This may be due to the increasing percentage of refugees in the AFDC-UP caseload who surely experience more barriers to employment than the average recipient.

These numbers have two implications. One is that since family size is down in AFDC-Basic, the number of people on welfare has increased at a less rapid rate than the number of welfare cases. This demographic shift helps to control growth in the number of people on welfare. The second is that welfare costs per case in AFDC-Basic are higher since OBRA because there is less offset of benefits by earnings. This is apparent in Table 4.5 since both the percentage of earners and the average amount each earns have decreased substantially with the onset of OBRA. The overall effect of OBRA on welfare costs depends on the extent to which the effect of measured costs per case has been offset by the effect of OBRA's stricter eligibility requirements.

Incidence of Welfare Dependence

Changes in the welfare caseload alone do not allow for a full understanding of the incidence of welfare dependence; demographic shifts also must be taken into account. Growth in the caseload must be contrasted with growth in the number of families in the population, while growth in the number of individuals in the caseload must be contrasted with growth in the number of individuals in the population. Table 4.6 suggests that 1972 is a good starting point for comparing growth in the number of people in the caseload with growth in the number of people in the population. The AFDC-Basic caseload explosion prior to 1972 has been explained primarily by rapid exhaustion of the welfare-eligible population. This occurred for reasons that are not clear. To attempt to explain caseload growth without including variables that account for exhaustion of the pool of eligibles would lead to misspecification of a model set to explain caseload growth.[23]

Table 4.6 presents people on welfare instead of cases and changes in the caseload since 1972 instead of 1970. Calculations also are presented with and without refugees in order to account for their impact on the incidence of welfare dependence in California. Without adjustment for refugees, population has grown 2.7 times faster than people on AFDC since 1972. But the number of children in AFDC families has grown more rapidly than the number of children in the general population. The consequence of this is relatively minor. The small proportion of children on assistance amounts to the difference between 15.8 percent (1985) and 15.6 percent (1972). If Southeast Asian refugees are not counted, the total number of people on AFDC has declined since that year and the number of children on AFDC has declined absolutely and as a proportion of all children in the general population.[24]

Table 4.6
Changes in Population and Dependence, 1972–85,
by Group

Population Component	Percentage Change 7/1/72–7/1/85
California Population	26.3%
California Population minus Southeast Asian Refugees	24.7
California Children	3.5
California Children minus Southeast Asian Refugee Children	0.9
Persons on AFDC	9.6
Persons on AFDC minus Southeast Asian Refugees on AFDC	-1.9
Children on AFDC	4.7
Children on AFDC minus Southeast Asian Refugee Children on AFDC	-8.1

Source: Calculation sources cited in text.

Note: Estimates of refugees on AFDC are for October 1984.

In summary, the aggregate caseload statistics suggest that the incidence of welfare dependence has not increased significantly since 1972. If Southeast Asian refugees are not included, the incidence of AFDC receipt within the general population and among children has declined absolutely. The recent surge in welfare dependence in the state can be associated principally with U.S. foreign policy. But while the data suggest that little ground has been lost, it is hard to find examples of significant improvement.

SUMMARY AND ISSUES

California has undergone demographic and economic changes over the past 13 years. The percentage of females of child-bearing age has grown much faster than the percentage of children in California. Family size is down, and California has experienced a large influx of refugees in recent years. On the other hand, the percentage of female household heads with children and the poverty rate for this group have remained virtually constant from 1976 to the present. Yet this group's poverty rate has always exceeded the poverty rate of households with children headed by males. Thus, although the categorically eligible sub-population has not become worse off over time, its economic situation has not improved.

Overall employment in California has been growing, but employment in certain types of industries hiring low-skilled workers for low wages has not grown as fast as the percentage of females of child-bearing age. If this trend continues it could have serious consequences for welfare recipients.

Thus far it has been shown that the AFDC caseload responds to some of the changes discussed above. The influx of refugees in recent years has had an impact on the AFDC caseload. The downward trend in family size in the general population is reflected in the AFDC caseload. If this latter trend continues, it will help to contain welfare costs.

The caseload probably has become more dependent since it contains fewer wage earners than in the past. If this trend continues, welfare costs per case will increase. If reducing welfare dependence is a policy objective, then viable economic alternatives to welfare need to be created. In real terms, minimum wage has fallen much more than welfare benefits in recent years. If minimum wage had kept up with inflation, a portion of the at-risk population might not have applied for welfare.

Many variables influence welfare accessions, terminations, and caseload size, and a multivariate model is required to sort out their individual effects. The specification of a model and the hypothesized effects of individual variables are discussed in Chapter 6. Chapter 5 examines the extent to which California's AFDC caseload and its demographic and economic context differ from that of the rest of the nation.

NOTES

1. Cited population figures are from unpublished estimates supplied by the California Department of Finance, Sacramento.

2. In the accessions equation in Chapter 6 the population at risk of welfare receipt (potentially welfare eligibles) is calculated by subtracting the number of females age 15 to 44 on welfare from the number of females in that age range in the general population. This is done because the number of accessions per month, not the caseload, is modeled. In this chapter the AFDC caseload is considered for the purpose of discussion. Consequently, all females age 15 to 44 in California are considered.

3. The percentage of female-headed households includes those on AFDC.

4. Demographic-economic status of the population was supplied by the California Department of Finance, Sacramento. These yearly figures are estimates developed from the Current Population Survey and are subject to sampling error proportional to the size of the population estimated.

5. For more information on refugees in California and on AFDC for October 1984 see California Health and Welfare Agency, Department of Social Services, *Refugees Receiving Cash Assistance Characteristics Survey* (Sacramento: July 1985).

6. Refugee totals are from California Department of Social Services for 1985. Estimates of total refugees in California are from California Department of Finance for 1985. Caseload data were supplied by the Department of Social Services.

7. Aggregate employment data for California were furnished by California Health and Welfare Agency, Employment Development Department, Employment Data and Research Division, Estimates and Economic Research Group, (Report LF101).

8. Ibid.

9. For details see Venti's study discussed in M.B. Sanger, *Welfare of the Poor* (New York: Academic Press, 1979), p. 39.

10. In 1980 receptionists' jobs constituted 0.8 percent of all California jobs. See California Employment Development Department, *Projections of Employment, 1980–1990, by Industry and Occupation* (Sacramento: 1985).

11. The CPI is used to deflate the wage index and minimum wage. The CPI includes medical costs and mortgage payments, thus reflecting the real purchasing power of those outside the welfare system.

12. The averages for the years 1978 and 1985 of minimum wage and wage index, both deflated by the CPI, were used to find the percentage decrease.

13. Taking the average AFDC plus food stamp benefits deflated by the CNI for a family of three for the years 1978 and 1985, the decrease is 7 percent.

14. For details see Appendix C.

15. In California some of OBRA's provisions were introduced in November, rather than October, 1981, as in most other states. Some states obtained a waiver from the federal government to delay implementation of OBRA's provisions; California did not. California statutes require that, unless urgent, any major changes in AFDC eligibility rules must be considered in a public hearing process. OBRA's provisions were introduced as needing urgent implementation, but this was opposed by some individuals and the matter was brought before the California Supreme Court. The California legislature subsequently passed two bills that allowed implementation of OBRA's provisions in November 1981.

16. All caseload numbers come from the California Health and Welfare Agency, Department of Social Services, Statistical Services Branch, *Aid to Families with Dependent Children: Cash Grant Caseload Movement and Expenditures Report* (Sacramento: January 1972 to December 1984, monthly reports). AFDC cases opened on behalf of children in foster care or group homes are not included.

17. For a discussion of this episode see C. Rence and M. Wiseman, "The California Welfare Reform Act and Participation in AFDC," *Journal of Human Resources* 13 (1978): 37–57.

18. Caution should be exercised in looking at the figures because of the exaggeration of caseload movements created by scaling. For example, the fluctuations apparent in Figure 4.6 involve changes of less than 10 percent in the total caseload.

19. For a discussion of OBRA's provisions see Chapters 2 and 3.

20. Growth of the AFDC-UP caseload in 1970–71 is attributable to the sharp post-Vietnam recession and a series of major strikes. The subsequent decline reflects economic recovery and tightening of eligibility rules. See Rence and Wiseman, "The California Welfare Reform Act," pp. 54–55.

21. For sources of refugee numbers see note 6.

22. Earnings received in AFDC-UP are subject to the same disregard procedures

as are applied in AFDC-Basic. As a result, OBRA might also be expected to reduce the incidence of employment in this program. Two factors reduce OBRA effects. The first is that earnings in AFDC-UP families are generally from the spouse of the principal earner and are insufficient to meet the needs of larger AFDC-UP families. Second, expected duration of AFDC-UP cases is shorter. Secondary earners in such families retain jobs even with low net immediate return because they expect their households to leave assistance in the foreseeable future.

23. See Rence and Wiseman, "The California Welfare Reform Act," pp. 54–55.

24. A few caveats are in order regarding Table 4.6. First, the state's Southeast Asian refugee count for July 1, 1985, was accepted. Second, as the table indicates, all of the estimates of refugees on welfare are actually for October 1984. The numbers probably are not changing fast enough for this to be a problem. Third, it is not known what proportion of the 335,000 refugees are children; it is assumed that half are. About 61 percent of refugees receiving any kind of assistance (not just AFDC) are children. Finally, for counts of refugees on welfare all members of refugee families, even children born in the United States, are included. The welfare dependence of U.S.-born children of refugees is considered to be part of the refugee problem, but these children apparently are not included in the state's estimate of total refugees in the population.

5

The Nation's AFDC Caseload
and Its Environment

In this chapter comparisons are made between the rest of the nation's AFDC caseload and California's. Since OBRA's provisions were implemented nationally with an expected reduction in the AFDC caseload, it is also of interest to compare the immediate reduction and subsequent recovery of caseloads in California and the rest of the nation.

Since the AFDC caseload is expected to be the outcome of complex interactions among demographic and economic developments and the welfare system, striking differences between caseload growth rates in California and the rest of the nation may be explained by these factors. In this chapter some of these factors are used to explain differences between caseload growth rates.

NATIONAL CASELOAD TRENDS AND THE EFFECTS OF OBRA

This section begins by comparing AFDC-Basic caseload growth rates for California and the rest of the nation in order to establish the appropriate time periods for comparison of demographic and economic developments. Both AFDC-Basic and AFDC-UP caseloads are examined, but the major focus is on the AFDC-Basic component. This is because all jurisdictions have the AFDC-Basic component, it constitutes the largest portion of the total caseload, and the empirical portion of the study analyzes only this component.

AFDC-Basic

Caseload trends for the nation's AFDC-Basic caseload are presented in Figure 5.1. The caseload numbers are cases receiving cash assistance during each month. The numbers of Foster Care cases are excluded from the numbers

Figure 5.1
Rest of the Nation AFDC-Basic Caseload: January 1970–December 1985

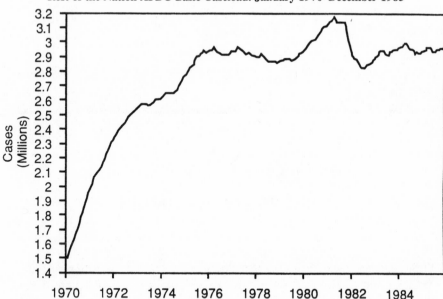

of AFDC-Basic cases. This is done everywhere in this study. In addition, these numbers exclude the number of cases receiving cash assistance in California. From 1970 to 1985 California's AFDC-Basic caseload ranged from a low of 12 percent to a high of 14 percent of the nation's AFDC-Basic caseload.

These data, reported to the federal government by each state on a quarterly basis, are the only numbers kept nationally. For the federal government, which is interested mainly in welfare expenditures, this information is adequate. Better suited to the purpose of studying welfare caseload dynamics, however, is the number of cases open at the beginning of each month.[1] This figure is used in the empirical portion of the present study.

Several factors should be noted in Figure 5.1. First, the number of families on AFDC-Basic across the nation rose by 100 percent from January 1970 to December 1985, reaching a maximum of about 3.2 million cases in March 1981, soon before passage of OBRA. As in California, in the early 1970s the rest of the nation's AFDC-Basic caseload grew at a very fast rate. From the beginning of 1970 to the end of 1971, the rest of the nation's AFDC-Basic caseload grew by 831,00 families, an increase of 56 percent in just two years. However, while rapid growth of the caseload in California had ended in summer 1971, the rest of the nation's caseload sustained a double-digit growth rate until early 1973. After this time, the growth rate of the national caseload substantially decreased.

Also evident from Figure 5.1, the remaining national AFDC-Basic caseload appears to be slightly seasonal and cyclically sensitive. However, the curve is smoother than the one previously shown for the California's AFDC-Basic caseload (see Figure 4.6). The combination of numerous states' caseloads is partially responsible for this smoothing effect. Also, a graph of the number of cases open during the month is smoother than a graph of the number of cases at the beginning of the month, and seasonal sensitivity in the caseload is not as easy to discern.[2]

The rest of the nation's AFDC-Basic caseload grew during a recessionary period, November 1973 to March 1975, by 6.1 percent year. From the time the nation's caseload recovered from this recessionary period to the beginning of the most recent recession it grew by only 1.7 percent per year. These figures closely resemble the corresponding figures for California.[3] Finally, during the last major recession, July 1981 to November 1982, the nation's AFDC-Basic caseload declined by about 7 percent per year. The main reason for this large unexpected decline in a recessionary period was OBRA.

Coinciding with the implementation of OBRA's provisions, the nation's AFDC-Basic caseload underwent an abrupt decline of 8.1 percent.[4] This immediate reduction in the caseload began in October because OBRA's provisions were signed into law in August 1981 and were to be implemented throughout much of the nation beginning in October of that year.[5]

The national AFDC-Basic caseload continued to decline after October 1981 as states implemented stricter eligibility criteria. From October 1981 to June 1982 the nation's AFDC-Basic caseload declined by over 10 percent. Since the caseload was not otherwise in a steady state during this period, this figure underestimates the actual effect of OBRA.[6] In fact, as in California, the nation was in the midst of a severe recession, when, all else equal, much caseload growth would be expected. Finally, in contrast to California's AFDC-Basic caseload, Figure 5.1 shows that as of the end of 1985 the nation's AFDC-Basic caseload had not recovered its previous high level. After an initial spurt in growth that slowed soon after the recession ended, it did not grow appreciably.

California's AFDC-Basic caseload grew more than twice as fast as the rest of the nation's after the initial effects of OBRA dissipated. This is apparent from comparing Figure 4.6 and 5.1, but calculations show that a striking difference in growth rates began during 1980. OBRA's effects obscure this difference somewhat but not entirely. Comparing the two figures suggests that the initial caseload drop due to OBRA was greater in the rest of the nation than in California. The percentage decline in California was one-half that in the nation, perhaps because California's caseload growth rate was double the rest of the nation's during the 1980s. This situation is in sharp contrast to growth rates found after the caseload explosion and recession in the 1970s. From mid-1975 to mid-1980 caseloads in California and the rest of the nation grew on average by 0.96 percent and 0.82 percent, respectively, per year. While the graphs suggest that the state's caseload grew a little more erratically during this period, these are the times when they resemble each other the most.

In sum, California's AFDC-Basic caseload generally has fluctuated in a fashion similar to that of the rest of the nation. Two periods of dissimilarity, however, stand out. First, after the welfare explosion in California, its caseload experienced a downturn not seen in the rest of the nation. Second, California's AFDC-Basic caseload now is growing at a much faster rate than the national average.[7]

Because of similarities and differences in caseload growth rates, the intervals between 1975-80 and 1980-85 provide an interesting backdrop for comparing developments in California with those in the rest of the nation. Since economic and demographic conditions also determine caseload growth, differences, if any, between the rest of the nation and California along these lines also will be examined.

AFDC-UP

Figure 5.2 presents the number of cases receiving cash assistance in the AFDC-UP program during each month. As in the previous figure, these numbers exclude the number of cases receiving cash assistance in California. From 1970 to 1985 California's AFDC-UP caseload constituted from about 26 percent to about 38 percent of the national AFDC-UP caseload.

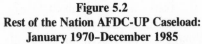

Figure 5.2
Rest of the Nation AFDC-UP Caseload:
January 1970–December 1985

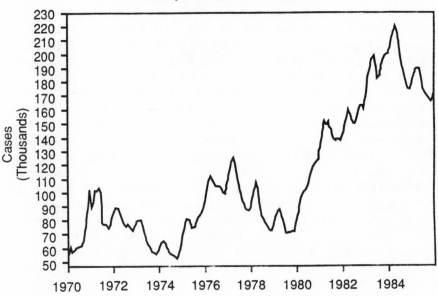

From 1970 to 1985 the rest of the nation's unemployed-parent component increased by almost 200 percent. Some of the growth in the number of AFDC-UP families can be attributed to the influx of refugees. To a lesser extent this increase may be attributed to the fact that during this time a larger number of states have added this component than have eliminated it.

When comparing Figure 5.2 with Figure 4.7, the resemblance between AFDC-UP caseloads in California and the rest of the nation is striking. As in California, the national AFDC-UP caseload shows considerable cyclical sensitivity and seasonality. The seasonality of the national AFDC-UP caseload leads to a peak in winter and a trough in fall. During the major recession of the 1970s the national caseload increased by one-half. During the 1980s recessionary period it increased by one-sixth. But the AFDC-UP caseload began to increase by a large amount prior to the beginning of the last recessionary period. From 1980 to 1984 the caseload increased by 150 percent. Statistical data for the U.S. show that other states have experienced an influx of refugees in the late 1970s. Most likely this influx has also affected the growth of AFDC-UP caseloads across the nation.[8]

The national AFDC-UP caseload most resembles California's in the 1980s. Both caseloads did not increase with the passage of OBRA but increased during the recession and the large influx of refugees. Without a full-scale statistical analysis the effects of multiple complex factors on the caseload cannot be separated.

Characteristics of AFDC Families

As discussed in Chapter 4, some of the characteristics of AFDC families in California changed over the last 14 years. Two of these in particular can affect caseload growth: the decline in family size and the decline in the percentage of recipient earners, which is a corollary of the implementation of OBRA.

The decline in family size reflects a nationwide change in the general population that is expected to continue.[9] The greatest decline has occurred among AFDC-Basic, rather than AFDC-UP families. From 1973 to 1982 the nationwide average AFDC-Basic family size, excluding California, decreased by 17 percent, from 3.46 persons per family to 2.86 persons per family. The picture is different for families on AFDC-UP, which, on the average, declined by only 11 percent during this period. Among these families the average decline was from 4.75 to 4.21 persons per family.[10]

In considering both the national AFDC-Basic and AFDC-UP components of the AFDC program, the overall decline in AFDC family size has been due primarily to the decline in the number of child recipients per family. In the rest of the nation, during 1986 the average AFDC family contained two children. After a steady decline throughout the 1970s, the number of children has stabilized at around two in the 1980s, with family size hovering at three persons.[11]

From the perspective of those concerned with welfare costs, the national decline in AFDC family size across the country throughout the 1970s and 1980s is a positive trend. Smaller families are less expensive to support. They also provide fewer obstacles when moving to employment or marriage, two main paths to self-sufficiency. The decrease in family size nationwide is evident also in California. The average number of adults and children in each assistance unit showed similar rates of decline. The only difference is that the average size of welfare households in California is very slightly smaller than the average for the rest of the nation. This has been true for the last 15 years. Since the decline in AFDC family size in California in the 1980s mirrors the national average, the gap between the two caseload growth rates is not explained by this factor.

An important nationwide change in the financial circumstances of AFDC recipients came about in recent years. In the rest of the nation, as in California, the percentage of earners on welfare has declined significantly as a response to OBRA. National statistics, adjusted to exclude California, show that prior to OBRA, while there was never a very large portion of recipients with earned income (usually about 12 percent), earnings accounted for over 83 percent of non-assistance AFDC income. As in California, recipients' earnings as a source of non-assistance income declined dramatically nationwide after passage of OBRA.[12]

In the rest of the nation the incidence of cases with any earnings declined sharply from 11.8 percent in May 1981 to 5.8 percent in May 1982. As would be expected, the largest decline during this period occurred among full-time earners, a decline from 6 percent to 1 percent. Moreover, lower non-assistance income levels were more typical in May 1982 than they were in May 1981. In May 1982 the percentage of earners with earnings of $200 or less represented 25 percent of cases, while 12 months earlier they represented 44 percent of families with earnings.[13]

From a cost savings perspective, it is not clear whether the higher welfare costs per case since passage of OBRA have been offset by savings incurred from caseload reductions. However, it is quite clear that OBRA had a substantial impact on the share of earners on AFDC across the nation. Overall, the financial circumstances of AFDC recipients in the 1980s in California did not deviate from the average elsewhere in the nation. Interestingly, the OBRA reforms seem not to have precipitated the accelerated growth rates of California's caseload during the 1980s. Even though the timing of the two events coincided, the cause of the burst in growth lies elsewhere. The difference in caseload growth between California and the nation still needs explaining.

Perhaps it is other characteristics that are strikingly different in California from the rest of the nation. Unfortunately, the information that the federal government gathers about other characteristics of welfare recipients is not separated by AFDC program component. This creates problems when analyzing changes in characteristics of recipients that are expected to affect one component more than another. In the case of the portion of earners on the AFDC-Basic rolls, the effect of OBRA may be underestimated since AFDC-UP earners are counted but theoretically should not be affected by the OBRA reforms.

Two AFDC family characteristics in California, namely, family size and percentage of earners, are not strikingly different from the rest of the nation. Due to lack of data, it is impossible to ascertain whether other characteristics of AFDC householders in California, such as the percentage of young mothers, the percentage of children whose parents are unmarried, or the percentage of children less than six years of age, were strikingly different from the national average. From demographic data on all California and United States residents, it appears that very few differences exist.

NATIONAL DEMOGRAPHIC TRENDS

Growth of the AFDC-Basic caseloads in California and in the rest of the nation has occurred in the context of changing economic conditions and demographic trends. The following discussion compares changes in total population, the size of the potentially welfare eligible population, and their respective birth rates in California and the rest of the nation. The influx of refugees to California also is placed in the larger context of the growth in refugee populations in the rest of the United States. The comparisons help to explain the differences observed in growth rates of AFDC-Basic caseloads and enable us to develop a sense of how typical the California experience is.

The Sub-populations

In 1985 California's AFDC-Basic caseload constituted about 14 percent of the total national AFDC-Basic caseload. This can be explained in part by the fact that for many decades California's total population constituted a larger share of the U.S. total population than any other state in the union. Moreover, for many years the state has sustained a much higher rate of growth in total population than the rest of the nation. From 1975 to 1985 California's growth rate was more than double that of the rest of the nation.[14]

From 1975 to 1985 growth in the number of females age 15 to 44, a measure of the potentially eligible welfare population, has been higher in California than in the rest of the nation.[15] During both five-year periods the rate of growth for this sub-population in California was about one and one-half times larger. In both the state and the rest of the nation, however, there has been a slowdown in the growth of the number of females age 15 to 44. All else equal, California's AFDC-Basic caseload would not be expected to grow more during the second five years of this period.

Changing fertility rates can offset the above effect. The fertility rate is the ratio of births to each 1,000 females of child-bearing age. Following a major slowdown in the 1960s, fertility rates in the rest of the nation have been fluctuating: from the mid-1970s to the early 1980s increasing slightly and thereafter decreasing to the mid-1980s. On a national scale the slight slowdown in fertility is helping to control welfare costs. In contrast, the picture in California is one of a continually rising fertility rate. At five-year intervals starting in 1975, fertility rates moved from 65.1 to 70.4 to 75.2 births per 1,000 females of child-bearing age.[16]

All else equal, a rising fertility rate should have exerted some upward pressure on California's AFDC-Basic caseload in the 1980s. In part, this trend may have helped the state's caseload to recover after passage of OBRA. The impact on the caseload is slight, however, because adding a child to a welfare family with children is not likely to increase the caseload, and these additional children are some of those counted in the increase in fertility.

A similar increase was not felt nationally. The increase in the number of women of child-bearing age was countered by a slight decline in fertility rates during the 1980s and it was never as large as in California. In the rest of the nation there has been less pressure on the AFDC-Basic caseload because of an increase in the number of women having children.

Finally, and very importantly, the larger influx of refugees into California in the 1980s may have contributed to the higher rate of growth in the AFDC-Basic caseload. In recent years more Southeast Asian refugees have migrated to California than to any other state. In 1980, 166,727 Southeast Asian refugees arrived in the United States, and almost 30 percent went to California. The state with the second largest number was Texas with 7 percent; most other states drew much fewer. The total number of refugee arrivals to the United States subsided over time, but California continued to receive much more than its share of refugees.[17] By September 1986 the total number of refugees on AFDC in the United States whose benefits were wholly reimbursed by the federal government amounted to 66,322. Of this California's share was 46,101 refugees on AFDC, while the rest of the country's share was only 20,211.[18] This large, disproportionately distributed sub-population exerted much upward pressure on California's caseload.

The above figures count only those refugees whose welfare payments are funded fully by the federal government. Since more than 70 percent of refugees on California's caseload in fiscal year 1984–85 were no longer fully supported by the federal government, the number of refugees on welfare in the state is more than three times the numbers cited above. This accounts for a large segment of the state's caseload growth after OBRA.[19]

In recent years the incidence of welfare dependence in California, more than any other state in the nation, may be associated with U.S. foreign policy. But since demographics is only one set of factors that may shape caseload growth, differences between the economic well-being of California and the nation are examined next.

NATIONAL ECONOMIC TRENDS

In Chapter 4 employment levels in several non-agricultural industries in California were examined. These industries were selected because they are relevant to the study of welfare caseload dynamics in California. In other states, the selection of other types of industries is perhaps more appropriate. Consequently, when comparing employment growth in California with that in the rest of the nation only aggregate measures of economic health should be used.

The following discussion begins by examining overall economic growth and proceeds by comparing growth of employment in various sectors of the labor market. The final section of this chapter compares unemployment rates in California and the rest of the nation. For each comparison, the analysis for the rest of the nation excludes California.

Employment

Table 5.1 presents percentage growth in employment in several sectors of the labor market that reflect the economic health of California as compared with the rest of the nation.[20] Several important facts stand out. First, over the past decade California's economic growth, as reflected by growth in total employment, has been above the national average. Indeed, from 1975 to 1985 the state's total employment grew over 70 percent faster than that of the rest of the nation. Moreover, California's employment grew faster not only in total employment, but also in both agricultural and non-agricultural industries and its sub-categories of service and manufacturing industries. Second, the service sector shows the largest increases during both periods, with California substantially outpacing the nation. Third, economic pictures for both California and the rest of the nation change as we move into the 1980s. Lately both have experienced a slowdown in aggregate growth of employment in all industries considered here. Nonetheless, California still out-performs the rest of the nation when these aggregate measures are used.

The relative economic health of California is further reflected by the average wage. In 1985 the average job in California paid about 16 percent more than the average job in the rest of the nation. Given this, it is not surprising that California's per capita personal income invariably exceeds the rest of the nation's. In 1985 per capita personal income was about 18 percent higher in California.[21]

Clearly, the state's population also is growing faster than the nation's. Thus, relevant to the study of AFDC caseload dynamics is the relative growth in the number of jobs in these selected industries to the sub-population of females of child-bearing age. Whereas it was previously found that from 1972 to 1985 growth in total employment in California only kept pace with growth in females of child-bearing age, in the sub-period 1975–80 it grew faster. Moreover, during this sub-period the sub-categories of agricultural and non-

Table 5.1
Percent Change in Selected Economic Data
for California and the Rest of the Nation, 1975–85

	1975–1980	1980–1985
Total Employment		
U.S.	14.6%	7.5%
CA	25.5	11.2
Total Non-agricultural Employment		
U.S.	16.8	9.7
CA	25.5	11.6
Total Agricultural Employment		
U.S.	9.6	2.1
CA	25.2	7.3
Manufacturing Employment		
U.S.	11.3	-5.9
CA	26.6	3.3
Service Employment		
U.S.	17.4	16.1
CA	37.3	22.4
Females of Child-Bearing Age		
U.S.	10.8	6.9
CA	17.4	9.5

Source: See Notes in Chapter 5.

agricultural employment, and the more specific employment levels in service and manufacturing industries, all grew at a faster rate than the number of females of child-bearing age. In particular, employment in service industries, the best performer, grew slightly more than two times faster. Healthy service industries are of particular importance since these industries employ a large portion of women. On the other extreme, the sector with smallest growth rate considered here was agricultural employment. In California it increased slightly less than one and one-half times faster than the number of females of child-bearing age. It is likely that this sector of the labor market is less relevant to those at risk of welfare since, at least in California, most welfare recipients reside in urban areas.

Overall, while a rosy picture is painted in California from 1975 to 1980, it should be kept in mind that the above are only aggregate measures of economic health and are not as relevant to those at risk of welfare receipt as employment in low-skill industries. Notwithstanding this, when comparing these aggregate measures to the growth in the number of females of child-bearing age in the rest of the nation (considered relative growths), the story is almost as encouraging as in California. Only total agricultural employment failed to grow as fast as the number of females age 15 to 44. California did a little better than the rest of the nation during this period. In examining the corresponding relative growth rates in employment in the rest of the country, growth in all of these industries except total non-agricultural lagged behind California. For service and manufacturing the lag was as much as 33 percent and 47 percent, respectively.

The picture changes as we move into the 1980s. During this period, for California and the rest of the nation, we find a slowdown in the relative growth of employment to females of child-bearing age in all but service industries. On the negative side, manufacturing industries are not keeping up with the growth in females of child-bearing age. While California managed to sustain a small amount of absolute growth in the employment in these industries, employment levels in these industries in the rest of the nation fell by almost 6 percent. Many low-skill jobs are in the manufacturing sector of the labor market. As shown in Chapter 4, from 1975 to 1985 the two low-skill manufacturing industries selected for analysis in California did not keep up with growth in the number of females at risk of welfare receipt.

On the positive side, in California and elsewhere relative growth in service employment in the first half of the 1980s exceeds that of the previous five years. Nationwide, service industries leaped upward 2.2 times as fast as the population of females of child-bearing age, a figure that closely resembles California's. On the whole, total employment and non-agricultural employment are still growing faster than those at risk of welfare receipt.

From 1975 to 1980 the economic situation in California was better than in the rest of the nation when considering growth in service, manufacturing, agricultural, and total employment in both absolute and relative terms. For the 1980s, however, the evidence is mixed. In total non-agricultural employment the state is not faring as well as the rest of the nation; in agricultural employment it is doing better. In service industries California lost its previous advantage, and the state and the rest of the nation are doing about the same. In manufacturing the state is keeping its advantage. This makes their relative economic pictures difficult to gauge, but the situation from 1975 to 1980, when jobs in the state were easier to find than in the rest of the country, probably is no longer the case.

One implication of these findings is that, everything else equal, California's

AFDC-Basic caseload from 1975 to 1980 should have been dampened by availability of jobs more than the rest of the nation's caseload. This was at a time when both caseloads were growing at about the same rate. In the 1980s, it is not likely that recipients in California who are trying to move from welfare to employment are finding jobs any more difficult to obtain than their counterparts nationwide. Given just these facts one might predict that, everything else equal, California's caseload in the 1980s would grow at about the same rate or perhaps somewhat faster than caseloads in the rest of the nation, but California's caseload has been growing much faster. Perhaps it is unemployment that explains the differences in caseload growth.

Unemployment

Figure 5.3 compares unemployment rates for California and the rest of the nation from 1972 to 1986. From 1972 until the end of the 1970s, the unemployment rate in California was consistently higher than in the rest of the nation, on the average by 1.6 points. Likewise, from November 1973 to March 1975, during the first recessionary period, California's unemployment rate exceeded the nation's by 1.8 percent per month.[22] Yet again, California's AFDC-Basic caseload was growing at about the same rate as the nation's

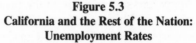

Figure 5.3
California and the Rest of the Nation:
Unemployment Rates

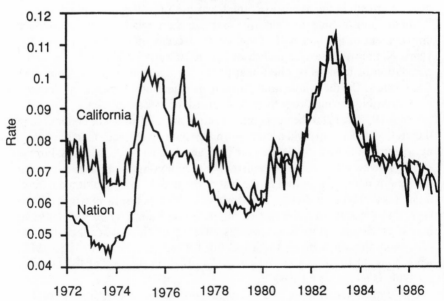

during this period, with growth rates of 5.2 percent and 5.9 percent, respectively.

As seen from Figure 5.3, since December 1979 the two unemployment rates have continued to mirror one another. However, as indicated previously, during the 1980s California's AFDC-Basic caseload grew slightly more than twice as fast as the rest of the nation's, suggesting that it is not the unemployment rate that is inducing California's caseload to grow much faster than the nation's. Sources of caseload growth in California are more likely to include both the increase in the number of females of child-bearing age and their increased fertility rate, coupled with the disproportionately large influx of refugees into California.

The aggregate measures of economic health used here do not support the notion that economic differences between California and the rest of the nation are contributing significantly to differences in caseload growth rates.

SUMMARY AND ISSUES

This chapter compared California's AFDC caseload, mainly its AFDC-Basic component, with that of the rest of the nation. The chapter began by showing that, although in some ways California's AFDC-Basic and AFDC-UP resemble their national counterparts, in recent years California's AFDC-Basic caseload has risen much faster.

In the 1980s several demographic changes may have exerted more pressure on California's caseload than changes in the state's economic health. Higher fertility rates may partially explain the state's faster growth in the AFDC-Basic caseload. The massive influx of refugees into California is an important explanation of the faster growth of its AFDC-Basic caseload.

This chapter's finding is consistent with the finding in Chapter 4 that the influx of Southeast Asian refugees is responsible for much of the recent caseload growth in California. An important issue here is how much financial responsibility for refugee support should be borne by California and other states with large refugee populations because of federal foreign policy. California has more than two-thirds of all refugees supported entirely by the federal government. Many of these families eventually will lose their entire federal support and still need state-supported welfare. More than three times the number of 100 percent federally supported welfare families are now the joint responsibility of the state and the federal government.

California's AFDC-Basic caseload now constitutes about 14 percent of the national caseload. This means that what happens in California has important federal and state fiscal consequences. It also means that sometimes California leads the way in welfare reform. Understanding how the state's welfare system and its caseload are unique or typical helps policy makers to judge the system's problems and successes better. Better policies can then be formulated.

NOTES

1. Nationwide AFDC caseload numbers were provided by the U.S. Health and Human Services Department, Social Security Administration, Office of Family Assistance, Washington, D.C. These numbers were adjusted to exclude Foster Care. The number of cases receiving assistance during a month is larger than the number of cases at the beginning of the month. This is because, at least in California, the number of cases open during a month includes all families receiving welfare at any time during that month, including those that are terminated during the month. Since the federal government simply requires the states to report the number of cases receiving payments during the month, it is not known exactly what each state reports. The numbers presented here thus may have different meanings in different states.

2. The graph using the number of cases during the month is smoother than the graph using the number of cases at the beginning of the month. This is because, for example, if a month has a net decrease of 15,000 cases, there will be a drop of 15,000 cases in the following month's stock of cases. However, the number of cases added the following month will offset the effect of this decline on the flow of cases. If 15,000 cases are added in the subsequent month, then the flow for that month would be the same as the flow for the previous month.

3. In Chapter 4 the number of cases at the beginning of the month was used for California. In this chapter, for comparative purposes it is necessary to use the number of cases receiving cash during the month. This slightly alters the growth numbers.

4. September 1981 to January 1982 is the period used to measure this decline.

5. Recall from Chapter 4 that OBRA's provisions went into effect in California in November 1981. For a full explanation see note 15, Chapter 4.

6. Steady state is taken to mean that the caseload is neither increasing nor decreasing more than usual.

7. Unfortunately, analyses of national caseload trends are somewhat limited. It would have been interesting to compare the rest of the nation's monthly accessions and terminations with those of California. This is not possible because the federal government does not gather these kinds of data separately for AFDC-Basic and AFDC-UP program components.

8. The statistics are from U.S. Commerce Department, Bureau of the Census, *Statistical Abstract of the United States, 1987*, 107th ed. (Washington, D.C.: U.S. Government Printing Office, 1986).

9. For a discussion of the decline in family size in California and in a comparative perspective see Kevin F. McCarthy and Burciaga R. Valdez, "California's Demographic Future," in *California Policy Choices*, vol. 2, ed. J.J. Kirlin and D.R. Winkler (Sacramento: Sacramento Public Affairs Center, 1985), pp. 37-62.

10. Data for the nation are from U.S. Health and Human Services Department, Social Security Administration, Office of Family Assistance, Office of Policy and Evaluation, *Findings of the May 1981-May 1982 Aid to Families with Dependent Children Study: Recipient Characteristics, Financial Circumstances—The Effects of the Omnibus Budget Reconciliation Act of 1981* (Washington, D.C.: Social Security Administration Publication No. 13-11731, 1985). In each case the data are adjusted to exclude California.

11. Ibid.

12. This information is from U.S. Health and Human Services Department, Social

Security Administration, Office of Family Assistance, Office of Policy and Evaluation, *Recipient Characteristics and Financial Circumstances of AFDC Recipients* (Washington, D.C.: U.S. Government Printing Office, 1986).

13. Ibid. The overall decline in the percentage of earners on AFDC was adjusted to exclude California; the decline for full- or part-time earners was not adjusted.

14. Resident population numbers by state from 1975 to 1985 are from U.S. Commerce Department, *Statistical Abstract of the United States, 1987*, Table 25.

15. The numbers of females age 15 to 44 for 1975, 1980, and 1985 for California were provided by the California Department of Finance, Population Research Unit, Sacramento. The numbers for California are used to estimate the numbers of females age 15 to 44 for the rest of the nation by taking the available numbers of females age 14 to 44 by state. These latter numbers are from U.S. Commerce Department, *Statistical Abstract of the United States, 1987*.

16. Fertility rates by state for 1970 are from U.S. Health, Education and Welfare Department, National Center for Health Statistics, *Summary Report: Final Natality Statistics, 1970*, Monthly Vital Statistics Report, vol. 22, no. 12, Supplement, Publication No. HRA-74-1120 (Rockville, Md.: Public Health Service, March 1974). For 1975 fertility rates are estimated by using births divided by females age 15 to 44. Births are from U.S. Commerce Department, *Statistical Abstract of the United States, 1987*. Fertility rates by state for 1980 are from U.S. Health and Human Services Department, National Center for Health Statistics, *Birth and Fertility Rates for States: United States, 1980*, National Vital Statistics System, series 21, no. 42, DHHS Publication No. PHS-84-1920 (Hyattsville, Md.: Public Health Service, September 1984). Fertility rates for 1985 are from U.S. Health and Human Services Department, National Center for Health Statistics, *Advance Report of Final Natality Statistics, 1985*, Monthly Vital Statistics Report, vol. 36, no. 4, Supplement, DHHS Publication No. PHS-87-1120 (Hyattsville, Md.: Public Health Service, July 1987). Trends in births or population estimates also are from U.S. Commerce Department, Bureau of the Census, *United States Population Estimates and Components of Change: 1970-1986*, Current Population Reports, series P-25, no. 1006 (Washington, D.C.: U.S. Government Printing Office, 1986).

17. Refugee arrivals by state are from U.S. Commerce Department, *Statistical Abstract of the United States, 1987*, Table 12.

18. U.S. Health and Human Services Department, Family Support Administration, Office of Refugee Resettlement, *Summary of Refugee Cash Assistance Caseload and Number of Recipient Assistants as of 9/30/1986* (Washington, D.C.: 4th QPRs, 1986).

19. The percentage of refugees on AFDC in California in 1984-85 who were no longer receiving federal assistance is from Michael Wiseman, "The Welfare System," in *California Policy Choices*, vol. 2, ed. J.J. Kirlin and D.R. Winkler (Sacramento: Sacramento Public Affairs Center, 1985), p. 195.

20. National employment and unemployment data for the nation were provided by the U.S. Labor Department, Bureau of Labor Statistics, Washington, D.C.

21. U.S. Commerce Department, *Statistical Abstract of the United States, 1987*.

22. Reference dates for the nation's recessionary periods are November 1973 to March 1975 and July 1981 to November 1982. The numbers for the 1980s recessionary period were taken from U.S. Commerce Department, Bureau of Economic Analysis, *Business Conditions Digest* (Washington, D.C.: U.S. Government Printing Office, 1982). The same source was used for the 1970s recessionary period.

6

An Approach to
Analyzing Welfare Dependence

This chapter presents a model for analyzing welfare dependence that consists of several mathematical identities and two linear regression equations. Taken together, the identities and regression equations make up a multiple equation, time-series, econometric model for use in analyzing and forecasting AFDC-Basic dynamics. A large portion of this chapter describes the exogenous variables later used to predict the endogenous variables in the component equations. The hypotheses associated with these variables are also delineated.

A MODEL OF AFDC-BASIC DYNAMICS

The model of caseload dynamics presented here is based on a simple accounting identity. This identity states that the AFDC-Basic caseload at the beginning of any month equals the cases at the beginning of the preceding month plus the difference between the previous month's additions and terminations. This is expressed in the following fundamental accounting identity:

$$C(t) = C(t-1) + CA(t-1) - CT(t-1) \qquad (6.1)$$

for any $t \geq 2$ where

$$
\begin{aligned}
t \;&=\; \text{1 corresponds to January 1972,} \\
C(t) \;&=\; \text{AFDC-Basic caseload at beginning of month } t, \\
CA(t) \;&=\; \text{total number of accessions to the caseload during month } t, \\
CT(t) \;&=\; \text{total number of terminations from the caseload during month } t.
\end{aligned}
$$

Note that the caseload numbers are stocks and have the dimension of cases. The caseload is assumed to be measured at the beginning of each month. Additions and terminations are flows and have the dimension of cases per month. Given an initial case count and the time path of additions and terminations, the development of the caseload itself is determined by the identity. The modeling effort will be devoted to developing theories of the determinants of additions and terminations.

Caseload Identities

From the fundamental identity given above, it is possible to construct a monthly time-series simultaneous equation model. This model, used to analyze and simulate the dynamics of the AFDC-Basic caseload, formally translates into a set of mathematical identities and component equations that are set forth below.

The idea underlying the model is that month-to-month changes in the caseload or its elements are the result of combinations of various flows. Together, three flows form any month's caseload accessions: cases added through restorations or new applications, cases transferring from AFDC-UP, and other additions. This is expressed in the following caseload accessions identity:

$$CA(t) = AD(t) + TB(t) + OA(t) \qquad (6.2)$$

for any $t \geq 1$ where

$AD(t)$ = number of new applications and restorations approved during month t,

$TB(t)$ = number of transfers from AFDC-UP to AFDC-Basic during month t,

$OA(t)$ = number of all other approvals during month t.

It would be possible separately to model the process of applications and acceptances that precedes admissions. For example, the number of new additions and restorations (AD) equaling the product of the number of families applying for welfare and the welfare acceptance rate could be examined, but this is not taken up here.

In the model of AFDC-Basic dynamics only two kinds of case closures are considered. These are closures due to individuals leaving the AFDC-Basic system and closures due to intraprogram transfers from AFDC-Basic to AFDC-UP. This translates mathematically to the case closures identity:

$$CT(t) = CL(t) + TU(t) \qquad (6.3)$$

for any $t \geq 1$ where

$CL(t)$ = number of cases closed during month t, excluding those transferring to AFDC-UP,

$TU(t)$ = number of cases transferring from AFDC-Basic to AFDC-UP
during month t.

All of the above identities, together with two linear stochastic component
equations, one for new cases added and restored (AD) and one for cases closed
(CL), comprise the entire time-series model.

Figure 6.1 summarizes the AFDC-Basic caseload movement process.[1] In
the next section linear equations are developed for each of the two components

Figure 6.1
AFDC-Basic Caseload Movement

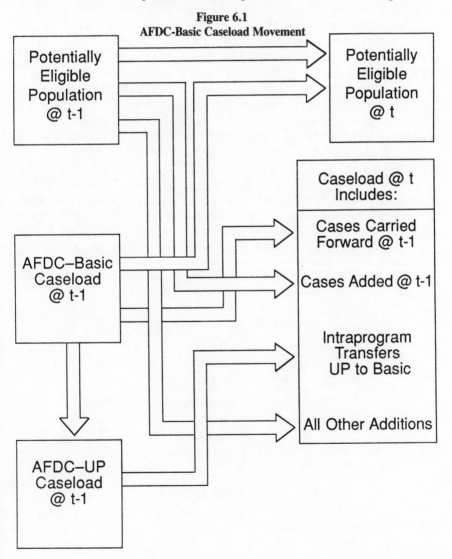

Potentially Eligible Population @ t-1

Potentially Eligible Population @ t

AFDC–Basic Caseload @ t-1

AFDC–UP Caseload @ t-1

Caseload @ t Includes:

Cases Carried Forward @ t-1

Cases Added @ t-1

Intraprogram Transfers UP to Basic

All Other Additions

of change. It is believed that intraprogram transfers from AFDC-UP to AFDC-Basic and vice versa (*TB* and *TU*), other additions (*OA*), and accounting errors (*ER*) that are used to adjust monthly caseload count, in theory, do not respond well to the exogenous variables selected for this analysis. In fact, as later discussed, most have a minor impact on either accessions or terminations because of their relatively small size.

Caseload Component Equations

Each of the component equations has a single dependent variable representing one of two major flows. For each month, one flow is the number of new cases added plus the number of cases restored (*AD*); the other is the number of cases terminated excluding those transferring to AFDC-UP (*CL*).[2] Each of the dependent variables in the component equations is considered to be a linear function of predetermined variables. These exogenous and lagged endogenous variables are selected on the basis of theory, past findings, or logic. Apart from seasonals, the independent variables fall into three major classes: labor-market conditions, program characteristics, and characteristics of households. The following sections describe the independent variables selected for each component equation.

Cases Added. California's caseload movement reports define two distinct classes of additions (see Appendix G). The number of cases added during any given month consists of those families who have not been on welfare for at least one year and those families who have returned to welfare within one year. However, in this analysis these two types of additions are lumped together as cases added (*AD*). The number of cases added is considered to be a linear function of the exogenous and lagged endogenous variables delineated below.

$$
\begin{aligned}
AD(t) = b_0 &+ b_1 \, TP(t) &&+ b_2 \, SN(t) &&+ b_3 \, MW(t-1) \\
&+ b_4 \, WI(t-1) &&+ b_5 \, U(t-1) &&+ b_6 \, U(t-2) \\
&+ b_7 \, U(t-3) &&+ b_8 \, U(t-4) &&+ b_9 \, F(t-1) \\
&+ b_{10} \, A(t-1) &&+ b_{11} \, NA(t-1) &&+ b_{12} \, B(t-1) \\
&+ b_{13} \, B(t-2) &&+ b_{14} \, B(t-3) &&+ b_{15} \, B(t-4) \\
&+ b_{16} \, K(t-1) &&+ b_{17} \, P(t-1) &&+ b_{18} \, CL(t-1) \\
&+ b_{19} \, CL(t-2) &&+ b_{20} \, CL(t-3) &&+ b_{21} \, CL(t-4) \\
&+ b_{22} \, DO(t) &&+ b_{23} \, JA(t) &&+ \ldots + b_{33} \, NV(t) \\
&+ e(t)
\end{aligned}
\tag{6.4}
$$

for any $t \geq 5$ where

$AD(t)$ = number of new applications and restorations approved during month t,

$TP(t)$ = total payments of AFDC maximum aid and food stamps for a family of three, deflated by the CNI ($6/1985 = 100$), at month t,

$SN(t)$ = AFDC income eligibility standard for a family of three (MBSAC), deflated by the CPI ($6/1985 = 100$), at month t,

$MW(t)$ = full-time minimum wage gross earnings, deflated by CPI ($6/1985 = 100$), at month t,

$WI(t)$ = full-time gross earnings wage index of operator receptionists, deflated by the CPI ($6/1985 = 100$), at month t,

$U(t)$ = number of seasonally unadjusted unemployed in California at month t,

$F(t)$ = number of workers in food and kindred products industries in California at month t,

$A(t)$ = number of workers in apparel and other textile industries in California at month t,

$NA(t)$ = number of workers in the rest of non-agricultural industries in California at month t,

$B(t)$ = number of births in California at month t,

$K(t)$ = number of children in California under age 18, excluding those on AFDC, at month t,

$P(t)$ = number of females in California age 15 to 44, excluding those on AFDC, at month t,

$CL(t)$ = number of cases closed during month t, excluding those transferring to AFDC-UP,

$DO(t)$ = dummy variable identifying the presence of OBRA policies during month t,

$e(t)$ = random error term at month t.

For variable sources and deflation indexes see Appendixes D and F.

The second through the fifth terms in Equation 6.4 contain variables selected on the basis of economic theory. According to economic theory, individuals choose between benefits available to them from income-maintenance programs and benefits available to them in the marketplace, namely, wages. Therefore, assuming that individuals opt for maximizing their income, individuals will choose welfare over work as welfare benefits (TP) increase, everything else being constant; in turn, the number of additions (AD) to welfare would increase. In order for a family to enter the AFDC system, its adjusted net income must fall below the income eligibility need standard (SN). It is therefore evident that as the standard of need reaches a higher level, everything else constant, more families will qualify for welfare, causing a greater number of additions.

Two variables representing the benefits available to welfare recipients in the marketplace are included in Equation 6.4. Earnings from full-time minimum wage (MW) employment represents the minimal standard of living provided by the private economy. Another measure of this type of benefit is the ongoing average gross wages of receptionists (WI). This occupation represents a slightly higher skill level than typical minimum wage employment.[3] Nonetheless, both these wage variables characterize jobs in which skill level is low and training is minimal. Contrary to the welfare system's benefit levels, when either wage variable reaches a higher level, everything else being constant, a smaller number of successful welfare applicants would be expected.

Underlying the above hypotheses is the tenet that, on the average, potential AFDC-Basic applicants make rational economic decisions by comparing the benefits in the marketplace to the benefits available to them in the welfare system. If the AFDC program provides them an overall better economic gain, some categorically eligibles will choose welfare over work. On the other hand, if the marketplace provides more benefits, they will stay or seek employment there.

Clearly the number of welfare additions cannot depend solely on the income alternatives available in the labor market and in the welfare system. Accessions to welfare also depend upon the choices available to potential recipients, including labor-market conditions. With this in mind, Equation 6.4 also contains a second set of terms designed to measure the demand side of the labor market.

The number of seasonally unadjusted unemployed (U) in California is one such measure assumed to affect welfare accessions. While levels marked by this general measure may understate unemployment in California and certainly understate the number of jobless among families at risk of becoming welfare dependent, it is possible that variations in the number of unemployed are highly correlated with variations in unemployment in the welfare-relevant labor sub-market.[4]

As the labor market ebbs, unemployment increases. Some, but not all, of this resulting pool of newly unemployed immediately will move onto welfare, causing welfare accessions to increase. As months pass, more of the categorically eligible individuals in this particular pool of unemployed eventually also will move onto AFDC. Ultimately, all of those in the pool who could be expected to move onto welfare due to their unemployment will actually do so. It is hypothesized that this process takes approximately four months before its effects on welfare accessions are exhausted. Consequently, starting with a one-month lag to account for a delayed response on the part of individuals seeking welfare or a delay in application processing, a linear four-month lag structure for the seasonally unadjusted unemployed variable is incorporated into Equation 6.4.

According to employment opportunity theory, it is assumed that successful matching of jobs to workers occurs in the marketplace. Therefore, since most of the welfare population is known to lack both extensive education and skills, the number of welfare additions should be determined in part by the demand for workers in low-skill, low-wage, and high-turnover industries. Employment levels in two types of non-agricultural industries, namely, apparel and other textile products (A) and food and kindred products (F), are selected to measure this specific type of market place demand. These two types of industries have a large number of women workers and are characterized as seasonal, low-wage, and low-skill.[5] It is hypothesized that, as the demand for employment in these two industries increases to a new level, everything else being constant, a lower level of welfare additions will result.

Clearly, since potential welfare recipients obtain jobs in industries other than the above two, another variable of the same kind is necessary. The employment level in non-agricultural industries other than the two cited previously (NA) is chosen. Here too a negative variation with welfare accessions is expected.

Next, welfare additions are hypothesized to be a linear function of a set of demographic variables. For a significant fraction of cases, the precipitating factor in welfare accessions is the pregnancy associated with the birth of a first child.[6] As the number of births to women not on welfare increases, the number of welfare accessions should also increase. Yet constructing an accurate functional form for births and measuring only births by potential welfare recipients out of total births in California is problematic. In California a woman may choose either to move onto welfare at any time during her pregnancy or to wait until sometime after the birth of her first child.[7] This implies that births could enter Equation 6.4 with some type of lead-lag structure. However, since calculations show that only about 1 to 3 percent of children on the caseload were not yet born at the time of entry and, more importantly, since some potential applicants may be unaware of this eligibility provision, no lead structure is deemed necessary. A four-month lag structure starting with a one-month lag should account for most of the underlying effect of births (B) on accessions. No satisfactory method of approximating births in the potentially eligible, but non-welfare population has been found; therefore, the number of births in the entire population is used.

Since one of the AFDC program's demographic eligibility requirements is that children are present, it is expected that the higher the number of children under age 18 and not on welfare (K), the greater the number of additions to the welfare rolls. Thus, the number of children less than 18 years old not already in a welfare-dependent family is also one of the demographic variables.[8]

Defining the population of potentially eligible recipients poses a serious empirical problem since potential welfare cases include not only the number of existing categorically eligible households that are poor but also households that are neither categorically eligible nor poor but have the potential of becoming both. Also, whatever the demographic measure selected, state population data at monthly intervals are very difficult to obtain. Nonetheless, it is essential to define this population at risk. For this study the number of females age 15 to 44 in the population not already heading dependent families is selected to be the population at risk (P). These females are of child-bearing age. As California's population grows, all else being constant, the number of potentially welfare eligibles is expected to vary positively with the number of cases added.[9]

Cases restored are included in the dependent variable of this equation. Although many welfare terminations return to the potentially eligible population and part of the potentially eligible population consists of individuals who have been on welfare within the past year, an additional independent variable included in the cases-added equation is cases closed (CL). Including cases closed as a predictor variable is warranted because recent welfare participants have some knowledge about regulations and experience less difficulty with the application process than do other applicants. A four-month, rather than a

Table 6.1
Expected Signs for Independent Variables in Accessions Equation

Symbol	Description	Hypothesized Sign
TP	Total Welfare Payments	$b_1 > 0$
SN	Standard of Need	$b_2 > 0$
MW	Gross Minimum Wage Earnings	$b_3 < 0$
WI	Gross Earnings of Receptionists	$b_4 < 0$
U	Seasonally Unadjusted Unemployed	$b_5 + ... + b_8 > 0$
F	Workers in Food and Kindred	$b_9 < 0$
A	Workers in Apparel, Other Textile	$b_{10} < 0$
NA	Workers in Other Non-agriculture	$b_{11} < 0$
B	Births in California	$b_{12} + ... + b_{15} > 0$
K	Children < 18 Not on Welfare	$b_{16} > 0$
P	Potentially Eligible Population	$b_{17} > 0$
CL	Number of Cases Closed	$b_{18} + ... + b_{21} > 0$
DO	Dummy Indicating OBRA	$b_{22} < 0$
	Seasonals	Indeterminate

Note: All variables valued in dollars, except for TP, are deflated by the CPI (6/1985=100). TP is deflated by the CNI (6/1985=100).

12-month, lag structure for this variable is incorporated into Equation 6.4 because it is assumed that restored cases return to welfare soon after they leave. In addition, a correlation of restorations with various lags of cases closed suggests a four-month lag structure starting with a one-month lag.[10]

Next OBRA is hypothesized to affect the flow of cases added. OBRA's provisions imposed a more restrictive assets-eligibility test and perhaps made the AFDC-Basic program less attractive to potentially eligibles by eliminating the $30 and one-third disregards after several months of employment. Consequently, a dummy variable measuring the presence of OBRA (DO) is expected to lower the number of additions to welfare.

Finally, the cases-added equation includes a set of seasonal monthly dummies. Although the variables discussed above cover many of the major influences on caseload accessions, some other social factors affect accessions, and, to the extent that these factors are systematically or seasonally changing caseload accessions, a set of seasonals is appropriate. Since some of these social factors are unknown, the sign of the coefficient of each seasonal variable is difficult to hypothesize. The seasonals are included in an additive rather than a proportional form since the model is a linear functional form.

The independent variables incorporated into the cases-added equation are summarized in Table 6.1 and are presented next.

Cases Closed. The flow of welfare cases that are terminated during a single month includes all those families who leave AFDC-Basic for any reason with the single exception of transferring to AFDC-UP. The linear functional form of this flow is given below. Definitions for any variables not defined in the list following the equation can be found in previous sections.

$$
\begin{aligned}
CL(t) = b_0 \ & + \ b_1 \, TP(t) & + \ b_2 \, E_r^{**}(t) & + \ b_3 \, MW(t-1) \\
& + \ b_4 \, WI(t-1) & + \ b_5 \, U(t-1) & + \ b_6 \, F(t-1) \\
& + \ b_7 \, A(t-1) & + \ b_8 \, NA(t-1) & + \ b_9 \, C(t-1) \\
& + \ b_{10} \, CA(t-1) & + \ b_{11} \, CA(t-2) & + \ b_{12} \, CA(t-3) \\
& + \ b_{13} \, CA(t-4) & + \ b_{14} \, FBU(t-1) & + \ b_{15} \, M_{20}(t) \\
& + \ b_{16} \, M_{30}(t) & + \ b_{17} \, C_5(t) & + \ b_{18} \, DS(t) \\
& + \ b_{19} \, DO(t) & + \ b_{20} \, DB(t) & \\
& + \ b_{21} \, JA(t) & + \ \dots + b_{31} \, NV(t) & + \ e(t)
\end{aligned}
\tag{6.5}
$$

for any $t \geq 5$ where

$E_r^{**}(t)$ = breakeven level for a family of three, deflated by the CPI (6/1985 = 100), at month t (referred to as the actual breakeven in Chapter 2),

$FBU(t)$ = average number of individuals on AFDC-Basic per case at month t,

$M_{20}(t)$ = number of mothers under age 21 on the caseload at month t,

$M_{30}(t)$ = number of mothers over age 29 on the caseload at month t,

$C_5(t)$ = number of children under age 6 on the caseload at month t,

$DS(t)$ = OBRA shock dummy at month t,

$DO(t)$ = dummy variable representing the presence of OBRA provisions starting in January 1982 at month t,

$DB(t)$ = interaction of E_r^{**} and DO at month t.

For variable sources and deflation indexes see Appendixes D and F.

Available literature suggests that certain welfare system features affect the likelihood of terminations by dependent families.[11] Accordingly, Equation 6.5 includes the basic AFDC guarantee plus food stamp benefits (TP) available to a family of three without any other income. It is expected that the larger the total benefits available to families already on welfare, everything else being constant, the smaller the number of terminations. The second AFDC system variable is the breakeven level (E_r^{**}) for the same family size. This breakeven accounts for changes over time in the amount of gross earnings, in real terms, that it takes for a family of three to become ineligible for welfare. This variable also is expected to vary negatively with terminations since the higher the breakeven the greater the net income of working recipients who combine work and welfare.[12]

The AFDC program's standard of need (SN) does not enter this equation since applicants' income must fall below this level to enter, but once they are on the rolls their income can exceed this level, sometimes by a great deal, and they still remain eligible. The taxpoint (E^*), which is the earnings at which benefits begin to be reduced, also is not included here since essentially no variation was obtained for this welfare parameter under the set of assumptions used to calculate total welfare payments and the breakeven level.[13] Since maximum aid, the taxpoint, the benefit reduction rate, and the breakeven level are related by a formula, and therefore are dependent, only three of these four variables can be considered in a single equation.[14] Here, instead of maximum aid, the total amount of welfare payments recipients face is included; thus, a variable highly correlated with maximum aid is included in the equation. The effect of the taxpoint is essentially integrated into the constant of Equation 6.5. The breakeven level is explicitly included in the equation; consequently, the benefit reduction rate cannot be included.

As in the cases-added equation, full-time gross earnings from minimum-wage employment (MW) and average gross earnings of receptionists (WI) are included to contrast the economic appeal of the welfare system compared to the private economy. Both of these variables are expected to vary positively with case closures.

The flow of case closures during the month is expected to be positively correlated with employment levels in selected industries. The number of case closures is a linear function of the number of workers in food and kindred products (F), apparel and other textile (A), and all other non-agricultural industries (NA). On the other hand, case closures are expected to vary negatively with the number of unemployed workers in California (U). Each variable has a one-month lag structure. Contrary to the four-month lag structure of the number of unemployed in the cases-added equation, in the case of terminations, there is no justification for such a multiple-lag effect because people on welfare are expected to respond quickly to changes in labor-market conditions.

Clearly, the larger the case caseload (C) in a month, all else being equal, the more terminations would be expected the next month. It is therefore posited that the caseload enters Equation 6.5 with a one-month lag structure. Similarly, several months of rather high case openings generally should be associated with higher than normal terminations. If the number of total cases added (CA) in recent previous months is strongly and positively associated with present terminations, then this suggests that a significant number of cases added are of short duration. Beginning with a one-month lag, a four-month lag structure for the total number of cases added is hypothesized to underlie the flow of the number of cases closed during the month. Indeed, the overall effect of these four terms on case closings should be positive; that is, the sum of these four coefficients should be positive.

As will be seen in Chapter 7, past analyses of AFDC dynamics using individual households have consistently found that certain characteristics related to household heads and their families are associated with the likelihood of case closure. As the size of the average number of recipients per case (FBU) reaches a higher level, the number of case closings, all else being constant, would be expected to fall. This is because the larger the family unit, the less likely is the private economy to provide a better standard of living than the welfare system to those recipients with limited education and work experience. Past research also has revealed that older welfare recipients tend to have a higher probability of closure.[15] Accordingly, the number of young females who are heads of households on AFDC-Basic [under 21 (M_{20})] and the number of older recipients [over age 29 (M_{30})] are expected to help determine the number of cases closed. Note that mothers between age 21 and 29 are excluded from the analysis. It is reasonable to expect that these three age groups and the caseload are collinear; therefore, all three age groups cannot be included. The younger age variable should vary negatively with case closures, while the older should vary positively.

Since children under school age can create barriers to employment or marriage, it is reasonable to incorporate into the case-closures equation a variable that measures this phenomenon. Two possible measures arise. One is the number of children under six years old who are on the caseload; another is the number of cases that include children under age six. This latter variable could not be incorporated into the analysis, unless estimated, since no data were available on the number of cases with children under age six. Moreover, it is not clear whether this latter variable is good since there are some cases with more than one child under age six. It is expected that the greater the number of children under age six in a family, the lower the probability of closure. Consequently, the absolute number of children under age six on the caseload (C_5) is incorporated into the closure equation. It is expected that the greater the number of these children on the caseload, the smaller the number of welfare terminations during any single month.

Next, several dummy variables are included in the case-closures equation. These variables reflect AFDC policy shifts accompanying OBRA. As noted in Chapter 2, one of OBRA's provisions in 1981 was to eliminate from welfare eligibility recipients whose non-welfare gross income exceeded 150 percent of the standard of need. Consequently, during November and December 1981 many more families than typically would be expected were terminated from the rolls. As seen in Figure 4.4, a huge spike occurred during November and December 1981 as a result of the implementation of the 150 percent gross income cutoff rule. In order to capture the effect of this rule, it was necessary to incorporate a dummy variable, titled dummy shock (DS), for the dramatic increase in case closures during these two months.

Another OBRA dummy (DO) is included in the termination equation. This variable, unlike the OBRA dummy in the previous component equation, begins taking effect in January 1982, after the effects of the dummy shock are over. This variable represents some of OBRA's provisions that the breakeven variable does not capture after November 1981. Recall that the breakeven variable in this study after the implementation of OBRA captures income cutoffs set at 150 percent of the standard of need from November 1981 until September 1984, and the 185 percent income cutoff henceforth. An OBRA dummy in the equation should represent the existence of other provisions accompanying OBRA that also could affect the number of welfare terminations. One such provision is the elimination of the $30 and one-third disregards after 4 months of employment from March 1982 until September 1984, and subsequently after 12 months of employment. Since it has traditionally been thought that such provisions create work disincentives by increasing the benefit reduction rate, the sign of the OBRA coefficient should be negative. That is, work disincentives accompanying OBRA and the near dollar-for-dollar benefit reduction may reduce overall terminations.

An interaction of the OBRA dummy and the breakeven (DB) is included in Equation 6.5. The reason for including an interaction term is that it is expected that the way in which a change in the breakeven level affects terminations will be different before and after OBRA. The sign of this interaction's coefficient is expected to be positive, while the sign of the breakeven's coefficient is hypothesized to be negative. This does not necessarily mean that after OBRA's implementation an increase in the breakeven is associated with an increase in the number of cases closed.[16] Rather, associated with a fixed increase in the breakeven, the post-OBRA decrease in the number of closures may only be smaller than the pre-OBRA decrease. In other words, the hypothesis that the coefficient of the interaction term is positive stems from a belief that after OBRA there will be less of a tendency on the part of recipients to combine work and welfare and in turn not to leave. Since the breakeven is a variable that reflects such a tendency, its coefficient should increase after passage of OBRA.

Finally, seasonal effects on closures not captured by the other independent variables are included in the equation. These seasonal trends may capture fluctuations in the number of marriages in California or serve as proxies for other variables not measured here.

Table 6.2 summarizes the independent variables.

Table 6.2
Expected Signs for Independent Variables in Closures Equation

Symbol	Description	Hypothesized Sign
TP	Total Welfare Payments	$b_1 < 0$
E_r^{**}	Breakeven (real)	$b_2 < 0$
MW	Gross Minimum Wage Earnings	$b_3 > 0$
WI	Gross Earnings of Receptionists	$b_4 > 0$
U	Seasonally Unadjusted Unemployed	$b_5 < 0$
F	Workers in Food and Kindred	$b_6 > 0$
A	Workers in Apparel, Other Textile	$b_7 > 0$
NA	Workers in Other Non-agriculture	$b_8 > 0$
C	AFDC-Basic Caseload	$b_9 > 0$
CA	Total Cases Added	$b_{10} + ... + b_{13} > 0$
FBU	Number of People per Case	$b_{14} < 0$
M_{20}	Mothers < 21 on the Caseload	$b_{15} < 0$
M_{30}	Mothers > 29 on the Caseload	$b_{16} > 0$
C_5	Children < 6 on the Caseload	$b_{17} < 0$
DS	OBRA Shock Dummy	$b_{18} < 0$
DO	Dummy Indicating OBRA	$b_{19} < 0$
DB	Interaction of E_r^{**} and DO	$b_{20} > 0$
	Seasonals	Indeterminate

Note: All variables valued in dollars, except for TP, are deflated by the CPI (6/1985=100). TP is deflated by the CNI (6/1985=100).

Variables Not Predicted

The system of Identities 6.1, 6.2, and 6.3 and Equations 6.4 and 6.5 consist of 40 variables, of which 35 need to be specified in order for the system of equations to determine the other five. Thus, there are only five endogenous variables in the model. These variables are the caseload (C), the total number of accessions (CA), the total number of terminations (CT), the number of cases added (AD), and the number of cases closed (CL). As explained in more detail in Chapter 9 and Appendix E, the actual, rather than predicted, values are taken for four welfare system variables. These are intraprogram transfers from Basic to UP (TU) and vice versa (TB), all other approvals (OA), and accounting errors (ER). The following sections briefly describe the reasons for not developing component equations for these four variables and thus treating them as exogenous.

Intraprogram Transfers. The number of cases transferring into AFDC-Basic from the AFDC-UP program (TB) constitutes on the average only about 4 percent of the cases added to the AFDC-Basic program each month. Furthermore, the number of AFDC-Basic cases that transfer to AFDC-UP (TU) each month is on the average only about 4 percent of the cases that terminate from AFDC-Basic. Thus, intraprogram transfers from AFDC-UP to AFDC-Basic and vice versa have a relatively minor impact on AFDC-Basic total additions and terminations. Furthermore, the overall impact of these intraprogram transfers on the AFDC-Basic caseload is minor because one type of transfer adds into the accession term and the other type of transfer adds into the termination term, which is then subtracted. This yields a change in the caseload of nearly zero because these transfers are about equal each month.

Intraprogram transfers from AFDC-UP to AFDC-Basic usually are the result of family separations or disability of at least one adult member of the household. Program changes from AFDC-Basic to AFDC-UP usually come about because of marriages or reunited couples. Due to the absence of monthly data on family separations, disabilities, marriages, or reconciliations in California and the small impact of these transfers on the number of AFDC-Basic cases added and terminated, intraprogram transfers are not predicted by exogenous variables.

Other Additions. A sizeable portion of other miscellaneous additions (OA) are corrections of administrative or recipient errors. Since the effect of institutional variables on caseload dynamics is not of interest in this study, no attempt is made to predict this variable.

Accounting Errors. Each month California's Department of Social Services discovers errors (ER) made sometime in the past by the counties. Each month these errors are added to the caseload count $[C(t)]$ in order to adjust its monthly value. These errors are probably random, and no attempt is made to predict them.

SUMMARY

In this chapter a model consisting of several mathematical identities and two linear regression equations was developed. Both regression equations will be used to test hypotheses about the effects of several sets of independent variables on accessions and terminations.

Apart from seasonals, the regression equations incorporate independent variables belonging to three classes. One class of variables deals with the AFDC system. This class includes the AFDC standard of need (SN), the AFDC guarantee plus food stamp benefits (TP), the AFDC breakeven level (E_r^{**}), and several dummy variables reflecting AFDC policy shifts. The benefits variable is included in both the accessions and the terminations equations, while the standard of need and the breakeven variables are included in the accessions and the terminations equations, respectively. SN represents income eligibility for entering and E_r^{**} for leaving the system. The dummy variables reflecting AFDC policy shifts enter both the accessions and the terminations equations.

The second class of variables in the model deals with California's economy. This class includes both the minimum wage (MW) and wage of a receptionist (WI) that are assumed to represent the level of benefits available to welfare recipients in the marketplace. This class of variables also includes unemployment and employment levels in selected industries. All of these variables are included in both the accessions and the terminations equations. It is assumed that potential recipients and welfare recipients respond in a fashion consistent with economic theory to changes in these variables.

The last class of variables in the model deals with characteristics of household heads and their families. Demographic variables such as births, number of children in California under age 18 not on welfare, and size of the potentially eligible population are assumed to affect welfare accessions. Variables such as the number of younger and older mothers on the caseload and the absolute number of children under age six are assumed to influence closures.

The selection of variables and the hypotheses associated with these variables rely on economic theory, past research, and logic. As will be shown in Chapter 7, past research in the area of AFDC dynamics included similar variables belonging to these three classes. The effects of these variables on AFDC dynamics as discovered by previous research are reviewed in the next chapter.

NOTES

1. The AFDC-Basic caseload movement process and the mathematical identities are based upon data provided by California Social Services Department, Statistical Services Branch, "Aid to Families with Dependent Children—Cash Grant Caseload Movement and Expenditures Report" (Sacramento: January 1972 to December 1984). An example of these monthly reports is furnished in Appendix G.

2. The model could have been specified in terms of rates instead of flows. Rates are not specified in the two equations because of the ambiguity involved in choosing appropriate denominators for some of the rate variables. For example, the number of cases added is chosen instead of the accession rate since, as discussed later on, the denominator of this rate, namely, the potentially eligible population, is not well defined. Moreover, if, for example, one of the selected independent variables, the employment level in food and kindred products, were to be measured using a rate, it is not clear whether its denominator should be the entire labor force, the number of workers in non-agricultural industries, or some other subdivision of the labor force. Because it is believed that a more accurate model results, rates are not chosen for the independent or dependent variables.

3. For explanations of the selected wage variables, see Chapter 4.

4. A seasonally unadjusted number of unemployed rather than an adjusted measure was taken in order to capture seasonal fluctuations affecting caseload movement.

5. For an explanation of employment levels in these two types of industries see Chapter 4.

6. See M. J. Bane and D. T. Ellwood, *The Dynamics of Dependence: The Routes to Self-sufficiency*, Contract No. HHS-100-82-0038 (Washington, D.C.: U.S. Health and Human Services Department, 1983), p. 18.

7. As mentioned in Chapter 3, California provides aid to pregnant women any time during their pregnancy, even after passage of OBRA. During the entire time interval under consideration in this study, a pregnant woman was considered categorically eligible for AFDC. Prior to passage of OBRA, however, a pregnant woman received full AFDC grants for herself and her unborn child. After April 1982, when OBRA provisions affecting payments for the unborn were implemented in California, a pregnant woman is still eligible for AFDC at any time during her pregnancy, but she receives an AFDC grant only for herself; for her unborn child she receives an additional special needs allowance rather than the full grant (in 1986 this allowance equaled $70). Furthermore, if a pregnant woman has other children, this special allowance is not paid until the third trimester of pregnancy.

8. See Appendix C for procedures for estimating the number of children not on welfare.

9. See Appendix C for procedures for estimating the number of potentially eligible.

10. Since cases closed for the past four months and the potentially eligible population, as previously defined, overlap somewhat, it is necessary to decrease the potentially eligible population in any month by the number of cases that closed during the previous four months. It is this slightly altered potentially eligible population, along with cases closed lagged four months, that is included in the accessions regression equation.

11. For discussion of the effects of welfare parameters on cases closed refer to Plotnick's, Wiseman's, and Hutchens' studies discussed in Chapter 7.

12. The breakeven variable used here is referred to as the actual breakeven variable in Chapter 2. It is deflated by the CPI. For discussion of the breakeven levels in California over time see Chapter 2.

13. Prior to OBRA's implementation work deductions were not standardized. Because an accurate estimate of work deductions could not be obtained for the purpose of calculating the taxpoint and the breakeven, it was assumed that work

deductions other than federal, state, and Social Security taxes equaled zero. Consequently, the taxpoint varies minimally over time. For further explanation of the breakeven, see Chapter 2 and Appendix B.

14. The benefit reduction rate is equal to maximum aid divided by the quantity of the breakeven minus the taxpoint, with, of course, all four variables calculated under the same set of assumptions. Within this set of assumptions, the taxpoint is essentially constant over the time interval considered in this analysis. No more than two of the three variables (the benefit reduction rate, breakeven, and maximum aid) may be used in any regression equation. If all three variables are used, a dependent set of variables would be incorporated into the equation.

15. For discussion of the effects of recipients' characteristics on case closures, refer to Bane and Ellwood's, Plotnick's, Wiseman's, and Hutchens' findings discussed in Chapter 7.

16. The coefficient of the breakeven after OBRA equals the coefficient of the breakeven plus the coefficient of the interaction. The latter coefficient is hypothesized to be positive so that the coefficient of the post-OBRA breakeven is greater than the coefficient of the pre-OBRA breakeven.

National Findings of Past Research

The previous chapter outlined a simple accounting framework for the study of welfare dynamics in California. The framework allows for the decomposition of the caseload into accessions and terminations. Thereafter, each component of the caseload is hypothesized to be a function of labor-market conditions, demographics, and welfare system characteristics.

This is not the first study of welfare dynamics. Other research has been conducted on a national scale or in other localities. In this chapter the literature on welfare dynamics is reviewed in order to highlight key hypotheses for testing and other issues for investigation. Moreover, since the value of the conclusions drawn about welfare dependence in California is partially dependent on how well the findings for California resemble the findings for other states, this review provides the basis for comparison.

The approach used to analyze welfare dynamics in the present study is uncommon. It can be characterized as "macro" in orientation; that is, it focuses on aggregate information such as the total number of accessions and terminations. In contrast, almost all past research on AFDC dynamics has been "micro" in perspective, focusing on the individual household as the unit of analysis. Specifically, past micro analyses of welfare dynamics have focused on how recipient characteristics, AFDC program parameters, or labor-market conditions influence the probability that a family will enter or exit the welfare rolls. Obviously this type of analysis requires data on the experiences and characteristics of individual households. Our understanding of welfare dependence is furthered both by these studies and by the relatively few studies that have analyzed aggregate responses of the caseload to changes in demographics, program characteristics, or labor-market conditions.

IMPACT OF RECIPIENT CHARACTERISTICS
ON AFDC DYNAMICS

An important question in micro analysis of AFDC dynamics is, holding other variables constant, what types of recipients or households are most likely to be welfare dependent? Are characteristics such as education, prior wages, labor-force attachment, age, race, or disability of heads of households associated with the likelihood that these individuals move to or from welfare? Is the size of recipients' families associated with the likelihood that recipients move to or from welfare?

In macro analysis of AFDC dynamics it is important to address the above questions in addition to others. In this type of study, the size of the population at risk is incorporated into a model of AFDC dynamics that is not considered in micro analysis. Researchers must tackle the problem of finding an appropriate definition of the population at risk and then attempt to determine the extent to which characteristics of that population affect welfare dependence.

The questions addressed in studies using micro data are also important and relevant to macro analysis. On a macro level these questions can be thought of in terms of the extent to which the number of individuals on welfare with particular characteristics (age, race, family size, and so forth) affect welfare dependence. Although these questions are important, they are not often addressed in the available literature.

The Literature

Individuals with certain characteristics in the general population have been known to have a greater chance of moving to welfare. When a women with children is the principal provider in the family, her chances of becoming poor and moving to welfare greatly increase. Analysis of Panel Study of Income Dynamics (PSID) data shows that changes in the composition of families is closely related to individuals' chances of falling into or climbing out of poverty.[1] Since most families in the AFDC-Basic program are headed by females, one would expect that growth in the number of female-headed families in the general population would be accompanied by growth in welfare accessions. Female-headed families in the population represent a high-risk group.

Plotnick and Lidman constructed a multivariate model for the single-parent AFDC caseload for Washington State using data for the years 1974 to 1983. The objectives of their research were to specify a model that explains caseload growth and to use this model to forecast the size of the caseload for 14 months in the future. No attempt was made to decompose the caseload into accessions or terminations equations. Thus, the dependent variable was the caseload, and the independent variables belonged to three classes: labor-market conditions, program characteristics, and demographics.

The authors claimed that in the initial stage of their analyses they used a set of demographic variables that would proxy the at-risk population. These variables included total births in the most recent 36 months, divorces, women age 15 to 34, and out-of-wedlock births. In the final stage of their historical simulation, they used only out-of-wedlock births. As expected, this variable is positively correlated with the caseload.[2]

Plotnick and Lidman did not use recipient characteristics as independent variables. However, since they specified a model of the AFDC caseload in order to improve future budgeting forecasts, if recipient characteristics were used as explanatory variables of the caseload, then these would need to be forecasted when extrapolating to the future. This would cause much unnecessary error.

Another macro analysis of AFDC dynamics was conducted by Jordan et al. in 1981, who analyzed the impact of the AFDC program's corrective actions on caseload size and expenditures in six U.S. jurisdictions. These researchers modeled the dynamics of the AFDC caseload from 1971 to 1979. Their approach was to decompose the caseload into several component equations, including as dependent variables the number of applications received, the processing rate, the rejection rate, and the closing rate. The exogenous explanatory variables in the component equations fell into four classes: institutional variables, including corrective actions; economic variables, including employment levels in selected industries; welfare system variables, including maximum aid for a family of four; and demographic and cultural variables, including the number of female heads of households in the population.[3]

The approach used by these researchers to decompose the AFDC caseload somewhat resembles the approach used in the present study, but rates, instead of flows, were used as dependent variables in all of the component equations except for that reflecting accessions. A flow rather than a rate was used as a dependent variable in the accessions equation because of the ambiguities involved in correctly defining the population at risk. A monthly estimate of the number of female heads of households in the population was sometimes used as one of the independent variables for the purpose of predicting the number of applications received. In Los Angeles County, this monthly estimate of the number of female household heads showed that from 1971 to 1979 an increase of 1,000 female-headed families was associated with 46 additional applications each month.[4]

One major problem is associated with using the number of female-headed families as an explanatory variable of the number of applications received. It is not clear whether only female-headed households in the population should be considered to be at risk. After all, because of rapidly changing circumstances, any females of child-bearing age, whether household heads or not, may become categorically eligible and apply for welfare.

Jordan et al. did not use other exogenous demographic variables or recipient characteristics in either their accessions or their terminations equations. Neither the number of births nor the number of children entered their accessions equation. Moreover, welfare recipient characteristics were not included in their terminations equations in any of the jurisdictions under consideration. As seen below, micro analyses of AFDC dynamics have shown that these variables predict both accessions and terminations.

The micro studies that consider the impact of AFDC recipient characteristics on entry and exit rates are in some accord and in some conflict over which variables are important in determining these rates. These studies differ in selected sample, variables controlled for in models, and the way in which the variables are measured. Although each study has some limitations, each furthers our understanding of welfare dynamics.

Plotnick[5] and Hutchens[6] considered the determinants of both entry and exit transitions in the AFDC program. Plotnick, analyzing a control group from the negative income tax experiment in Denver, included characteristics of female heads of households such as age, race, ethnicity, education, and disability as determinants of AFDC entry. As expected, he found that aging slowed the entry rate, implying that, as the population at risk ages, the number of applications to AFDC would decrease. The remaining variables were statistically insignificant in determining AFDC entry, yet each varied positively with this rate.

Hutchens, using PSID data, included various measures of individual characteristics such as the number of children of female household heads, age of the youngest child, and race in both his entry and exit models. He found them all to be insignificant and eliminated them from his logistic models. Leaving other characteristics of female household heads, such as age and education, in some models, he found that, as age increases the probability of entry decreases in three of his four models.

Plotnick and Hutchens both found that aging seems to have an inverse effect on entry. This is not surprising since older females are less likely to have young children or new births and more likely to be living in intact families. Both Hutchens and Plotnick examined the effect of recipients' prior wages on probability of entry. In addition, Plotnick incorporated in the entry model an economic variable representing any attachment to the labor force prior to welfare receipt. As expected, Plotnick and Hutchens found that higher wages strongly reduced entry rates. More importantly, Plotnick found that any attachment to the labor force prior to welfare receipt highly reduced the probability of entry.

Much interest among researchers has centered on the impact of recipient characteristics on the probability of case closure. Bane and Ellwood used PSID data to examine the nature of welfare spells and the determinants of exit probabilities for AFDC female household heads during a 12-year period.[7] A spell was defined as the number of consecutive years, not necessarily consecutive months, on welfare with an annual welfare income of more than $250. However, a great deal of turnover may be masked in one year's time, and Bane and Ellwood's results do not differentiate between people who are continuously on welfare during a year and those whose cycle on and off.

Bane and Ellwood included time in their logit model and time may have served as a proxy for other variables correlated with it. Time could stand for either a recipient's age or the age of her child. Their findings showed that the probability of leaving the welfare rolls is greatest during the first two years and the sixth year of welfare receipt. The tendency to leave welfare after six years may be due to the youngest child entering school making it possible for the mother to accept employment. In fact, Bane and Ellwood found that for 90 percent of recipients exiting in the sixth year, the youngest child had just reached school age; thus, time on welfare served as a proxy for age of the youngest child.

Recipients leave the welfare rolls by two main routes: when a change in family structure occurs, such as marriage, which makes the recipient categorically ineligible; or when earnings increase and eligibility is terminated. According to Bane and Ellwood, while a few AFDC recipients (12 percent) entered the rolls because of a decrease in earnings, a greater percentage (32 percent) left the rolls because of an increase in earnings. About one-third of those leaving welfare leave because of an increase in earnings; a third leave through reconciliation or marriage; and most of the remaining third leave because they become categorically ineligible.[8]

Several researchers besides Bane and Ellwood have distinguished between different exit routes when they assessed the effect of recipient characteristics on probability of exit. Plotnick censored his data in order to ensure that income rather than marriage determined the end of a spell.[9] Hutchens, who examined PSID data, also looked at exits via the route of income rather than marriage.[10]

In micro analysis of AFDC dynamics it seems essential to differentiate between types of closures, especially if economic variables such as wages or employment of recipients are used as predictors of closure rates; otherwise, these variables seem to have the unenviable task of predicting both types of exits.

Recipient's wage rates prior to welfare receipt, recipient's age, and number of children are variables that have yielded some agreement among researchers. Both Hutchens and Plotnick found that previous earnings allowed recipients to leave the welfare rolls faster. Hutchens, using PSID data for the years 1970 and 1971, examined the probability of exiting welfare by including the average hourly wages of recipients over the five years prior to his study. In his logit model he controls for other variables such as region, program parameters, and age of female household head. The hourly wage was found to be a significant factor in lowering the probability of stay. The greater the wage rate, the higher the probability of closure.

Plotnick, who examined economic variables as determinants of exit via the route of income, considered both expected wage and whether people received or did not receive wages prior to entering the rolls. The expected wage was not significant in its ability to predict exit; however, whether one had worked did appear as an important determinant in AFDC exit. Plotnick concluded that if a client accrued any wages prior to welfare receipt, then the probability of exit was greater. It should be noted that including wage as a discrete variable, as Plotnick did, disregards the importance of the amount of income accrued by earnings.

Wiseman, in his analysis of Alameda County welfare recipients, included employment history, but not prior wage rate, as a variable in his logit model.[11] Bane and Ellwood included recipients' earnings for the year prior to the beginning of the welfare spell. As expected, these researchers found that recipients with no prior earnings had longer expected spell length than those with some earnings.

The fact that female household heads with more children have a lower propensity to leave welfare has been a matter usually of accord but sometimes of conflict among researchers. Hutchens claimed that he did not include the number of children in his final logit model because he initially found that the coefficient of the number of children was statistically insignificant. Because the welfare guarantee increases as family size increases, one could argue that in some micro analytic studies of AFDC dynamics the guarantee measures the effect of family size on probability of closure. However, although the guarantee is proportional to family size, it does not exactly measure family size since a base line is inherent in the guarantee. Since the guarantee is correlated with number of children, when both the guarantee and number of children are entered in micro analysis, the reliability of both of their coefficients may be questioned. Mingling of the effects of the guarantee and family size can be prevented if a guarantee for a fixed-size family rather than the guarantee for a particular family is taken. Wiseman used the guarantee for a fixed-size family.

Hutchens and Plotnick did not include number of children in their final analyses. Wiseman found number of children to be statistically insignificant but positively correlated with closure probability.

Other researchers found that number of children had an effect on the length of stay. Coe and Bane and Ellwood, both using PSID data, did not control for any program parameters in their models and found that the greater the number of children in a family, the lower the probability of exit and the longer the stay on welfare.[12] Coe's analysis included other welfare recipients besides those on AFDC.[13] Bane and Ellwood's findings showed that AFDC mothers who started welfare with one child are twice as likely as mothers with three children to exit via the route of earnings. Obviously, it takes more money to support larger families; thus, closure via the route of earnings is more difficult for AFDC recipients with large families. Rydell et al. who examined some correlates of case openings, closings, and lengths of welfare stays in New York City, found that AFDC cases with two or more children had significantly longer stays than cases with fewer children.[14] In essence, some evidence suggests that an increase in number of children increases length of stay on the welfare rolls. Often this occurs because both the guarantee and the breakeven point are higher, inducing recipients to stay longer.

The evidence that aging increases the likelihood of exit is reasonably good. Both Hutchens and Plotnick found that the older the AFDC female head the greater the likelihood of exiting. The same is true of Wiseman, although his result is statistically insignificant at the .05 level. Hutchens suggests that this may occur for two reasons. The first is that older women tend to have older children and thus are more able to participate in the labor force and pursue economic self-sufficiency. The second is that older women often have a longer work history and thus are able to exit via the route of earnings more easily. Hutchens' second explanation is somewhat tenuous since Plotnick found that aging increased the probability of exit regardless of a recipient's work history. Hutchens, on the other hand, found that aging increased the probability of exit only for women with work histories. Bane and Ellwood did not find that a recipient's age, when she begins a welfare spell, increases the probability of exit. Most of the evidence suggests that aging increases closure probabilities.

Whether exit probabilities are functions of race is a matter of controversy filled with contradictory results. Bane and Ellwood found that race is a determinant factor of length of stay on the rolls. Their findings show that while white high-school graduates under age 30 have an expected AFDC spell of 4.3 years, non-whites with the same education and of the same age have an expected spell of 6.2 years. While the expected length of stay on AFDC is longer for both whites and their counterparts who did not complete high school than for those who completed high school, again such non-whites have a longer expected stay on welfare. Overall, they found that when non-whites are compared to whites with similar characteristics, non-whites stay longer on the rolls.

Bane and Ellwood controlled for numerous variables when they looked at transition rates of different groups. Variables observed at the beginning of a spell included income relative to need, marital status, regional variation, and age. Although these researchers controlled for regional variation, they did not control for programmatic variation within these regions. If program parameters in regions with more whites on welfare are associated with greater closure rates, then on the average non-whites would be found to have lower transition rates.

Wiseman, who analyzed AFDC dynamics in Alameda County, controlled for program parameters in his model and found that, other things being equal, blacks had a lower probability of closure than whites. Wiseman's and Bane and Ellwood's finding that non-whites have a lower probability of closure does not concur with either Plotnick or Hutchens, who found race to be statistically insignificant in predicting closure. Both Wiseman and Bane and Ellwood examined exits via the route of both marriage and earnings, while Hutchens and Plotnick did not. Bane and Ellwood found that the probability of closure substantially decreases for non-whites via the route of marriage but not as much via the route of increase in earnings. This, in part, may explain the lower probability of closure for non-whites.

In fact, if a disproportionate number of non-whites are long-term recipients, and if for many the likelihood of achieving a state of independence is less than for their counterparts, this is an important issue. Female headship has always been more pronounced among black families than among other groups.[15] Irrespective of race, female-headed families are often poor, yet the chances of long-term poverty are more prevalent among black female household heads. Duncan and Coe's descriptive analyses of short- and long-term welfare recipients also found this to be true. Although they considered welfare to include AFDC, food stamps, and Supplemental Security Income, their results are relevant. Their findings from PSID data showed that the characteristics of the persistently welfare dependent closely resemble those of the persistently poor.[16]

The fact that there is an unbalanced ratio of black females to black males in our society has been a cause for growth in household headship among black females.[17] Other explanations may be offered for the finding that black females have a lower probability of exiting the rolls via the route of marriage. Many black males encounter some economic insecurity, making marriage an unattractive economic alternative for some black females. Remarriage rates for blacks in the general population are significantly lower than those for whites and lengths of separation are much longer.[18] Unfortunately for some black female household heads, marriage could offer an escape not only from welfare dependence but also from poverty. About half of women who escape poverty do so by getting married.[19] According to Bane and Ellwood, rates of leaving welfare via the route of earnings increase are not much lower for black than for white female-headed families.

Summary and Issues

The evidence is fairly strong that prior and expected earnings of household heads influence entry and exit transition rates. In the studies discussed above, prior earnings represent either the existence of any prior earnings or the amount of prior earnings. The amount of recipients' prior earnings seems to be a better measure since it reflects the quality and duration of their past employment. The findings of these studies lend support to policies that invest in increasing the earning power of recipients.

There is fairly strong evidence that older recipients have a greater probability of closure. The rise in teenage pregnancy in recent years has many social and psychological consequences of which persistent welfare dependence is only one. Birth of a child to a young mother increases both the likelihood of long-term dependence on welfare and the likelihood of falling below the poverty threshold after leaving the rolls.

There is strong evidence that the number of children in a dependent family is a good predictor of AFDC closure. Studies consistently show that female heads with many children have a lower probability of welfare exit than those with few children. When measuring the effect of the number of children on the probability of closure, and using individual families as the unit of analysis, there is a need to find a way to isolate the effects of the guarantee from the effects of family size so that each can be better understood. These effects can be isolated if the guarantee included in the analysis is not the actual guarantee but rather the one for a fixed family size as was included in Wiseman's analysis and in the present study.

There is mixed evidence about the extent to which disability, education, and race affect welfare dependence. It appears that the effects of race on closure can be better understood when exit routes via marriage or increase in earnings can be differentiated and integrated into models that control for program parameters.

All of the evidence presented thus far is taken from studies using individual families as the unit of analysis. In macro studies, evidence indicates that the extent to which the population at risk affects caseload movement or size is only as good as the researcher's definition of the population at risk. In the studies reviewed there has not been a consistent definition of the at-risk population.

Recipient characteristics such as the number of young female household heads on the rolls, the number of children under school age, or family size can be, but usually have not been, integrated into aggregate models. As seen in Chapter 6, these variables are included in the component equations used in the present study. Since a large number of welfare recipients exit via the route of marriage, seasonal variables are expected to serve as proxies for marriages. All of the variables in the aggregate equations in the present study are hypothesized to vary in a fashion consistent with the cited findings.

IMPACT OF PROGRAM CHARACTERISTICS
ON AFDC DYNAMICS

Micro and macro studies consider the effects of AFDC program characteristics on entry or exit behaviors or on the entire caseload. The variables considered in these analyses consist of one or more of the following AFDC program characteristics: the guarantee (maximum aid), the benefit reduction rate, or the breakeven level. Using economic theory as a guide, researchers have hypothesized the effect of each variable on entry or exit behaviors. There is one set of common questions addressed by researchers: Does the benefit reduction rate, the guarantee, or the breakeven level affect entry or exit behaviors as posited by economic theory? If so, how large are the effects of changes in a particular variable on entry or exit behaviors?

Since some program characteristics, such as the AFDC guarantee and the benefit reduction rate, are also associated with work incentives, and since employment while on welfare allows some recipients to gain economic self-sufficiency, past research has paid particular attention to the ways in which these variables affect recipients' work efforts. Much past research has centered on the effects of these variables on movement to employment while on welfare rather than on movement from employment to closure. Here the relevant set of important questions concerns the extent to which these variables affect the labor supply of recipients. Do changes in the benefit reduction rate or guarantee affect the labor supply of recipients in a fashion consistent with economic theory? If so, by how much does the labor supply of this population change?

Program Characteristics and Employment: The Literature

Researchers have been concerned with the degree to which the welfare guarantee and the benefit reduction rate affect the labor supply of recipients. Some researchers perceive a change in labor supply to mean a change in whether an AFDC participant is employed. Others perceive this to mean a change in work hours during a fixed interval of time.

Garfinkel and Orr used national cross-sectional data on AFDC recipients to measure the effects of the guarantee and the benefit reduction rate on AFDC recipients' employment rate.[20] Employment rate was defined as the ratio of working AFDC participants to all participants in the program. Findings have confirmed what economic theory posited, namely, that an increase in the guarantee and a decrease in the benefit reduction rate would lower the employment rate of AFDC participants. Specifically, research has shown that an increase in the guarantee by 40 percent lowers the employment rate by 5 percent, and a 35 percent decrease in the benefit reduction rate increases the employment rate by 5 percent; thus, quite large percentage changes in program parameters lead to small changes in the employment rate of AFDC participants.

Since Garfinkel and Orr examined AFDC data in 1967, they were not able to study the effects of the $30 disregard and the 67 percent implicit tax imposed on earnings that were implemented across the nation in 1968. Yet variations in both the guarantee and the benefit reduction rate imposed on welfare recipients prevailed across the states because states paid recipients welfare benefits according to different benefit structures. Additional variations among states existed because of the differing amounts of allowed work deductions and because of the different ways states deduct in-kind benefits; however, benefit reductions of in-kind benefits such as Medicaid and food stamps were not considered in Garfinkel and Orr's analysis.

Interdependence among the benefit reduction rate, taxpoint, guarantee, and breakeven level creates some problems in the interpretation of Garfinkel and Orr's results. A decrease in the benefit reduction rate can raise the employment rate of recipients, but since it increases the breakeven level it may also increase the number of working recipients, allowing more of them to combine work and welfare and stay on the rolls rather than become ineligible. Consequently, a decrease in the benefit reduction rate and the resulting increase in the breakeven captures both the greater number of recipients on the rolls who assume employment due to the decrease in the benefit reduction rate and the greater number of working recipients who are not made ineligible for welfare under a higher breakeven level. An increase in the guarantee also increases the breakeven, with the former decreasing the employment rate of recipients and the latter allowing more workers to stay on the rolls, possibly lowering terminations. When Garfinkel and Orr increased the guarantee in their study, they implicitly increased the breakeven, consequently biasing their results.

Changes in AFDC program characteristics can affect the economic behaviors of those already on welfare and of those not participating but categorically eligible. While lower benefit reduction rates can increase work efforts among participants, they can have different effects on categorically eligible non-participants who may leave the labor market and enter the welfare system. But Garfinkel and Orr did not observe all categorically eligible female household heads. It seems that they should have either used cross-sectional data with a different dependent variable, such as the employment rate of the categorically eligible population, or observed recipients' behaviors over time. Observing employment behaviors of both non-participants and participants over time would limit the accompanying problems of changes in the breakeven level. Garfinkel and Orr should have examined the employment rate of all female household heads.

Garfinkel and Orr recognized the existence of interstate variability in work requirements and manpower training for welfare recipients that influence employment rates, and they accounted for this in their model; yet there are many other sources of interstate variation, particularly conditions of the labor market relevant to the welfare population for which they did not control. Garfinkel and Orr's study provides only a gross approximation of how individuals behave when confronting changes in program parameters.

While Garfinkel and Orr used cross-sectional data to analyze the employment rate of AFDC recipients, Wiseman examined the effects of program parameters on AFDC recipients' work efforts by employing historical variations in welfare parameters in Alameda County, California, from 1968 to 1981.[21] Participants selected for analysis at different time periods were assumed to be comparable since they were randomly selected from welfare records and an array of variables were controlled for in the model. Participants were observed at the end of each of two consecutive three-month periods, and a person was counted as employed if she was employed at either of those two sampling times. Wiseman assumed that he could adequately capture recipients' transitions to employment; however, his discrete two-point measurement of employment may have masked some additional transitions to and from employment. For example, capturing short seasonal work in which some AFDC recipients engage would be difficult.

Wiseman used a logit model with the dependent variable being the probability of employment of jobless recipients and the independent variables consisting of program parameters, local unemployment rate, and recipient characteristics. The guarantee in his model included the cash value of food stamps. The taxpoint included both the earnings disregard and variant work expenses. The time variable in Wiseman's model represented the time at which particular recipients were observed. This time variable could serve as a proxy for variations in administrative stringency in enforcing work requirements over the years.

Wiseman's results, as expected, showed that the welfare benefit, the taxpoint, and the breakeven point had the anticipated sign effects on the probability of obtaining employment. A 10 percent increase in the benefit level reduced the probability of gaining employment by 25 percent when all other variables were held constant, while a 10 percent increase in the breakeven point increased the probability of employment by 25 percent.

Wiseman and Garfinkel and Orr examined the effect of variability in program parameters on the work efforts of only AFDC household female heads. Levy, using PSID annual data for 1978, examined the labor supply of all female household heads with children.[22] Levy assumed that tradeoffs exist when a decrease in the benefit reduction rate increases participants' work efforts since this also motivates more non-participants to apply for welfare, thus decreasing their labor supply.

Levy's rationale for using annual work hours rather than simply observing whether women gained employment during the year was well founded since a year's time can mask many transitions to and from employment. Moreover, by looking at annual hours Levy was able to capture the seasonal employment often taken by low-income workers. After gathering data on annual hours of work by female household heads, Levy made his dependent variable discrete by dividing hours of work into three cells. These cells were defined as "little" (0–400 hours); "some" (400–1,500 hours); and "full time" (more than 1,500 hours). The second cell is quite large, measuring discretely too much variation in hours worked.

Levy examined how variant program parameters affect the probability of being in one of the earning cells. Later he compared actual versus predicted results to see whether female household heads fell into the appropriate earning cell. Since essentially no one was accurately predicted to be in the second cell, Levy was left with two cells. His predictions were accurate 58 percent of the time, but given only two cells, 58 percent is not much better than chance.

It would have been interesting if Levy also had accounted for variations in eligibility standards across the states as these also determine the number of low-income applicants allowed to enter the welfare rolls.

Levy concludes that "any AFDC parameter shift which increases the program's breakeven point will decrease the woman's expected hours of work."[23] No doubt there are tradeoffs, and, while an increase in labor participation among AFDC recipients as a response to a change in program parameters may result in a decrease in labor participation among non-participating female heads, it is not clear whether the former group's work efforts increase much more than the latter group's work efforts decrease. In addition, Levy's contention that a low marginal tax is not an appropriate goal is not based on good empirical evidence. Nonetheless, Levy should be given credit for examining all categorically eligible female household heads rather than only AFDC participants.

Summary and Issues: Program Characteristics and Employment

There is strong evidence that an increase in the guarantee and a decrease in the benefit reduction rate reduce AFDC participants' work efforts. Moreover, since a decrease in the benefit reduction rate increases the breakeven level, an increase in the breakeven increases the probability of employment on the part of participants. However, there is some disagreement among researchers concerning the magnitude of the effect of a particular program characteristic on employment. Differences in researchers' findings often are due to different samples, different definitions of the dependent variable, different variables controlled for in the model, and some oversights.

Although the evidence is limited, it has been shown that, while a decrease in the benefit reduction rate can increase the work efforts of participants, it may lower the work efforts of the at-risk population. More studies need to investigate this effect by taking into account the responses of all of the categorically eligible population to changes in program parameters.

Program Characteristics and Accessions and Terminations: The Literature

Program parameters affect not only rates of transition to employment, they also affect rates of transition to and from the welfare system. Policy makers hope that the work incentives accompanying low benefit reduction rates will result in movement to closures, that is, that once participants gain employment while on welfare they also will move out of the system. Whereas Garfinkel and Orr, Wiseman, and Levy examined the effects of welfare parameters on labor supply. Plotnick and Hutchens examined their effects on entry to and exit from welfare. Only Wiseman examined the relationship between gaining employment while on welfare and moving out of the system.

Plotnick examined AFDC turnover among households in the control group for the Seattle-Denver income-maintenance experiment.[24] In his analysis of AFDC turnover, some of the variation in the guarantee was simply due to family size, which is a poor indicator of a larger transfer payment motivating people to work less. As the guarantee increases with family size, so does the need of the family. Furthermore, another source of variation in the guarantee was that Colorado increased welfare benefits once during the experiment. Plotnick's findings revealed that, the greater the size of the guarantee, the lower the probability of closure and the higher the probability of entry. His findings show that a 10 percent increase in the guarantee increases the probability of closure by 6.4 percent and lowers the average time off welfare by 8.2 percent. However, given the problem with this variation, interpretation of the effect is somewhat questionable.

Hutchens, using PSID data for 1970 and 1971, examined the probability of entry to and exit from the welfare rolls as a function of program parameters.[25] Since PSID data are annual, a good deal of movement to and from welfare is masked. Hutchens assumed that recipients at one point in time are representative of the welfare population; however, since at any single time there are substantially more long-term than short-term recipients, his assumption is questionable. As expected, Hutchens' findings revealed that the higher the level of benefits, the higher the probability of entry and the lower the probability of closure. Hutchens found that a 10 percent increase in benefits yields small changes in entry and exit probabilities but results in an increase in AFDC participation rates of almost 17 percent. In addition, he found that the higher the breakeven point, the greater the probability of exit; yet given the large standard error in the breakeven point, the results are questionable. Hutchens was disappointed with the sign of the breakeven since he hypothesized that the higher the breakeven the lower the probability of closures.

Policy makers have sought to induce recipients to leave welfare by building work incentives into welfare benefit computations. Wiseman tested the hypothesis that obtaining a job while on welfare would increase the probability of closure.[26] He found that working while on welfare significantly increases the probability of closure. Other researchers have examined the effects of working prior to welfare on the probability of closure, but this variable has a meaning different from obtaining work while on welfare. The difference is important because welfare work incentives are aimed at inducing jobless recipients to obtain employment and thereby leave welfare.

Wiseman's findings demonstrated that the higher the breakeven point, the greater the probability of closure, and that the lower both the taxpoint and the guarantee, the higher the probability of closure. His findings show that a 10 percent increase in benefits decreases the probability of closure by about one-fifth. Although an increase in the breakeven point can mean that families who would have earned their way off welfare over a lower breakeven point are still eligible under a higher breakeven point and, presumably, remain on welfare for longer periods of time, Wiseman's findings revealed otherwise. His findings concur with Congressman Wilbur Mills' expectation that welfare recipients will eventually work themselves off welfare when the marginal value of work is increased.

Thus far, all of the studies reviewed in this section use micro analytic techniques to determine probabilities of entry to and exit from welfare. The extensive macro analysis of the determinants of the AFDC caseload by Jordan et al. examined the effect of the AFDC guarantee relative to prevailing wages on both welfare accessions and terminations in some of the six jurisdictions studied.[27] Since these researchers used a rate rather than a flow as a dependent variable in the closure equation, a benefit-to-wage ratio seemed appropriate. However, they ignored remaining welfare features that may affect AFDC turnover, such as the breakeven level. As expected, in Los Angeles County the number of applications received varied positively with the guarantee. In this county the guarantee was not included in the closure equation. In other counties where the guarantee was included in the closure equation, applications received varied negatively with the guarantee.

When Plotnick and Lidman analyzed the determinants of the AFDC caseload in the state of Washington, they included the AFDC guarantee for a family of three.[28] Moreover, they initially incorporated the guarantee divided by average real earnings in the service sector. This latter variable subsequently was discarded due to lack of statistical significance. Also included were dummy variables representing programmatic changes that accompanied both the Omnibus Budget Reconciliation Act of 1981 and the Deficit Reduction Act of 1984. Plotnick and Lidman found that as the welfare guarantee increased by 1 percent the caseload increased by 0.1 percent in the next 12 months. These two researchers did not include other AFDC program characteristics that are theoretically relevant.

Summary and Issues:
Program Characteristics and Accessions and Terminations

The evidence is strong that an increase in the guarantee increases welfare accessions and decreases terminations. There is some evidence that an increase in the breakeven increases the probability of closure. Although both Hutchens and Wiseman found this, Hutchens' finding was contrary to his hypothesis. The hypothesized direction of the breakeven depends on one's belief. If it is believed that a higher breakeven resulting from a lower benefit reduction rate allows recipients to combine work and welfare as a first step toward independence, then the hypothesized sign of the breakeven in a termination equation should be positive. If it is believed that a higher breakeven allows people to enjoy higher incomes by combining work and welfare, in turn reducing the likelihood of closure, then the hypothesized sign of the breakeven should be negative.

The studies reviewed here using aggregate data exclude all other program characteristics except for welfare benefits. The evidence from these studies reveals that an increase in a fixed size of the guarantee results in a greater number of accessions, a lower number of terminations, and a larger caseload. Although these studies ignore the effects of eligibility standards at both point of entry and exit, that is, the standard of need and breakeven, respectively, these variables are not ignored in the present investigation. In the present study, it is hypothesized that prior to OBRA the breakeven varies negatively with the number of closures, since it is believed that higher breakevens allow more people to combine work and welfare, thus reducing the number of people who exit through earnings increase.

IMPACT OF LABOR-MARKET CONDITIONS ON AFDC DYNAMICS

Controlling for labor-market conditions is essential in examining the impact of AFDC program characteristics on either AFDC recipients' labor supply or welfare turnover, since for some individuals the economic appeal of the welfare system is weighed against the availability of jobs and the level of wages in the marketplace.

Questions relevant to assessing the impact of these conditions are: Does the aggregate unemployment rate affect entry or exit transitions? Does the demand for employment in industries assumed to employ welfare or potential welfare recipients affect AFDC transitions? Do ongoing wages available to welfare or potential welfare recipients affect AFDC transitions?

The Literature

In the micro analytic studies discussed earlier, Hutchens, Levy, and Bane and Ellwood did not control for labor-market conditions in their models. The other micro studies did include local unemployment rates in their equations. In both Plotnick's and Wiseman's findings, the aggregate unemployment rate always had an unexpected sign and a statistically insignificant coefficient.

Venti argues that the aggregate unemployment rate does not necessarily reflect the experiences of the welfare population in the marketplace.[29] Rather, the author claims, the demand for low-skilled labor and its variation in terms of gender and race all affect the demand for welfare. For the most part, welfare recipients face low-wage occupations, often in low-wage industries. Moreover, even when low-wage industries provide stable employment, rising above the poverty line is often difficult, if not impossible, for low-skilled workers, and the demand for welfare may still exist.

Jordan et al., when examining the impact of quality control on aggregate response of the AFDC caseload, attempted to control for the aggregate unemployment rates and employment levels in selected industries across six jurisdictions. Variables were included in the final equations only if they had the correct sign and were statistically significant.[30]

In their macro analyses of AFDC dynamics, Jordan et al. found the aggregate unemployment rate to be a significant predictor of both accessions and terminations in some jurisdictions. For example, in both Los Angeles and Alameda counties in California, as the aggregate unemployment rate increased, the number of closures decreased. In Los Angeles County, an increase in this rate of one percentage point resulted in a decline of nearly seven-tenths of a percentage point in the rate of case closures. In Los Angeles County the unemployment rate had the correct sign in the accessions equation but this was not found in Alameda County. The researchers claim that the unemployment rate is expected to vary negatively with closures not only because of more limited employment opportunities but also because during difficult economic conditions welfare departments usually adopt a more lenient attitude toward recipients and, in turn, fewer cases are closed.

Jordan et al., believing that employment levels in selected industries would be good predictors of AFDC accessions and terminations, selected low-wage, low-skill industries for the six jurisdictions under consideration. In Los Angeles County, the change in employment level in eating and drinking establishments was found to be a good predictor of AFDC accessions. Its coefficient suggests that for every 1,000 additional jobs in this sector, there will be 112 fewer applications for welfare. However, this variable was not a good predictor in either the accessions or closures equations in Alameda County or in the closures equation in Los Angeles County.

As opposed to Jordan et al., Plotnick and Lidman did not include employment levels in low-wage, low-skill industries as predictors of the AFDC caseload. They did include the total employment level in all non-agricultural industries and found it to be strongly negatively associated with caseload growth.

Whereas wages of recipients prior to welfare entry were appropriately included in studies using household data, the ongoing wages of welfare recipients were included in the study by Jordan et al. but not in Plotnick and Lidman's study. In the former study a ratio was constructed reflecting welfare benefits to wages net of taxes. The disposable income variable was created from average wages in low-skill, high-turnover industries weighted by relative employment levels and numbers of female workers in these industries. Their results are as expected. As benefits increased relative to wages, accessions increased and terminations decreased.

Summary and Issues

Past research reveals some accord and some conflict over whether selected variables are good predictors of AFDC dynamics. Although the evidence is mixed, it seems reasonable to include the aggregate unemployment rate in a model, if only for the purpose of statistical control.

The evidence that demand for employment in low-skill, high-turnover industries has the expected impact on AFDC receipt is good, yet limited. More research is needed to determine both the kinds of industries employing those at risk of welfare receipt and their impact on AFDC dynamics. Overall, both aggregate unemployment and demand in certain low-skill industries should be included. Clearly, demand in these industries is in part dependent upon the aggregate unemployment rate. When the unemployment rate is high, demand may be low.

Not much evidence exists concerning the effects of ongoing wages on AFDC turnover. The limited evidence suggests that, on the average, potential recipients do weigh the alternatives available to them in the marketplace against those available in the welfare system.

SUMMARY

Almost all of the studies reviewed in this chapter investigated the determinants of AFDC receipt using household data. Studies using aggregate data are in short supply. Yet regardless of the nature of the data used, researchers analyzing welfare dependence choose three classes of independent variables. These three classes relate to characteristics of household heads or their families, characteristics of the welfare system, and conditions of the labor market. All of the researchers tackle a major problem, namely, choosing appropriate variables from these three classes. Some choose an array of variables and discard some from their final analysis on the basis of the coefficients' statistical insignificance. Others maintain their initial variables by using theory as a guide. Conclusions drawn from the former studies should be viewed with caution due to the high probability that the variables' coefficients have attained statistical significance by chance.

As seen in Chapter 6, the independent variables chosen for investigation in this study also fall into the above three classes. The reasons for selecting each of the variables are based on findings from past research and theory.

The model of AFDC dynamics is specified and the effects of welfare system characteristics, labor-market conditions, and household characteristics on welfare dependence in California are discussed in Chapter 8. Whether these effects differ from past research conducted on the national level or in other locations remains to be seen.

The model constructed in this study will be used in Chapter 9 to analyze the consequences of California's welfare benefit levels and the Omnibus Budget Reconciliation Act. The results of this analysis and comparisons between the effects of OBRA on AFDC caseloads in California and in the rest of the nation will also be discussed in Chapter 9.

NOTES

1. On the dynamics of poverty and changing family composition, see G. J. Duncan and R. D. Coe, "The Dynamics of Welfare Use," in *Years of Poverty, Years of Plenty: The Changing Economic Fortunes of American Workers and Families*, ed. G. J. Duncan et al. (Ann Arbor: University of Michigan, Institute for Social Research, 1984), pp. 17–24.

2. See R. Plotnick and R. M. Lidman, "Forecasting Welfare Caseloads: A Tool to Improve Budgeting," unpublished manuscript, Contracts 2000–46181 and 6500–52438 (Seattle: Washington State Social and Health Services Department, 1986).

3. The component equations were not functions of the same variables for all six

jurisdictions. An exogenous variable entered a jurisdiction's component equations if, upon theoretical considerations, it seemed appropriate to incorporate it and if it was found significant. For example, a variable such as the number of female-headed households was included in the applications-received equation for upstate New York because it was found significant but was excluded from the applications equation for New York City because there it was found insignificant. For more detail see P. Jordan et al., *Corrective Action and AFDC Dynamics: An Empirical Study in Six Jurisdictions*, Grant No. 5-21474 (Boston: Boston College, Social Welfare Institute, Public Assistance Data Analysis Laboratory, 1981).

4. Ibid. Jordan et al. constructed monthly estimates of the number of female-headed families for an area using 1960 and 1970 census data and current population surveys.

5. R. Plotnick, "Turnover in the AFDC Population: An Event History Analysis," *Journal of Human Resources* 18 (1983): 65–81.

6. R.M. Hutchens, "Entry and Exit Transitions in Government Transfer Programs: The Case of Aid to Families with Dependent Children," *Journal of Human Resources* 16 (1981): 217–237.

7. Bane and Ellwood, using logit regression equations, empirically predicted exit transitions via different routes but examined the reasons for entry to the AFDC program only in tabular form. For details see M.J. Bane and D.T. Ellwood, *The Dynamics of Dependence: The Routes to Self-sufficiency*, Contract No. HHS-100-82-0038 (Washington, D.C.: U.S. Health and Human Services Department, 1983).

8. Ibid.

9. Plotnick, "Turnover in the AFDC Population."

10. Hutchens, "Entry and Exit Transitions."

11. Michael Wiseman, *Work Incentives and Welfare Turnover*, Working Paper 84-01 (Berkeley: University of California, Department of Economics Welfare and Employment Studies Project, 1984).

12. See R.D. Coe, "A Preliminary Empirical Examination of the Dynamics of Welfare Use," in *Five Thousand American Families: Patterns of Economic Progress*, vol. 9, ed. M. Hill, D. Hill, and J. Morgan (Ann Arbor: University of Michigan, Institute for Social Research, 1981).

13. In his analysis of the dynamics of welfare receipt, Coe included recipients receiving aid from AFDC, Supplemental Security Income, the Food Stamp program, or General Assistance.

14. C. Rydell et al., *Welfare Caseload Dynamics in New York City*, Report No. R-1441-NYC (New York: Rand Institute, 1974).

15. The proportion of female household heads among white families rose in the United States from 9 percent in 1965 to 12 percent in 1980; during the same period, the proportion of female heads for blacks rose from 25 percent to 40 percent. For more information see W. Darity and S. Myers, "Exploring Black Welfare Dependency: Changes in Black Family Structure—Implications for Welfare Dependency," *American Economic Review* 37 (1983): 59-64.

16. Duncan and Coe describe the incidence of welfare use and the characteristics of recipients. See Duncan and Coe, "Dynamics of Welfare Use."

17. See Darity and Myers, "Exploring Black Welfare Dependency."

18. See H. Ross and I. Sawhill, *Time of Transition: The Growth of Families Headed by Women* (Washington, D.C.: Urban Institute, 1975).

19. Ibid.

20. I. Garfinkel and L. L. Orr, "Welfare Policy and the Employment Rate of AFDC Mothers," *National Tax Journal* 27 (1974): 275–284.

21. Wiseman, *Work Incentives and Welfare Turnover*.

22. F. Levy, "The Labor Supply of Female Household Heads, or AFDC Work Incentives Don't Work Too Well," *Journal of Human Resources* 4 (1979): 76–97.

23. Ibid., p. 87.

24. Plotnick, "Turnover in the AFDC Population."

25. Hutchens, "Entry and Exit Transitions."

26. Wiseman, *Work Incentives and Welfare Turnover*.

27. Jordan et al., *Corrective Action and AFDC Dynamics*.

28. Plotnick and Lidman, "Forecasting Welfare Caseloads."

29. For a discussion of Venti's study see M. B. Sanger, *Welfare of the Poor* (New York: Academic Press, 1979), p. 38.

30. Jordan et al., *Corrective Action and AFDC Dynamics*.

8

Regression Results

The model of AFDC-Basic dynamics presented in this volume is designed both to test hypotheses about the effects of independent variables and to forecast additions, terminations, and thus the entire caseload. In this chapter each individual equation for California is examined with respect to its theoretical reasonableness and the extent to which it concurs with findings of research conducted elsewhere. In addition, each equation is examined with respect to the statistical significance of its coefficients and its overall fit.

REGRESSION RESULTS

The model for predicting the AFDC-Basic caseload has two regression equations, each containing a single dependent variable: one for the number of accessions, which consists of new additions and restorations (AD), and the other for the number of cases closed (CL), which excludes intraprogram transfers. The results for each of the regression equations are discussed below. The level of significance chosen for discussion is set a priori at the 0.10 for all one-tailed t-tests.

Cases Added

The estimated equation for welfare accessions is presented in Table 8.1. Because the initial regression analysis had a Durbin-Watson statistic that showed the presence of significant autocorrelation, the Hildreth-Lu rho correction procedure for first-order autocorrelation was applied. The rho corrected results are shown in Table 8.1 and exclusively used throughout the analysis of cases added. This rho corrected ordinary least square (OLS) regres-

Table 8.1
Regression Results for Accessions Equation, Rho Corrected

From 5/1972		Until 12/1984		
Observations		152	Degrees of Freedom	118
R Squared		.75	Rbar Squared	.69
SSR		88750000	SEE	867.2
Durbin-Watson		2.2	Rho	.4615
F(34, 118)		487.7	Significance Level	.0000

Variable	Lag	Coefficient	t-Statistic	Mean
Constant	0	2720	0.1518	2720
SN	0	4.530	0.3824	610.0
TP	0	6.174	0.5538	673.1
DO	0	-1006	-1.252	0.2500
WI	1	10.61	1.225	1250
MW	1	-5.490	-1.347	726.3
U	1	0.8072	0.4424	861.8
U	2	-1.800	-1.055	860.4
U	3	0.04545	0.02727	859.3
U	4	-1.398	-0.7952	857.7
NA	1	-2.830	-1.392	8693
F	1	-30.37	-1.414	178.5
A	1	-104.7	-1.980	100.7
K	1	0.02275	3.959	3754000
B	1	-0.4810	-2.617	30740
B	2	-0.1369	-0.7115	30660
B	3	0.2397	1.327	30570
B	4	0.01010	0.1048	30470
P	1	-0.007714	-1.000	4890000
CL	1	0.08307	1.872	22350
CL	2	-0.03893	-0.8412	22310
CL	3	0.08940	1.927	22240
CL	4	0.01943	0.4137	22170
JA	0	-144.7	-0.2550	0.07895
FB	0	-1534	-1.984	0.07895
MR	0	-475.2	-0.5791	0.07895
AP	0	-413.6	-0.3913	0.07895
MY	0	-198.7	-0.2060	0.08553
JU	0	-232.7	-0.2678	0.08553
JL	0	493.8	0.6973	0.08553
AG	0	2614	3.328	0.08553
SP	0	3073	2.451	0.08553
OC	0	4548	3.929	0.08553
NV	0	1024	1.761	0.08553

Sources, definitions, and deflation: See Appendix F.

Notes: U, NA, F, and A are in thousands. TP, SN, WI, and MW are in real terms (6/1985=100).

sion explains about 70 percent of the variance in monthly accessions. The standard error is 5.2 percent of the 16,612 average monthly new and restored additions.[1]

Apart from seasonal trends and multiple lags, the accessions equation contains 13 predictor variables. Despite some of the correlation between two independent variables in the equation, namely, the AFDC and food stamp benefits for a family of three (*TP*) and the AFDC program's standard of need (*SN*), both variables have the expected sign. These findings concur with past findings, which also showed that an increase in the guarantee or the income eligibility cutoff increases accessions. In contrast to past research that used the actual guarantee of selected families, thus mingling effects of the guarantee and family size, the AFDC maximum aid (guarantee) and the standard of need used here are for a fixed family size. Although both of these variables have the expected sign, neither alone nor together do these variables' coefficients attain statistical significance at the 0.10 level.

With the onset of OBRA, new cases added and cases restored decreased from their historical monthly average of 16,658 from May 1972 to November 1981 by about 1,006 additions per month. This is a decrease of about 6 percent.

As for the ongoing benefits available to welfare recipients in the marketplace, the minimum wage (*MW*) variable, but not the wage of receptionists (*WI*), has the expected sign, and its coefficient attains statistical significance. The coefficient of this variable suggests that in response to a hypothetical 10 cents per hour increase in the minimum wage about 95 cases per month remain off the rolls. It should be kept in mind that a 10 cents per hour increase in the minimum wage is a realistic increase.[2] These findings would not be expected in past micro research since these studies used the household head's prior wages as determinants of accession. Although past macro research did not incorporate either the minimum wage (*MW*) or the wage index (*WI*) established here, these studies find that increasing selected wages available to recipients in the marketplace lowers the number of welfare accessions.

The variables in the equation reflecting the relationship between other labor-market conditions and accessions are jointly significant predictors. All of the employment levels in the selected non-agricultural industries (*A, F,* and *NA*) have the expected sign and individually or jointly are found to be statistically significant. This implies that, if in any given month the employment level in selected industries increases by 1,000 workers, welfare accessions decrease by about 138 cases. From examining both the magnitude of the apparel coefficient (*A*) and its level of statistical significance, it appears that employment in this industry, or in one that fluctuates in a similar fashion, has a large impact on cases added.

The finding that accessions decrease as employment levels in selected industries increase concurs with the Jordan et al study of welfare dynamics.[3] Although these researchers used other industries as determinants of welfare accessions, they also found that accessions decreased as employment levels in certain low-skill industries increased. It should be kept in mind that, in contrast to the present study, not all of the selected industries in that study had the expected effect. For example, out of several selected low-skill industries in Los Angeles County only the employment level in drinking and eating establishments had the expected sign. This suggests that in the present investigation, and perhaps not in others, suitable industries were selected for the analysis.

The aggregate unemployment (U) variable is not statistically significant.[4] Since past findings regarding the effect of aggregate unemployment on welfare accessions are mixed, the statistical insignificance of this variable's coefficient lends support to the fact that aggregate unemployment is a poor predictor. The contention of other researchers that demand for employment in low-wage industries is a better reflector of welfare recipients' experiences in the marketplace than aggregate unemployment is substantiated here.

When examining all of the demographic variables, the coefficient of only the number of children in California not on welfare (K) both has the expected sign and is found to be statistically significant. The coefficient of K suggests that a monthly increase of 1,000 in the number of children not on welfare results in an increase of about 23 accessions. The remaining coefficients of the demographic variables reveal unexpected signs. A joint F-test on the lagged set of births (B) reveals statistical significance; however, overall their signs are unexpected (the sum of the coefficients' signs is negative). This anomaly exists for two major reasons. First, the number of children not on welfare (K) and the lagged set of births (B) overlap. Second, since the number of births (B) is a highly seasonal variable, it is correlated with the seasonal dummies.[5] To somewhat alleviate the problems associated with this variable, another measure of births might have been used. This measure would include only the number of out-of-wedlock births. As mentioned in Chapter 7, Plotnick and Lidman used both seasonals and out-of-wedlock births in their caseload equation, producing the expected sign and statistical significance for the coefficient of the latter variable.[6]

Next, the number of cases closed (CL) in this equation is not jointly statistically significant at the 0.10 level, yet jointly it has the expected sign.[7] The sign suggests that as the number of case closures increases in the last four months so does the number of new and restored additions; however, due to statistical insignificance this result is questionable.

Lastly, the set of seasonal dummies has a strong impact on accessions. The significant impact of seasonals on the AFDC caseload also was found by Plotnick and Lidman. The present study's findings and Plotnick and Lidman's results suggest the importance of integrating seasonals into an analysis of AFDC dynamics. However, in this study little can be made of the month-to-month variation in accessions as indicated by the seasonals' coefficients because of the seasonal nature of births already incorporated in this component model.

Table 8.2
Joint F-Tests for Accessions Equation

Variables	df	F Value	Level of Significance
TP, SN	2, 118	0.6386	0.5298
WI, MW	2, 118	1.192	0.3071
NA, F, A	3, 118	3.968	0.0098
U Lags 1 to 4	4, 118	0.6555	0.6242
U, NA, F, A	7, 118	2.974	0.00657
P, K	2, 118	12.17	0.00002
B Lags 1 to 4	4, 118	2.183	0.07502
B, P, K	6, 118	6.023	0.00002
CL Lags 1 to 4	4, 118	1.619	0.1740
Seasonals	11, 118	7.717	0.00000

Sources, definitions, and deflation: See Appendix F.

Table 8.2 summarizes the joint F-statistics for groups of theoretically related variables.

Cases Closed

The second regression equation in the AFDC-Basic model has as a dependent variable the number of cases closed (CL) excluding intraprogram transfers. This equation was not rho corrected since an insignificant amount of first-order serial correlation is present. The OLS regression explains 87 percent of the variance in monthly case closures. The standard error of estimate is 4.8 percent of the average of 22,667 cases closed per month. Table 8.3 presents the regression results.

Table 8.3 reveals that the total welfare benefits (TP) variable has the expected sign. This suggests that as total welfare payments increase, closures decrease. This finding is consistent with past research, which also indicates the same effect. However, in this study this variable is statistically insignificant at the 0.10 level.

The other AFDC program feature, the AFDC breakeven level (E_r^{**}), needs to be interpreted along with the coefficient of another variable, namely, the interaction between the OBRA dummy and the breakeven level (DB). Both variables are found to be statistically significant with the hypothesized sign. Interpretation of these coefficients reveals that a monthly increase of \$1 in the breakeven prior to OBRA results in about five cases remaining on the welfare rolls that otherwise would have terminated. However, a monthly \$1 increase

Table 8.3
Regression Results for Closures Equation

From 5/1972	Until 12/1984		
Observations	152		
R Squared	0.89	Degrees of Freedom	120
SSR	142000000	Rbar Squared	0.87
Durbin-Watson	1.7	SEE	1088
F(34, 118)	2047	Significance Level	.0000

Variable	Lag	Coefficient	t-Statistic	Mean
Constant	0	-7574	-0.2956	-7574
TP	0	-5.165	-0.4065	673.1
E_r^{**}	0	-4.974	-1.374	1147
DO	0	-9469	-1.517	0.2368
DS	0	14160	8.049	0.01316
DB	0	8.953	1.483	202.0
WI	1	4.134	0.7335	1250
MW	1	2.887	0.8476	726.3
U	1	-3.445	-1.752	861.8
F	1	1.198	0.05058	178.4
A	1	156.2	4.259	100.7
NA	1	-1.034	-1.148	8693
FBU	1	-1997	-0.4064	2.974
C	1	0.007260	0.5236	411400
CA	1	0.09409	1.445	23210
CA	2	0.1568	2.945	23180
CA	3	0.1988	3.719	23090
CA	4	0.09424	1.591	23040
C_5	0	0.01118	0.8620	321600
M_{20}	0	0.09128	2.691	57210
M_{30}	0	0.04491	1.485	181800
JA	0	423.6	0.7648	0.07895
FB	0	-82.69	-0.1343	0.07895
MR	0	1158	1.745	0.07895
AP	0	1383	2.275	0.07895
MY	0	2369	4.383	0.08553
JU	0	2358	3.948	0.08553
JL	0	2675	4.731	0.08553
AG	0	3616	6.026	0.08553
SP	0	2077	1.914	0.08553
OC	0	2036	1.960	0.08553
NV	0	326.0	0.5398	0.08553

Sources, definitions, and deflation: See Appendix F.

Notes: U, NA, F, and A are in thousands. TP, SN, WI, MW, and E_r^{**} are in real terms (6/1985=100).

in the post-OBRA breakeven level results in an increase of about four case closures. This phenomenon probably is due to the fact that prior to OBRA an increase in the breakeven level resulted in more individuals combining work and welfare and not leaving the system. On the other hand, when OBRA's provisions are in effect, the breakeven's effect on case closures is reversed. This means that an increase in the breakeven actually results in closure of cases that otherwise would remain open. Under OBRA, perhaps some of those people who are motivated by this hypothetical $1 increase in the breakeven to increase their work efforts work themselves off welfare since they anticipate the major reduction in income that will occur with elimination of the $30 and one-third disregards.

Similar findings about the opposite effects of the breakeven on closures prior to and after passage of OBRA are not found in past research. The present finding about the effect of the breakeven prior to OBRA is inconsistent with the findings of Wiseman[8] and of Hutchens,[9] which showed that an increase in the breakeven results in an increase in closures.

OBRA has certain provisions other than those captured by the breakeven variable itself and its interaction. Some of these are captured by both the dummy shock (DS) and the OBRA dummy (DO) variables explained in Chapter 6. The coefficient of the OBRA dummy indicates that in the presence of OBRA, other things equal, there is a significant monthly average of 9,469 fewer case closures than the historical monthly average of 22,074 case closures from 1972 until the inception of OBRA. This large impact of OBRA on case closures could be associated with work disincentives accompanying it. As discussed in Chapter 4, during this time period the number of earners on the rolls has been much smaller than in prior years. These facts suggest that OBRA reduced the number of closures via the route of increased earnings.

The dummy shock, as expected, significantly affects the number of cases closed in November and December 1981. Its coefficient indicates that, on the average, during each of these months 14,160 cases closed, mainly due to the imposition of the 150 percent income eligibility standard. The impact of both the OBRA and shock dummies should be kept in perspective; that is, they should be interpreted only in conjunction with other OBRA variables.

On the surface, the effect of OBRA's provisions on case closures seems mixed. On the one hand, we have seen that OBRA increased case closures by both its interaction with the breakeven and the effect of the shock. On the other hand, we have observed by the OBRA dummy that the long-term effect of OBRA on case closures is to decrease them. In the next chapter, where the effects of OBRA are analyzed using forecasting techniques, a clearer picture of the consequences of this policy for case closures is presented.

In the closure equation, both wage variables (WI and MW) revealed the expected sign; that is, both show that an increase in ongoing wages increases closures. This again concurs with past studies that used other wage variables in their equations. These studies also show that selected wage variables do indeed affect welfare terminations. However, in the present investigation both variables are statistically insignificant at the 0.10 level.

On the other hand, both the aggregate number of unemployed and employment levels in apparel industries are found to be statistically significant with the expected hypothesized sign. Moreover, a joint F-test of all non-agricultural industries and the aggregate unemployment variable is found to be statistically significant. An increase of 1 percent in the unemployment rate over the estimation period would result in about 450 additional cases per month remaining on the roles. This calculation takes into account the effect on case closures of an increase in the aggregate unemployment rate and of the extra jobs lost in non-agricultural industries due to this 1 percent increase in the unemployment rate.[10]

Overall, the effect on closures of employment levels in low-skill industries is strong in this study. This is consistent with some past findings but not with others. For example, it is consistent with the findings of Jordan et al. in Los Angeles County but inconsistent with their findings in other counties. Again it should be recognized that these researchers used industries other than the ones selected here to reflect welfare recipients' experiences in the marketplace. The fact that aggregate unemployment by itself is a good predictor of welfare is inconsistent with most past findings, which have shown it to vary in an unexpected way or to be statistically insignificant.

Caseload characteristics such as the average number of people per case (FBU), the size of the caseload (C), and the number of cases added within the last four months (CA) are found to have the expected signs. The fact that case closures decrease as average family size increases is quite consistent with past findings, which suggest that the larger the family, the more difficult it is to attain economic self-sufficiency. However, although this variable has the hypothesized sign, it is statistically insignificant.

The number of cases added (CA) to the caseload in previous months is found to be a statistically significant predictor of cases closed. This finding is consistent with the Jordan et al. finding for Los Angeles County. Here the coefficients of cases added indicate that in any given month an increase of 100 in the number of cases added the previous month results in about 9 more case closures. Together the coefficients of cases added suggest that if the number of cases added in each of the past four months increased by 100 cases there would be about 54 extra case closures in the current month.

Two coefficients associated with recipients' characteristics have unexpected results. The number of non–school-aged children (C_5) and the number of mothers under age 21 (M_{20}) have unexpected signs. The anomalous finding that case closures vary positively and significantly with both age groups of mothers on welfare is unexpected. The latter finding is contrary to past findings discussed in Chapter 7, which showed that the younger the mother the lower the probability of closure.

Finally, seasonal trends reveal that the greatest number of case closures occur from spring to late fall. These trends may be proxies of the effects of

Table 8.4
Joint *F*-Tests for Closures Equation

Variables	df	F Value	Level of Significance
TP, E_r**, DB	3, 120	2.297	0.08113
WI, MW	2, 120	0.8071	0.4486
NA, F, A	3, 120	6.683	0.00033
U, NA, F, A	4, 120	10.60	0.00000
CA Lags 1 to 4	4, 120	9.079	0.00000
C, CA Lags	5, 120	7.264	0.00000
C_5, M_{20}, M_{30}	3, 120	2.820	0.04187
Seasonals	11, 120	7.546	0.00000

Sources, definitions, and deflation: See Appendix F.

other variables not in the model, such as marriages. As in the accessions equation and as in Plotnick and Lidman's finding, seasonals greatly impact AFDC dynamics.

Table 8.4 summarizes the results of the *F* values and statistical significance for groups of variables in this equation.

SUMMARY AND CONCLUSIONS

In this chapter the individual coefficients of both the accessions and terminations equations were analyzed. Excluding seasonals, the variables belong to three classes. For the most part, the effects of the variables on either accessions or terminations appear reasonable on theoretical grounds and substantiate research findings conducted on a national scale.

Judging from the signs of the coefficients and their level of statistical significance, welfare system variables are better predictors of closures than of additions. This is perhaps because once individuals are on the rolls they are better able to weigh their alternatives than when they are off welfare and probably not as familiar with the system.

As for labor-market conditions, aggregate unemployment was a better predictor of closures than of accessions. However, employment levels in low-skill industries are good predictors of both accessions and terminations. An interesting fact is that the employment level in apparel and other textile products industries is a very strong predictor of both accessions and terminations. This suggests that this type of industry employs welfare recipients in California. Careful selection of the types of industries that employ welfare recipients seems to be important.

The findings regarding demographics and recipients' characteristics are mixed; some had the expected sign and others did not. Perhaps this is because there is some correlation between them.

Of the two regression equations, the number of cases closed is predicted the best. The independent variables in this equation explain the largest amount of variance in the dependent variable, and many independent variables both have the expected signs and attain statistical significance. Moreover, this equation has a small standard error of estimate relative to the mean number of cases closed. The number of cases added is more difficult to predict by the three classes of variables selected here. Perhaps the number of additions is also a function of administrative discretion and of personal life circumstances that are difficult to measure on an aggregate level.

In time series analysis using simultaneous equations, the model's ability to replicate actual data is not completely determined by the R^2 of the individual regression equations or by the statistical significance of its coefficients. The model thus needs to be analyzed by other statistical criteria. Simulation results for the model are presented next, followed by the results of several forecasting experiments using the AFDC model.

NOTES

1. New additions and restorations initially were analyzed separately. Because the number of cases restored was not predicted well by the selected welfare parameters and most economic variables in the marketplace, new and restored cases ultimately were combined into one equation. These variables have unexpected signs and are statistically insignificant. The only good predictors of the number of cases restored are the lagged number of cases closed and the aggregate number of unemployed. All of the independent variables explain only 52 percent of the variance in monthly restorations.

2. The minimum wage variable is deflated, as are other variables valued in dollars. Minimum wage is deflated by the California Consumer Price Index (6/1985 = 100). In real terms, the reported average monthly minimum wage value in Table 8.1 and in subsequent tables is substantially larger than the actual present monthly minimum wage value. This is because minimum wage was not raised for a long time, making the actual present value for 1985 less than the average. In the 1970s the minimum wage value was larger than it was in 1985. The monthly minimum wage is created by multiplying the hourly minimum wage by 173 hours per month. For source see Appendix F.

3. P. Jordan et al., *Corrective Action and AFDC Dynamics: An Empirical Study in Six Jurisdictions*, Grant No. 5-21474 (Boston: Boston College, Social Welfare Institute, Public Assistance Data Analysis Laboratory, 1981).

4. The sum of the coefficients is found to be negative (-2.345), which means that if aggregate unemployment were to increase by 1,000 people and remain at this level for four months, about two cases would not be added to the rolls. This is contrary to expectations.

5. Ideally, the number of children not on welfare should have included children older than five months so that the lagged set of births and this variable would not have overlapped. Unfortunately, monthly data are not available on the number of children not on welfare less than five months old. That the number of births is seasonal is demonstrated by other calculations showing that the number of births can be predicted with an $R^2 = 0.99$ from a set of seasonals and a cubic polynomial in time.

6. R. Plotnick and R. M. Lidman, "Forecasting Welfare Caseloads: A Tool to Improve Budgeting," unpublished manuscript, Contracts 2000-46181 and 6500-52438 (Seattle: Washington State Social and Health Services Department, 1986).

7. When the number of cases restored was predicted separately from new additions, the number of cases closed in the last four months was statistically significant at the .05 level.

8. Michael Wiseman, *Work Incentives and Welfare Turnover*, Working Paper 84-01 (Berkeley: University of California, Department of Economics Welfare and Employment Studies Project, 1984).

9. R. M. Hutchens, "Entry and Exit Transitions in Government Transfer Programs: The Case of Aid to Families with Dependent Children," *Journal of Human Resources* 16 (1981): 217-237.

10. By taking as a reference the average number of persons in the labor force over the estimation period, an increase of 1 percent in the unemployment rate is associated with 107,000 more individuals unemployed. Using the coefficient of the number of unemployed (U), a monthly increase of 1 percent in the unemployment rate in California yields about 370 additional cases per month remaining on the roles. A 1 percent increase in the unemployment rate means that extra jobs are lost in non-agricultural industries. It is assumed that all of the increase in the number of unemployed results from lost jobs in non-agricultural industries, with each of the three types of industries (F, A, NA) bearing their proportional share of extra lost jobs. The extra jobs lost in non-agricultural industries due to a 1 percent increase in the unemployment rate would yield an additional 83 fewer case closures.

9

The Simulations

This chapter evaluates the overall fit of the model, which then is used to forecast the consequences for the AFDC caseload of changes in payments and in certain labor-market conditions. The model also is used to analyze the consequences of the Omnibus Budget Reconciliation Act. Comparisons are made between the findings for California and those of national studies.

HISTORICAL SIMULATION

In a simulation process a simulation step is taken to be the prediction of a set of endogenous variables from one given month to the next. In the simulations used in this study all endogenous variables are predicted from actual values of exogenous variables. This means that all of the exogenous variables take on their real values and are not predicted in any simulation step. Aside from the three classes of independent variables and seasonals used in the regression equations, there are four variables, each with minor impact on the AFDC-Basic system, for which actual rather than predicted values are used. These four variables are the number of accounting errors (ER), transfers to and from AFDC-UP (TU and TB, respectively), and all other approvals (OA).[1] In this model these are also considered exogenous variables. Endogenous variables in the model are the AFDC-Basic caseload (C), total number of accessions (CA), total number of terminations (CT), number of cases added (AD), and number of cases closed (CL).[2]

Briefly, the welfare caseload is simulated in a succession of months. Simulated values of endogenous variables from any earlier month and actual values of exogenous variables in the current month or earlier months are entered into the system of equations given in Chapter 6. Out of this come forecasts of the endogenous welfare variables during the current month. This procedure iterates month to month, producing a forecast of the welfare caseload, caseload accessions, and caseload terminations over a period of time. For a detailed description of this process, see Appendix E.

When a model predicts the historical or actual series well, one would expect the simulated series to resemble the historical series closely. A historical simulation is performed in order to evaluate the model's ability to replicate historical data. This historical simulation begins in May 1972 and ends in December 1984.[3]

Performance of the model must be measured by determining how well each endogenous variable tracks its known historical values. Several statistics are available for measuring this, including root mean square (rms) percent error, mean percentage errors, and several Theil statistics.[4]

Calculations show that cases closed has a slightly smaller root mean square deviation (4.7 percent) than cases added (5.4 percent), meaning that the deviations of the simulated values from the historical values of cases closed are smaller in percentage terms than the same deviations of the other regression equation. The caseload's simulated values stay very close to the historical values, as evidenced by the caseload's root mean square percentage error of 0.7 percent. This is partially due to the fact that simulated caseload values are composed not only of the two endogenous variables predicted by regression equations, cases added (AD) and cases closed (CL), but also of four exogenous welfare system variables (ER, TU, TB, and OA). Using actual values for these exogenous variables limits error. The size of these variables relative to the endogenous variables is, however, small. Of greater consequence is the substantial cancellation of errors between the accessions side and the terminations side of the model.

Further analysis reveals that in all cases the mean percentage errors are much smaller than the root mean square percentage error. This indicates that each simulated endogenous variable oscillates through its historical values and there is not much consistent overestimation or underestimation in any endogenous variable.

Theil's U statistic can be decomposed into three statistics, one analogous to the mean of the simulated series, another to its standard deviation, and a third to the covariance of the historical and simulated series. Overall, the Theil statistics used demonstrate that, for the three endogenous variables, the simulated series and the historical series have very similar means, standard deviations, and covariances. In particular, all of the series have high Theil's covariance statistics varying from 0.95 to 0.99. This indicates that the shapes of the historical and simulated series resemble one another very closely.

A graphic representation of the simulated and historical time series is one way to judge the ability of the simulated series to capture abrupt, steep, or frequent changes. The dotted lines and the solid lines in Figure 9.1 represent the simulated and historical time series, respectively. This figure shows that

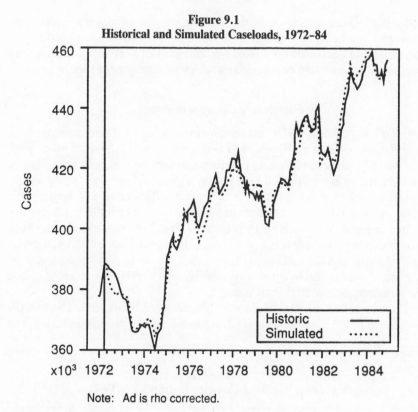

Figure 9.1
Historical and Simulated Caseloads, 1972–84

Note: Ad is rho corrected.

the simulated caseload replicates the historical caseload quite well. Every sharp increase or decrease is captured. The poor performance of the simulated caseload during 1972 is due to underestimation of the number of cases added (*AD*) and overestimation of the number of cases closed (*CL*) in the initial months of the simulation.

Overall, it seems that the entire model is valid for predicting AFDC-Basic caseload dynamics as evidenced from the results of regression equations and the simulation statistics. Given the validity of this model, it can be used to forecast changes in benefits or unemployment and analyze the consequences of OBRA.

FORECASTING CHANGES IN
BENEFITS AND UNEMPLOYMENT

The following two sections examine whether the model responds to changes in several exogenous variables in a manner consistent with economic theory and with previous observations of the relationship between selected variables and AFDC-Basic dynamics. In this first section, in separate forecasts, total payments available to a family of three and aggregate unemployment are increased and decreased by a fixed percentage. The goal is to compare with the historical series two new simulated series reflecting these variations.

Forecasting Changes in Benefits

For this experiment AFDC maximum aid for a family of three, in real terms, is raised and lowered by 10 percent. Food stamp benefits, the standard of need, and AFDC breakeven levels, in real terms, are changed accordingly. That is, total payments are calculated with new maximum aid and food stamp values reflecting a change in benefits. In addition, since the standard of need historically has been raised in much the same way as welfare benefits, it is necessary to increase and decrease it by 10 percent as well. The breakeven level, which in part depends on the level of maximum aid, is recalculated with appropriate federal, state, and Social Security tax rates. It should be recognized that a 10 percent change in real benefits is substantial, representing over three standard deviations of its historical variation.

The new values for total payments (TP), the standard of need (SN), and the breakeven (E_r^{**}) variables are used to produce a new simulated series. The

Table 9.1
Forecasting Results of Changing Benefits by 10 Percent

Period	Variable	Percent Change in Means	
		10% Increase	10% Decrease
Pre-OBRA	Accessions	2.70%	-3.20%
5/72 to 10/81	Closures	-1.80	1.40
	Caseload	13.20	-13.20
Post-OBRA	Accessions	3.80	-3.00
11/81 to 12/84	Closures	2.10	-1.30
	Caseload	1.39	-0.49
Entire Period	Accessions	3.10	-3.30
5/72 to 12/84	Closures	0.02	-0.09
	Caseload	15.00	-15.00

Figure 9.2
Effects of Increasing and Decreasing Maximum Aid

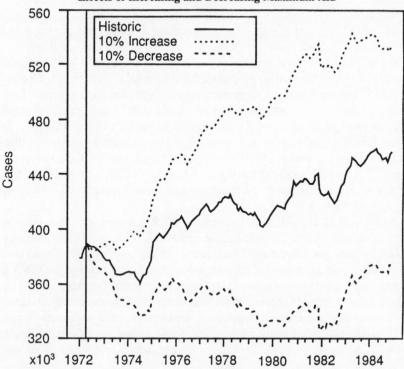

Note: Total payment is increased and decreased by 10%.

actual values of all other exogenous variables and the coefficients of each variable found in the historical regression equations also are used. Now the effect of an increase and decrease in benefits on the caseload and its components is captured by a new simulated series. This new simulated series is compared to the historical series in Table 9.1. The consequences of changes in benefits for the caseload and its components are measured over three estimation periods by the percentage change in the means of the simulated series relative to the historical series. A graphic representation of the resulting simulated caseload is provided in Figure 9.2.

Three time periods, namely, pre-OBRA, post-OBRA, and the entire simulation period are presented in Table 9.1. From the given data, it is apparent that OBRA has a profound effect on how variations in payments influence AFDC dynamics. That is, changes in benefits produce opposite net effects on case closures, before versus after OBRA.[5] For the pre-OBRA period, an increase in benefits increases accessions, decreases closures, and thereby increases the caseload. A decrease in benefits produces exactly the opposite situation. This is consistent with the notion that increasing the payments standard makes welfare more attractive and thereby produces more additions and fewer closures.

But there is another effect—that of increasing or decreasing the breakeven level. When the guarantee increases, so does the breakeven level; when the guarantee decreases, the breakeven follows suit. Changes in the breakeven due to changes in the welfare guarantee have a strong impact on case closures. Recalling the results of the regression equations presented in Chapter 8, the effects of the breakeven on case closures prior to OBRA are opposite to those after its passage. Prior to OBRA an increase in the breakeven decreases closures. This result affects the outcomes presented in Table 9.1. Prior to OBRA an increase in payments, which increases the breakeven level, decreases closures. This is consistent with the notion that prior to OBRA an increase in the breakeven is associated with more recipients combining work and welfare and not leaving the system.

After passage of OBRA an increase in the breakeven increases closures. This result also affects the outcomes presented in Table 9.1. During the post-OBRA period an increase in payments, which increases the breakeven, increases closures. This result supports the idea that after passage of OBRA an increase in the breakeven is associated with more people working themselves off the rolls as they anticipate a major reduction in income with elimination of the income disregards. Recalling from Chapter 8, the total payments variable (*TP*) has the expected negative sign in the closures equation. Consequently, the present finding is due to the breakeven effects dominating the total payment effects when payments are changed.

As opposed to welfare closures, welfare accessions change in the same fashion prior to and after passage of OBRA. Over the entire simulation period, accessions change much more than closures as a response to percentage changes in welfare payments (Table 9.1). But this comparison is deceiving since the apparently small impact on closures is due to the differing pre-OBRA and post-OBRA effects canceling out one another.

As further observed in Table 9.1, when payments are raised or lowered by equal percentages, the caseload or its components also rise or fall by almost equal percentages. Since the model is composed of linear functional forms, a 10 percent increase in any variable will produce the same absolute proportionate change in outcomes as a 10 percent decrease in that variable. However, this does not happen here for two reasons. First, the new simulated series is compared to the historical rather than the simulated series shown in Figure 9.1. If a comparison were made between two forecasted models, one with all exogenous variables taking their actual historical values and the other with all variables affected by the 10 percent change taking their new values and with the remaining exogenous variables taking their actual historical values, then a 10 percent increase in benefits would produce the same absolute proportionate change in outcomes as a 10 percent decrease. This is not done here.

The second reason for the unequal absolute proportionate change in outcomes is due to the recalculation of the breakeven variable. Since the breakeven is recalculated to adjust for changes in welfare payments and since federal and state taxes are not exactly linear, a 10 percent increase in benefits may not produce absolute changes in the breakeven variable exactly proportionate to a 10 percent decrease. The breakeven is a non-linear function of total payments.

As observed in Table 9.1, over the entire simulation period, the percentage change in the caseload is far larger than the percentage change in either accessions or closures. This shows that relatively small percentage changes in accessions and closures have a strong impact on the caseload. During the pre-OBRA period an increase in the caseload due to an increase in welfare benefits is associated with a cumulative month-to-month effect of the additional people who move to welfare as well as a cumulative month-to-month effect of people who otherwise would have left but do not leave. After passage of OBRA, accessions slightly dominate closures. Consequently, the caseload increases in response to an increase in benefits even though both accessions and closures increase. Overall, during the entire simulation period, the 15 percent increase in the caseload would have dramatic effects on welfare expenditures, since both payments per person and the number of individuals on welfare would increase.

Key Findings and Policy Implications. From this simulation exercise and previous regression results several key findings should be emphasized. Increasing benefits may either increase or decrease case closures. From the regression results in Chapter 8, it was seen that increasing total payments was associated with an increase in accessions and a decrease in terminations from 1972 to 1984. Yet benefits may play another role because the consequence of a change in benefit levels is a change in the breakeven. Prior to passage of OBRA, increasing benefits and the resultant increase in the breakeven had the joint effect of decreasing closures. After its passage, increasing benefits resulted in two opposite effects of decreasing closures because of increased total payments and increasing closures because of a resulting increase in the breakeven. In the current system the effect of the breakeven on closures dominates the effect of total payments.

These findings about the effect of the breakeven suggest that, prior to OBRA, an increase in the breakeven results in more individuals combining work and welfare and not leaving the system. On the other hand, after passage of OBRA, an increase in the breakeven results in more people working themselves off the rolls. As expected, no longer are those with relatively high earnings able to remain eligible for welfare due to the income cutoffs or elimination of the disregards.

Thus it seems that in the current system, if the breakeven point increases as a response to an increase in benefit levels or some other factor, it is now less likely that a large number of working recipients will prolong their stay in order to maximize combined income from work and welfare. This does not mean, of course, that recipients should not be provided with incentives to find jobs.

The current system provides fewer work incentives through its welfare payment formulae than were provided prior to 1981. However, once obtaining jobs, working recipients now are able to work themselves off the rolls more easily. In the absence of work incentives after the first four months of employment, employment programs that increase recipients' skills and assure that recipients find jobs are more likely to result in welfare terminations now than before 1981. All else being equal, employment programs that are successful in placing recipients in jobs are more likely to result in welfare terminations since once recipients have increased their earned income they are more likely to leave welfare.

The results of this exercise suggest that, under the current rules regarding eligibility and payments, major growth in the caseload would not be anticipated if benefit levels were raised. Since the Reagan administration's reforms, the overall impact on caseload growth of increasing benefit levels is minimal even with an increase as large as 10 percent. Costs would increase, but not primarily from an increase in the caseload. Increasing real benefit levels would help those already on welfare. If, on the other hand, the welfare system were to return to its pre-OBRA rules and if real benefit levels were raised, a major increase in the caseload would be anticipated, probably with substantial fiscal consequences.

Illustrating the key role that change in turnover plays in shaping the welfare caseload is the finding that even a small change in the amount of caseload turnover can have substantial effects on caseload growth. When accessions or terminations change minimally as a response to changing benefit levels, the overall effect on the entire caseload can be large. This implies that any welfare policy designed to change either accessions or terminations needs to be considered in light of its total effect on the caseload.

Forecasting Changes in Unemployment

In this experiment the aggregate unemployment level is increased and decreased by 10 percent and employment levels in selected industries are changed accordingly.[6] In the case of an increase in the number of unemployed, the number of additional jobs in selected industries is estimated. In apparel industries, the share of jobs lost due to the rising unemployment level is taken to be a percentage of the number of additional unemployed. This percentage equals the percentage of apparel jobs out of all non-agricultural jobs.[7] New values for the aggregate number of unemployed and employment levels in selected industries are used to produce a new simulated series. The actual values of all other exogenous variables and the coefficients of each variable found in the regression equations also are used. Now the effect of an increase

Table 9.2
Forecasting Results of Changing Unemployment by 10 Percent

	Percent Change in Means	
Variable	10% Increase	10% Decrease
Accessions	1.02%	-1.04%
Closures	-0.461	0.518
Caseload	5.47	-5.53

Note: Changes in employment levels are proportional to total non-agricultural employment.

or decrease in unemployment on the caseload and its components is captured by the new simulated series. This new simulated series is compared to the historical series in Table 9.2.

As seen in this table, again the percentage changes in the caseload and its components are about equal. This happens only because a comparison is made between the historical and new simulated series.[8] As further observed in Table 9.2, accessions again are more sensitive to these changes than are closures. The caseload is affected by these changes more than either accessions or closures alone. In the case of a 10 percent increase in aggregate unemployment, this is due to the cumulative impact on the caseload of an increase in additions and a decrease in closures. Overall, changes in the caseload and its components are as expected. The effects of the caseload of changes in aggregate unemployment are presented in Figure 9.3.

Changes in economic conditions do not appear to have as dramatic an impact on the caseload as changes in benefits. But to compare a 10 percent change in unemployment to a 10 percent change in the real value of benefits is unfair. The latter change is much less likely to occur than the former. A 10 percent change in real benefits represents about three standard deviations of its historical fluctuation, whereas a 10 percent change in unemployment represents only a little over 0.4 standard deviations of its historical fluctuation. A 69.4 percent increase in unemployment is comparable to a 10 percent change in real benefit levels. That is, a 69.4 percent change in unemployment, on the average, is equal to about three standard deviations of this variable. It should be realized that a 69.4 percent increase in unemployment would increase the average unemployment rate from 8 percent to more than 13.5 percent during the forecasting interval. A 69.4 percent decrease in unemployment produces an unemployment rate of only 2.5 percent during the same interval. During the

Figure 9.3
Effects of Increasing and Decreasing
Unemployment Level

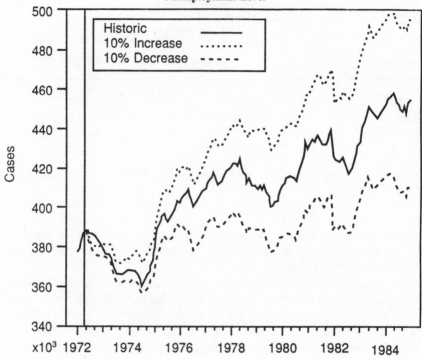

Note: Unemployment is increased and decreased by 10%.

forecasting interval, maximum and minimum unemployment rates were 11.9 percent and 5.6 percent, respectively.

For this last experiment, California's unemployment is increased and decreased by 69.4 percent, employment levels in selected industries are adjusted accordingly, and a new simulation is run with only these exogenous variables differing from their historical values. Results show that accessions vary by about 6 percent, closures by about 3.5 percent, and the entire caseload by about 36 percent. Thus, changes in benefits do not have as dramatic an impact on the caseload as changes in certain labor-market conditions.

Key Findings and Policy Implications. Two findings from the above analyses should be emphasized. First, given comparable percentage changes, the impact of labor-market conditions on the caseload and its components is much greater than that of benefits. These findings suggest that, all else being equal, in a recessionary period with a double-digit unemployment rate caseload growth should be expected and dealt with accordingly. For example, emergency assistance to families under the AFDC program should be given more readily during a recessionary period than at other times. In addition, during recessionary periods, government intervention intended to improve the economy, if successful, should have an added side effect of controlling caseload growth.

The findings further suggest that, if the welfare caseload were to decrease substantially, expanding the supply of jobs to low-skilled individuals should be an important policy objective. Employment opportunities in low-skill, low-wage industries should be expanded, and recipients should be helped to gain marketable skills that meet the needs of growing industries.

The second key finding shows that economic conditions affect accessions more than terminations. This suggests that focusing on expanding the supply of jobs for low-skilled individuals may help prevent welfare dependence. Clearly, as more individuals from the at-risk population assume jobs, fewer will enter the welfare rolls. Moreover, expanding job opportunities for low-income individuals may in some cases prevent marital dissolution, in turn, perhaps, preventing welfare dependence. Research has shown that families often separate because the principal earner is unable to find a job.

EFFECTS OF OBRA

To analyze the effects of OBRA on AFDC-Basic caseload dynamics, all the OBRA dummies and interaction variables are simply turned off. The breakeven variable in Equation 6.5 also must be altered. The imputed values substituted for this variable were calculated with pre-OBRA benefit formulae throughout time so that OBRA's effects are absent from this variable. This variable, titled pre-OBRA breakeven (E_o**), is presented in Figure 2.5.

Since OBRA affects no other exogenous AFDC program variables, such as the standard of need or benefits, it is unnecessary to alter any other exogenous variables. With the above-mentioned alterations, the new simulation begins in November 1981 and ends in December 1984.

As seen earlier, the historical simulation series replicates actual historical data quite well. In addition, the accessions and closures equations have many significant variables strongly associated with caseload movement. Given these facts, the model is taken as a valid representation of the system during OBRA. Turning off the OBRA dummies and altering the breakeven variable should represent the AFDC-Basic caseload had OBRA not been implemented.

Figure 9.4 shows the AFDC-Basic caseload with and without OBRA's provisions. The dotted lines represent the caseload in the absence of OBRA and the solid lines show the actual series. The vertical line indicates the month prior to the inception of OBRA. As seen from Figure 9.4, in the absence of OBRA the caseload would have been larger. The magnitude of the difference is exaggerated by the perspective of the figure as the simulated caseload is

Figure 9.4
AFDC-Basic Caseload with and without OBRA

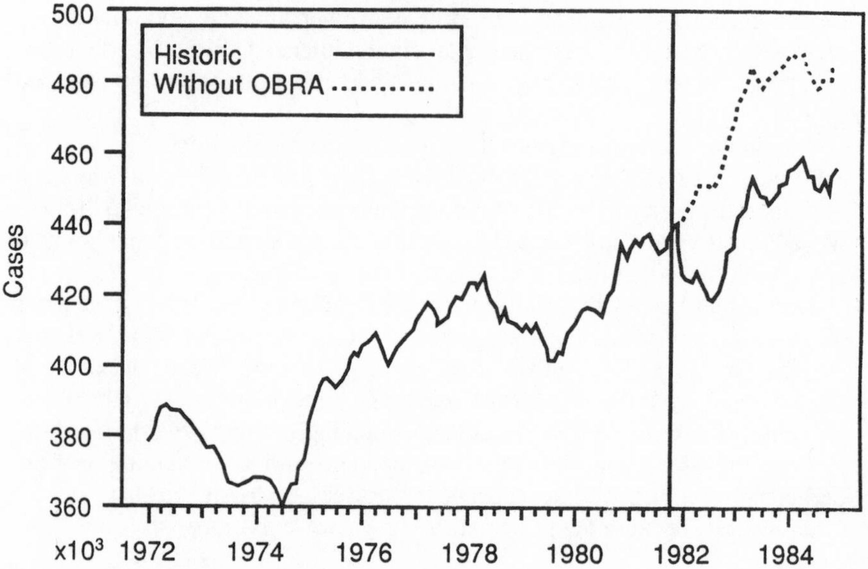

Note: OBRA dummies equal zero.

only 7 percent larger than the actual caseload. In the absence of OBRA, the caseload would have grown during the recession in 1982–83. During this time the actual caseload fell dramatically mainly because of the passage of the 150 percent income cutoff rule. Furthermore, in the absence of OBRA the caseload would have continued to grow, slightly reducing as the economy began to recover.

Further analyses reveal several important effects of OBRA on the components of the caseload. First, on the average, in the absence of OBRA there would have been more accessions from November 1981 until May 1984. On the accessions side, the actual and simulated series begin to merge in April 1984. Second, in the absence of OBRA closures would have decreased in 1982 when California's unemployment rate was high. On the closures side, simulated closures exceed historical closures from June 1982 until May 1984, after which time the opposite is true. Table 9.3 presents the averages for the simulated and historical series for two distinct periods.

From Table 9.3 it is evident that, in the absence of OBRA, from November 1981 to December 1984 accessions would have been greater but closures would have been about the same. On the other hand, if one were to discount

Table 9.3
Forecasting the Impact of OBRA

Variable and Time	Actual	Simulated	Percent Change from Actual
11/81 to 2/84			
AD	16444	17481	6.31%
CL	23790	23647	-0.60
C	441677	470732	6.58
1/82 to 12/84			
AD	16453	17541	6.61%
CL	22951	23697	3.25
C	442161	472438	6.85

the dramatic decrease in the historical caseload during November and December 1981, it appears that in the absence of OBRA both accessions and terminations would have been greater. The large decrease in the historical caseload during these months may have contributed to fewer closures from 1982 onward, yet this could have been, but was not, compensated by a greater number of accessions. It appears that, if fewer cases had been eliminated from the rolls in November and December 1981, in the absence of OBRA those made ineligible during these months might have left the system gradually, and over time welfare turnover would have been greater from 1982 to 1984.

When OBRA was first implemented, its effects seem to have been to eliminate a significant portion of the caseload and thereafter to isolate the caseload from the full impact of the recession. Calculations show that in the initial months after OBRA's implementation, 4.9 percent of AFDC-Basic cases closed because of OBRA's provisions, excluding the elimination of the disregards. With elimination of the disregards, another 1.2 percent of cases were closed. Over the entire OBRA period most of the people initially made welfare ineligible do not seem to have returned quickly to the rolls. If most of those initially eliminated had returned quickly, one would expect the historical curve to show steeper growth than the simulated curve beginning sometime after July 1982.

It could be argued that growth of the historical and simulated caseloads from July 1982 to April 1983 might be caused by two different sets of people. For the historical caseload, growth could be the result of a return to the rolls of people initially made ineligible due to OBRA. For the simulated caseload, growth could have been due mainly to families who would be ineligible for welfare under OBRA's provisions. But this would imply dramatic increases in restorations or other approvals during this period, which did not occur. Since growth rates for simulated and historical caseloads are nearly identical after July 1982, most of those initially made ineligible for welfare probably did not return after April 1983, the last month of the steep increase in the historical caseload.

Calculations show that the simulated caseload grew at about the same rate as the historical caseload from July 1982 until December 1984. This means that after the initial effects of OBRA had dissipated, the difference between the number of cases added and those terminated each month would have been almost the same whether or not OBRA existed. Further calculations suggest that the difference between historical and simulated caseloads is slowly becoming smaller. This difference is not apparent from the graph. The difference has decreased by about 15 percent from November 1983 to December 1984. If this trend continues, then historical and simulated caseloads gradually will merge and OBRA's effects will have washed out.

Comparison with National Studies

Several studies have analyzed the effects of OBRA on the AFDC caseload or its components on a national scale. Although these studies differ from the present study in both methodology and sample, some obtained relevant findings.

One study was conducted by Griffith and Usher.[9] Employing a quasi-experimental design, these researchers assessed the effects of OBRA on case closings and reopenings. Two national probability samples were drawn from cases active in the base months of September 1980 and September 1981. These two samples were followed for a year. Since the researchers relied on case records, they were able to examine recipients' characteristics such as employment status and benefit amounts and differentiate the effects of OBRA policy changes on caseload characteristics. As did the present study, Griffith and Usher found that OBRA did not increase the probability of reopening for either earners or non-earners. As expected, they found that families with earners comprised most case closings. After OBRA's implementation, over a 12-month period, about 10 percent more cases closed due to OBRA. Consistent with the present findings, most of the case closings were in the early months after OBRA's implementation rather than equally distributed throughout the year. The researchers found that by the third month after OBRA's implementation, about 9 percent of cases closed due to OBRA. This figure is higher than that found for California.

The advantages of the Usher and Griffith study include its national scope and examination of case characteristics. However, the study has some limitations. First, the effect of OBRA on accessions was not studied. Second, among other factors, the researchers did not control for economic conditions that can affect participation, although they claimed they attempted to control for the unemployment rate, which proved to be an insignificant predictor.

Other studies also present relevant findings. A study conducted by the U.S. General Accounting Office (GAO) examined case records in Boston, Dallas, Memphis, Milwaukee, and Syracuse. This study revealed that OBRA reduced the caseload from 7 to 14 percent. Consistent with the findings for California, most case closings occurred within the first few months of OBRA's implementation. Moreover, more than any other provision, the 150 percent income cutoff rule affected case closures. This study's limitations included a short follow-up period and failure to separate the effects of OBRA from those of the economy.[10]

In order to separate the effects of OBRA and of the recession on the AFDC caseload, a microsimulation study by Mathematica Policy Research (MPR) was conducted on a national scale.[11] Using data from the March 1981 Current Population Survey, MPR created four scenarios simulating a weak or strong economy with or without OBRA over a period of one year. It was assumed that all of OBRA's provisions were implemented immediately, which exaggerates the actual effects during fiscal year 1982.

Unlike Usher and Griffith's study, the MPR findings reveal that the recession increased the AFDC caseload by about 5 percent. Yet unlike Usher and Griffith, MPR included the unemployed-parent component in their analyses, which responds to business cycles. In fiscal year 1982 the net effect of the recession and OBRA was a reduction in the national AFDC caseload of about 8 percent.

Another study assessing the effects of OBRA on the AFDC caseload was conducted by Moffit and Wolf.[12] Using a national quality control sample of the AFDC caseload drawn in May 1981, they determined the separate effects of several of OBRA's provisions on those who lost or retained eligibility. Only OBRA's effects before four months of work were assessed. The consequence of eliminating income disregards was not considered for the caseload. Furthermore, the data sample did not allow an estimate of stepparent income. The key finding of this study was that about 5 to 11 percent of the national caseload lost eligibility due to OBRA. The upper bound is an overestimate since it assumes that all families with stepparents lose eligibility. Of all the provisions measured, the one with the largest impact (4 percent of the caseload) was the 150 percent income cutoff rule. As expected, OBRA's greatest effects were on earners, with about 35 percent of those who work losing eligibility. Overall, the lower estimate of OBRA's initial reduction of cases closed is in agreement with the findings for California.

From comparing the present study with those conducted on a national scale, it seems that in California, as elsewhere, OBRA's effects on the caseload were limited primarily to the early months after implementation. However, the initial impact of OBRA's provisions on case closings seems less in California than nationwide. This may be because California is a high-benefit state with a high need standard, and recipients may retain eligibility with higher levels of income in California than in median-benefit states. Consequently, it is expected that the impact of OBRA on case closings would be less in California and other high-benefit states with high standards of need.

The studies discussed here further our knowledge of the impact of OBRA because they separate the impact of different OBRA provisions on case closures or on the caseload and they analyze case characteristics. The present study used aggregate data and was not able to discern these effects. But unlike the present study, these other studies did not examine the effects of OBRA on both accessions and terminations. Moreover, not all studies controlled for economic conditions, among other factors that can affect the caseload. Finally, the importance of discerning long-term effects is recognized by some of the studies even if OBRA's most obvious effects were limited to the early months after implementation.

Policy Implications

In previous chapters it was shown that in California, as elsewhere, AFDC-Basic caseload growth has been moderate since the end of the caseload explosion in the early 1970s. Findings presented in this chapter indicate that nationally OBRA's provisions dampened caseload growth. All studies point out that for the most part the effect had run its course within a few months after OBRA's implementation. As expected, OBRA's provisions resulted primarily in the elimination of wage earners. Now the nation's welfare caseload is composed of a more dependent group of recipients. Various ways of dealing with this dependent welfare population have been proposed. Several states, including California, are experimenting with or expanding programs aimed at helping the dependent population to find employment. Often these programs are mandatory. In the near future the main avenue for controlling the size and composition of the caseload probably will be through these employment programs. Radical measures to curtail eligibility substantially, such as those implemented under OBRA, do not seem necessary.

Studies show that, at least initially, major case reopenings did not occur. This suggests that former recipients somehow are managing without welfare. Extending medical benefits likely has been helpful, but further study is needed to assess the economic situation of this population. If for the most part these former recipients have adequate resources at their disposal, then the effects of OBRA have not been as drastic as perceived by some.

NOTES

1. Accounting errors do not explicitly appear in any of the equations but are taken into account by adjusting monthly caseload count. Moreover, values for this variable are assumed to be known.

2. For a discussion of endogenous and exogenous variables see Chapter 6.

3. See Appendix E for an explanation of the simulation process, which illustrates why the simulation begins in May 1972.

4. See Appendix E for a brief explanation of the statistics used to evaluate the historical simulation.

5. For the post-OBRA period, these changes are calculated by performing a simulation beginning when OBRA was implemented. This is done to separate pre-OBRA from post-OBRA effects.

6. For reference, an increase or decrease of 10 percent in the number of unemployed would raise or lower the average unemployment rate over the forecasting interval from 8 percent to 8.8 percent or 7.2 percent, respectively.

7. When unemployment was increased by 10 percent, the employment level in apparel industries was adjusted as follows:

$$A(t) - U(t) * (0.10) * A(t) / TA(t)$$

where

$A(t)$ = employment level in apparel industries at month t,

$U(t)$ = number of unemployed in California at month t,

$TA(t)$ = employment level in total non-agricultural industries at month t.

A similar procedure is followed for the other two industries and for when unemployment decreases. Most likely, this procedure slightly overestimates the impact of changing unemployment levels in these industries because it assumes that all jobs lost from the rising unemployment level come from non-agricultural industries instead of the entire labor force.

8. Comparison between the initial simulated series and the new simulated series showed that a 10 percent increase in unemployment produced the same absolute proportionate change in outcomes as a 10 percent decrease.

9. J.D. Griffith and C.L. Usher, "A Quasi-experimental Assessment of the National Impact of the 1981 Omnibus Budget Reconciliation Act (OBRA) on the Aid to Families with Dependent Children (AFDC) Program," *Evaluation Review* 10 (1986): 313-333.

10. See U.S. General Accounting Office, *An Evaluation of the 1981 AFDC Changes: Final Report* (Washington, D.C.: U.S. Government Printing Office, 1985).

11. For details see U.S. House of Representatives, Committee on Ways and Means, Subcommittee on Oversight and Subcommittee on Public Assistance and Employment Compensation, *Effects of the Omnibus Budget Reconciliation Act of 1981 (OBRA) Welfare Changes and the Recession on Poverty*, prepared by Mathematica Policy Research, Inc., under contract to the Congressional Research Service (Washington, D.C.: U.S. Government Printing Office, 1984).

12. R. Moffit and D.A. Wolf, "The Effect of the 1981 Omnibus Budget Reconciliation Act on Welfare Recipients and Work Incentives," *Social Services Review* (June 1987): 247-260.

10

Policy Objectives

Earlier chapters have demonstrated that welfare caseload turnover responds to changes in welfare policies as well as to economic and demographic developments. This chapter addresses possible policy objectives and means of attaining them.

BENEFITS

As already noted, California is a relatively high-benefit state where, since the early 1970s, benefit levels have kept up with price changes more than in almost all other states. The consequence of this is that welfare recipients in California are economically better off than their counterparts in most other states, even in the face of Reagan administration policies and a recent slight decline in benefit levels.

Maintaining adequate benefit levels should continue to be an objective in California and in other high-benefit states. Changing benefits only to reflect changing prices probably will have a neutral impact on caseload growth, assuming that alternative incomes in the marketplace also keep up with inflation.[1] The government at least should assure that the minimum wage is adjusted upward as prices increase.

Low-benefit states should guarantee an adequate standard of living to poor families by raising benefit levels. This may increase caseloads by increasing accession and decreasing termination rates, but states need not fear that higher benefits will support many of those who are not truly needy. Providing adequate benefits helps those with no outside income, while current welfare rules prevent recipients from combining high earnings with welfare income. Increasing benefit levels in low-benefit states will allow similarly situated families across the nation to achieve similar economic conditions.

U.S. welfare systems also need to coordinate multiple programs in which recipients participate. Multiple benefits, such as food stamps and AFDC payments, significantly impact recipients' economic well-being and play an important role in shaping the welfare caseload. When AFDC policies are subject to change, they should not be considered in a vacuum. The combined effect of AFDC and other benefits always needs to be considered. Under current welfare rules, working welfare recipients face very high combined benefit reduction rates, which can be strong work disincentives and in some instances may undermine the goals of employment programs.

Medical benefits are very important to low-skilled workers, who often do not receive them in the work place. The current practice of extending medical benefits to those terminated from the rolls because of the elimination of the income disregards should be continued.

This book has shown that some interaction exists between the AFDC-Basic and AFDC-UP components of the welfare system. An important objective for those states that do not already do so is to extend benefits to intact families. Although there is little evidence that the absence of AFDC-UP programs increases marital dissolutions, those participating in this program are in dire need of assistance, and this in itself justifies the extension of benefits to them. States that offer this program should consider eliminating the 100-hour rule. This restriction, which stipulates that recipients be eliminated from the rolls if they work more than 100 hours a month, seems unfair. Applied without regard for wages earned, the rule provides incentives not to seek work.

REFUGEES

California has assumed a larger share of refugees than the rest of the nation. Welfare dependence among refugees needs to be addressed jointly by federal and state officials. From the state perspective, it may be desirable for the federal government to commit itself to the sole support of refugees for more than three years. An open-ended commitment by the federal government to support refugees may be appropriate.

State and federal efforts should focus on dealing with identified problems of refugees. No doubt, some of these problems include language barriers and cultural adjustment. The Office of Refugee Resettlement currently provides an employment program for refugees. Although it is too early to assess the program's effects on recipients' well-being, providing employment and training that fulfill refugees' unique needs seems to be a goal worth pursuing.

EMPLOYMENT AND WELFARE

The findings of this study strongly suggest that, if the AFDC-Basic caseload is to be decreased, employment opportunities in low-skill, low-wage industries should be expanded. The lack of employment opportunities for low-skilled individuals who are not on welfare also warrants attention. Several studies have shown that economic problems are related to marital instability and the incidence of female household headship. Joblessness among black males accounts for some of the rise in female household headship among black families.[2]

The above findings are especially disconcerting because nationwide employment levels in manufacturing industries, some of which are low-skill industries, have declined substantially in the 1980s. Stimulating growth in low-skill, low-wage, high-turnover industries or providing incentives to employers in these industries to hire welfare recipients would be beneficial, perhaps reducing the incidence of welfare dependence. Yet stimulating growth in low-skill industries has the side effect of increasing the inflation rate.

Creating job opportunities by establishing public jobs programs is another way to tackle welfare dependence and the general problems of poverty. Aside from philosophical opposition to the notion of government intervention in the marketplace, this alternative is accompanied by practical opposition. Some union members oppose the creation of low-wage jobs. Yet aside from their expense, if high-wage public jobs were created, the very poor might find themselves competing with middle-class workers who also may find these jobs attractive. Another problem associated with public job creation is displacement. Those hired to fill public jobs may displace workers who otherwise would have been hired. Worse yet is the situation in which a currently employed worker is laid off in order to be replaced by a subsidized worker.[3]

Employment opportunities for welfare recipients or other economically disadvantaged groups can be expanded by helping them gain marketable skills that meet the needs of growing industries. Over the past two decades, there has been a fair amount of federal involvement in employment and job training programs targeted at welfare recipients and other economically disadvantaged groups. The Comprehensive Employment Training Act (CETA) of 1973 consolidated many training programs of the late 1960s. This Act was replaced in 1982 by the Job Training Partnership Act (JTPA), which also emphasized training for the most disadvantaged in the labor force. A program specifically targeted at welfare recipients has been the Work Incentive Now (WIN) program, which required eligible recipients to register for work placement and provided job training to some.[4]

Research findings on the impact of employment programs on welfare turnover, however are inconclusive. In the absence of experimental designs, the impact of employment programs on recipients' income is difficult to determine.[5] Nonetheless, the demand for employment programs targeted at welfare recipients typically has exceeded the supply of public services provided.[6]

California and some other states recently have been implementing compulsory job-taking programs for welfare recipients. California's program is titled Greater Avenues to Independence (GAIN). From the perspective of some, the expenses of compulsory work programs outweigh the benefits and the programs are seen as punitive and degrading. Others see these programs as providing recipients with necessary skills and work habits as well as helping discouraged recipients who have been out of the labor force for a long time. The impact of compulsory work programs on welfare turnover is not clear.

One employment policy option is to target long-term welfare recipients for employment and training programs. Long-term welfare recipients often are the most disadvantaged. Bane and Ellwood's study showed that welfare receipt is transitory for many recipients, but for some welfare is a long-term state of affairs.[7] It is toward these recipients, who are most disadvantaged in the marketplace and who face a small chance of finding jobs, that efforts need to be geared.

The challenge of employment programs lies in keeping costs at a minimum while providing recipients with skills needed in the marketplace and helping them to find jobs that pay more than welfare. Sometimes expectations are too high and dedication to providing recipients a worthwhile experience is lacking.

There are no simple solutions to job problems facing economically disadvantaged groups. Increasing the supply of jobs and helping recipients to find jobs are not sufficient if those jobs do not provide families with a decent standard of living. The government should assure that the minimum wage keeps up with general price changes. Nationwide, in real terms, the minimum wage has declined substantially in recent years. A lower real level of minimum wage compared to welfare benefit levels is likely to make welfare a more attractive income alternative. This study's findings suggest that welfare accessions increase when the minimum wage decreases.[8] If the downward trend in the minimum wage continues, those in need will tend to see welfare as a more attractive alternative, perhaps necessary for survival.

Finally, encouraging recipients to become economically self-sufficient by building work incentives into the welfare benefit formula should be an important welfare objective. Nationwide, welfare systems provide fewer work incentives now than they did prior to OBRA. The present welfare system's high benefit reduction rates should be of concern not only because of their effects on work efforts, but also because in some cases the system does not adequately reward those who work. This should be of special concern in low-benefit states.

ILLEGITIMACY AND SINGLE PARENTHOOD

The incidence of female-headed families and illegitimacy is intertwined with the incidence of poverty and welfare dependence. Policies dealing with problems of welfare receipt need to address more general problems of illegitimacy and single parenthood.

During the 1960s the percentage of female-headed families began to increase among all racial groups. From 1960 to 1985 the incidence of female-headed families increased from 22 percent to 44 percent among blacks and from 8 percent to 13 percent among whites.[9] Among whites the major reason for the increase has been marital dissolution. The major reason for the large increase in female-headed black families has been the illegitimacy rate.[10]

In 1984, 59 percent of births to black females were illegitimate. The corresponding figure for whites was 13 percent.[11] The increase in the percentage of illegitimate births has been accompanied by a decline in marriage and marital fertility. Moreover, among blacks and whites, the illegitimacy rate among females age 15 to 19 has risen considerably from 1970 to 1980.[12]

By 1985 about one in five families with children less than 18 years old were female headed. While only 15 percent of white families with children were headed by females, the corresponding percentage for blacks was 50 percent.[13] These figures are alarming since children living in female-headed households face a greater probability of living in poverty and receiving AFDC benefits. Of special concern should be the rise in illegitimacy among teenagers. Bane and Ellwood's study showed that women who became female household heads by having a child or who are non-white or young are more likely to be long-term welfare recipients. About 30 percent of those on welfare nationwide have an illegitimate child at the beginning of their welfare spells.[14] For the welfare system the implication of rising illegitimacy among teenagers is that the caseload may include a larger portion of very dependent recipients, because the at-risk population contains a larger portion of individuals who are likely to be long-term recipients.

Employment and training programs for welfare recipients should focus on identifying and helping those who can be expected to be long-term recipients, for example, the very young and those who enter the system with an illegitimate birth. But among other factors, the problem of illegitimacy involves social values, including acceptance of the notion of single parenthood. Social values are difficult to change, but it seems essential to integrate into the education system information about the consequences of single parenthood, especially for teenagers.

In general, female headship often results in economic and social problems irrespective of the woman's age. Policy makers should be concerned about recent changes in family structure and provide programs to help families cope both socially and economically. One policy option is to establish and enforce strong child support laws for all children, whether welfare dependent or not.

Another policy option, which may prevent family dissolution and perhaps welfare dependence in some cases, is to provide employment opportunities to intact families. Economic insecurity has been shown to affect the decision to divorce or separate, and for females divorce often results in poverty, if not welfare dependence. Employment opportunities for the poor seem to be of utmost importance if some welfare dependence is to be prevented.

While these policy options may prevent some from becoming welfare dependent, there need not be concern about the effect of welfare benefits on family structure. A study conducted by Ellwood and Summers revealed that family structure and benefit levels are unrelated.[15] Benefit levels do not seem to affect illegitimacy rates, the percentage of divorces, or the percentage of children living in single-parent families.

Overall, in attempting to understand and deal with problems of welfare dependence, we need also to deal with general economic problems of the poor, marital dissolutions, and illegitimacy.

NOTES

1. Conclusions about the impact of welfare benefits on accessions should be viewed with caution. For the accessions equation the joint F-statistic for SN and TP variables is not statistically significant. The sign of the coefficients is not in doubt since it is virtually certain upon theoretical grounds that the coefficients of both SN and TP are positive. The reliability of the magnitude of the coefficients, however, can be questioned.

2. For more information see M. Hoing, "AFDC Income, Recipient Rates and Family Dissolution," *Journal of Human Resources* 9 (1974): 303–322; H. Ross and I. Sawhill, *Time of Transition: The Growth of Families Headed by Women* (Washington, D.C.: Urban Institute, 1975); and I. Sawhill et al., *Income Transfers and Family Structure* (Washington, D.C.: Urban Institute, 1975).

3. For details see Edward M. Gramlich, "The Main Themes," in Sheldon H. Danziger and Daniel H. Weinberg, eds., *Fighting Poverty: What Works and What Doesn't* (Cambridge, Mass.: Harvard University Press, 1986).

4. See J. Laurie Bassi and Orley Ashenfelter, "The Effect of Direct Job Creation and Training Programs on Low Skilled Workers," in *Fighting Poverty*, ed. Dangizer and Weinberg, pp. 133–172.

5. Ibid.

6. See Michael Wiseman, "The Welfare System," in *California Policy Choices*, vol. 2, eds. J.J. Kirlin and D.R. Winkler (Sacramento: Sacramento Public Affairs Center, 1985), pp. 133–202.

7. Bane and Ellwood's study is discussed in Chapter 7.

8. Only on the accessions side is the real value of the minimum wage a statistically significant predictor.

9. The figures are from Table 68, U.S. Commerce Department, Bureau of the Census, *Statistical Abstract of the United States: 1987*, 107th ed. (Washington, D.C.: U.S. Government Printing Office, 1986).

10. See William Julius Wilson and Kathryn M. Neckerman, "Poverty and Family Structure: The Widening Gap between Evidence and Public Policy Issues," in *Fighting Poverty*, ed. Danziger and Weinberg, pp. 232–259.

11. The figures are from Table 68, U.S. Commerce Department, *Statistical Abstract of the United States: 1987*.

12. Wilson and Neckerman, "Poverty and Family Structure."

13. U.S. Commerce Department, *Statistical Abstract of the United States, 1987*.

14. See M.J. Bane and D.T. Ellwood, *The Dynamics of Dependence: The Routes to Self-sufficiency*, Contract No. HHS-100-82-0038 (Washington, D.C.: U.S. Department of Health and Human Services, 1983).

15. See David T. Ellwood and Lawrence H. Summers, "Poverty in America: Is Welfare the Answer or Problem?" in *Fighting Poverty*, ed. Danziger and Weinberg, pp. 78-105.

APPENDIX A

Calculation Procedures and Sources for Countable Income and Breakeven

This section provides a historical account of how countable income (CI) and break-even (E^{**}) changed from 1971 to 1985. Symbols are defined at the end of this appendix. As in most other states, in California during the interval considered the AFDC payment (P) calculation stayed the same:

$$P = \max (0, M - CI).$$

Some of the formulae furnished below are derived from Michael Wiseman, *Work Incentives and Welfare Turnover*, Working Paper 84-01 (Berkeley: University of California, Department of Economics Welfare and Employment Studies Project, 1984).

CALCULATIONS OF COUNTABLE INCOME (CI) FROM 1971 TO 1985

For 10/1971 to 10/1981 during all months of work

$$CI = \max [0, E - X - 30 - 1/3\,(E - 30)] + I.$$

For 11/1981 to 8/1982 during the first four months of work

$$CI = \max [0, E - x_o - 30 - 1/3\,(E - x_o - 30)] + I.$$

For 9/1982 to present during the first four months of work

$$CI = \max [0, E - X - 30 - 1/3\,(E - X - 30)] + I.$$

For 11/1981 to 8/1982 when the $30 and one-third disregards were eliminated

$$CI = \max (0, E - x_o) + I.$$

For 9/1982 to present when the $30 and one-third disregards are eliminated

$$CI = \max (0, E-X) + I.$$

For 10/1984 to present when the $30 disregard is retained and the one-third disregard is eliminated (from the fifth month to the twelfth month of work)

$$CI = \max (0, E-X-30) + I.$$

CALCULATIONS OF BREAKEVEN (E^{**}) FROM 1971 TO 1985

For 10/1971 to 10/1981 during all months of work

$$E^{**} = (M + x_o + 20 - I) / (2/3 - x_e).$$

For 11/1981 to 8/1982 during the first four months of work

$$E^{**} = \min (3M + 2x_o - 3I + 60) / 2, 1.50 \ SN].$$

For 9/1982 to 9/1984 during the first four months of work

$$E^{**} = \min \{ [M + 2/3x_o - I + 20] / [2/3 (1 - x_e)], 1.50 \ SN \}.$$

For 10/1984 to present during the first four months of work

$$E^{**} = \min \{ [M + 2/3x_o - I + 20] / [2/3 (1 - x_e)], 1.85 \ SN \}.$$

For 11/1981 to 8/1982 when the $30 and one-third disregards are eliminated

$$E^{**} = M + x_o - I.$$

For 9/1982 to present when the $30 and one-third disregards are eliminated

$$E^{**} = (M + x_o - I) / (1 - x_e).$$

For 10/1984 to present when the $30 disregard is retained and the one-third disregard is eliminated

$$E^{**} = (M + x_o + 30 - I) / (1 - x_e).$$

CALCULATIONS ILLUSTRATING HOW MUCH OBRA REDUCES AFDC PAYMENTS

Let P_g be the amount of benefits received when the one-third disregard was out of gross income, as was true prior to the passage of OBRA. Similarly, let P_n be the benefits when one-third disregard is out of net income, as is now true during the first four months of work. Assuming the recipient retains eligibility, the payment and appropriate countable income formula above give

$$P_g = M - 2/3E + 20 + X - I$$

and

$$P_n = M - 2/3E + 2/3X + 20 + X - I.$$

If the two equations are subtracted,

$$P_g - P_n = 1/3X.$$

This shows exactly how much OBRA lowers payments over pre-OBRA levels during the first four months of work, provided one has the same amount of deductions before and after OBRA. Of course, OBRA capped child care deductions and standardized work deductions. The above calculation does not account for these effects and consequently is probably an estimate of the impact of OBRA on the change in payments.

In the same way, if we let $P_{1/3}$ and P_{30} be the benefits when the one-third and \$30 disregards are eliminated, respectively, then

$$P_g - P_{1/3} = 1/3E - 10$$

and

$$P_g - P_{30} = 1/3E + 20.$$

These results are the basis for the comments made in Chapter 3 about the impact of OBRA on benefits across states.

NOTATION

SN = standard of need or minimum basic standard of adequate care.

M = maximum aid or guarantee.

E = gross earnings of household members.

I = household income from sources other than earnings.

x_o = work deductions for child care or transportation expenses.

x_e = deductions such as federal, state, and Social Security taxes.

X = $x_o + x_e$.

E^{**} = breakeven.

APPENDIX B

Welfare System Variable Calculation Procedures and Sources

Data on AFDC and food stamp benefit calculation procedures were used to construct the numbers in Tables 2.1, 2.2, 2.3, 3.1, and 3.2. These data also were used to construct the total payments (*TP*) variable and the breakeven (*E***) variable in the time-series equations. This appendix summarizes the sources of this information and the assumptions employed in carrying out the computations.

AFDC

Sources and calculation procedures for AFDC without earnings, AFDC with earnings, and the breakeven variable are described in this section.

AFDC without Earnings

Data for California's AFDC maximum aid by family budget unit size are from California Health and Welfare Agency, Department of Social Services, *Manual of Policies and Procedures: Eligibility and Assistance Standard*, Section 44-315.411. The basic reference was the manual for June 1985; figures for dates before and after this were taken from later or earlier issues as appropriate. For cases both with and without earnings it is assumed the recipient family receives no other outside income.

Data for July 1985 maximum aid in all other states and Washington, D.C. were obtained from U.S. Department of Health and Human Services, Social Security Administration, Office of Family Assistance, Washington, D.C. For Table 3.1 changes in AFDC maximum aid are for a family of four and taken from U.S. House of Representatives, Committee on Ways and Means, *Background Material and Data on Programs within the Jurisdiction of the Committee on Ways and Means* (Washington, D.C.: U.S. Government Printing Office, 1986).

AFDC with Earnings

In calculating AFDC benefits with earnings in California, the procedures set out in the California Social Services Department, *Manual of Policy and Procedures*, section 44-300, are followed. For Texas and Pennsylvania similar procedures are followed, except these two states do not pay their full AFDC need standard. To obtain maximum aid for these states, need standards were reduced by appropriate percentages. After these reductions, payment calculation procedures are identical to those for California. For Tables 2.2 and 3.2 it is assumed that child care expenses equal $160 in the case of full-time employment, and 50 percent of that for part-time employment. All appropriate cases in Tables 2.2 and 3.2 receive $75 for work expenses. Revised OBRA regulations grant a "flat" $75 in work expenses other than mandatory withholdings; prior to OBRA work expenses were granted only if documented and then only for certain types of expenses. Thus the "pre-OBRA" cases in Tables 2.2 and 3.2 may exaggerate or underestimate the generosity of the system prior to November 1981.

For mandatory federal withholdings, the rates used are reported in U.S. Internal Revenue Service, *Employers' Tax Guide*, Publication 15, various issues. Federal withholding taxes were calculated using the income tax withholding—percentage method for a single/head of household of three persons. California state tax withholdings, which in most cases were inapplicable, are from California Health and Welfare Agency, Employment Development Department, Employers' Tax Guide: Unemployment Insurance Code of California. Withholding taxes were calculated using the exact calculation method for an unmarried head of household of three persons. Pennsylvania state tax withholdings were provided by the Commonwealth of Pennsylvania, Department of Revenue, Bureau of Business Trust Fund Taxes, *Instructions for Employer Withholding of Pennsylvania Personal Income Tax*, 1987. Texas has no state income tax. Social Security rates are from U.S. House of Representatives, Committee on Ways and Means, *Background Material and Data on Programs within the Jurisdiction of the Committee on Ways and Means* (Washington, D.C.: U.S. Government Printing Office, 1984), pp. 58-59, plus updated information received from the Social Security Administration.

The applied benefit computation formulae are those set out in Michael Wiseman, *Work Incentives and Welfare Turnover*, Working Paper 84-01 (Berkeley: University of California, Department of Economics Welfare and Employment Studies Project, 1984). The computation formulae are adjusted to account for the assumptions imposed above about work expenses and non-welfare income, and for recent alterations in income disregards.

For Table 3.2, the Earned Income Tax Credit (EITC) is included only for those cases in which no welfare payments are received. The administration attempted in OBRA to assume that all earners received the EITC irrespective of whether they actually did. This provision was subsequently eliminated in a court challenge. Without automatic presumption there is no incentive for a working recipient on welfare to collect the EITC unless the EITC exceeds the AFDC benefits, since the EITC reduces welfare benefits dollar for dollar. Even in cases in which the EITC exceeds AFDC, the recipient may prefer to retain AFDC eligibility. There is an incentive for the state to ensure that working recipients collect the credit, since EITC dollars are all federal, while welfare dollars cost the state 50 cents. In most cases it still appears not to be worth the administrative effort. In practice, food stamp benefits in California are not affected by receipt of the EITC.

AFDC Breakeven

In Figure 2.5 one version of the breakeven (E_r**) uses actual welfare benefit computations in effect during the appropriate month. The second version of the breakeven (E_o**) was calculated under the assumption that OBRA's provisions were not in existence. Consequently, pre-OBRA welfare benefit computations in effect in October 1981 were used for this variable from November 1981 onward.

In order to calculate both time-series versions of the breakeven only gross earnings and maximum aid for a family of three were considered. That is, it was assumed that welfare payments are for families with no outside unearned income and no child care or work deductions, except for federal and state withholding taxes and Social Security taxes. Moreover, it was assumed that the Earned Income Tax Credit equaled zero. For tax withholdings and payment sources, see the section in this appendix titled "AFDC with Earnings." Both breakeven variables capture changes in maximum aid, taxes, and inflationary effects over time.

The breakeven computation formulae and sources are those shown in Appendix A. The computation formulae are adjusted to account for the assumptions imposed above about work expenses and non-welfare income and for recent alterations in income disregards.

FOOD STAMPS

Food stamp benefits were calculated for Tables 2.1, 2.2, 2.3, 3.1, 3.2 and for the variable titled total payments (TP) used in the regressions or simulations. The source for basic food stamps benefits data is California Health and Welfare Agency, Department of Benefit Payments, *Manual of Policies and Procedures: Division 63, Food Stamp Regulations*. The basic reference was the manual for June 1985.

In order to calculate food stamp benefits the calculation procedures for net income were taken from the manual. Information for dates before and after this was taken from earlier or later issues or revisions, as appropriate. No issues were found prior to 1974, the year food stamps were distributed nationwide. Consequently, the net income formula for 1974 was used.

Thrifty Food Plan amounts were used to calculate the amount of food stamps allotted to a family of three. The Food Stamp program allows deductions for "excess shelter costs" and for child care expenses. Currently a maximum deduction is allowed for both items combined.

In Table 2.1 food stamps are calculated both by assuming no excess shelter cost or child care deduction and by assuming that the maximum is granted. For Table 3.1, food stamp benefits are computed using maximum deductions. The standard household deduction of $95 and maximum allowable deduction for excess shelter or dependent child care of $134 are assumed in the 49 contiguous jurisdictions. In Alaska, the standard household deduction is $162 and maximum allowable deduction for excess shelter or dependent child care is $233; in Hawaii the corresponding figures are $134 and $192. In the 49 contiguous jurisdictions maximum food stamp benefits for family of three were $208; in Alaska, $294; and in Hawaii, $319.

In some states part of the AFDC grant has been designated as an energy payment and is disregarded in calculating food stamp benefits. In 1985 the following states designated these amounts as energy aid: Maryland, $43; New York, $53; Oregon, $118; Rhode Island, $127; and Washington, $46. This raises food stamp benefits in these states.

Tables 2.2, 3.1, and 3.2 were constructed under the assumption that households received the maximum food stamp deductions. In construction of the total payments (*TP*) variable used in the simulation series, the shelter or child care deduction was assumed to equal zero. This necessary assumption was made since prior to 1979 these deductions were itemized rather than capped. Consequently, it was not possible to develop a satisfactory time series on average deductions granted to AFDC recipients receiving food stamps. Without this information, it has been necessary to calculate food stamp benefits for the simulation model given no deductions.

The poverty standard used in Chapters 2 and 3 in the 49 contiguous jurisdictions in July 1985 was $738. In Alaska and Hawaii it was 25 percent and 15 percent higher, respectively.

The Thrifty Food Plan, poverty standard, and food stamp deductions were provided by the U.S. Department of Agriculture, Food and Nutrition Service, Washington, D.C.

Benefit Reduction Rates

For Table 2.3, benefit reduction rates are taken to be the ones between the taxpoint (E^*) and the breakeven (E^{**}) for each of the three welfare systems. Thus, the benefit reduction rate in each case is the negative of the difference between the food stamp benefit, for gross earnings equal to the breakeven, if any, and if taken into account, and maximum aid plus the food stamp benefit, if taken into account, divided by the difference between the AFDC breakeven and the taxpoint.

The assumptions employed when calculating benefit reduction rates are that a family of three receives $75 in work deductions and the maximum food stamp deductions. No child care deductions are considered. Aside from the $30 and one-third disregards, Social Security taxes and federal and state withholding rates are the only other deductions considered.

For breakeven calculations see Appendix A. The taxpoint (E^*) formulae are: during October 1981 prior to OBRA

$$E^* = \max[(x_o + 20 - I)/(2/3 - x_e), 0];$$

during July 1985 for the first four months of work

$$E^* = \max[(2/3x_o + 10 - I)/(2/3 - 2/3x_e), 0];$$

and during July 1985 after 12 months of work

$$E^* = \max[(x_o - I)/(1 - x_e), 0].$$

For a more complete explanation of the taxpoint, see Michael Wiseman *Work Incentives and Welfare Turnover*.

DEFLATION

Constant dollars are used in the analyses for every variable valued in dollars. Welfare benefits for a family of three are deflated by using the California Necessities Index, or CNI (see Appendix D for source). The CNI also is used to deflate the AFDC standard of need (SN) only for Figures 2.2 and 2.4 so that it can be compared to total payments (TP). In all other instances the standard of need is deflated by the California Consumer Price Index, or CPI (for source see Appendix D). The breakeven variable and its two versions (E_r^{**} and E_o^{**}) are deflated by the CPI.

Since it includes medical costs and mortgage payments, the CPI is used to deflate the AFDC standard of need and both versions of the breakeven (E_r^{**} and E_o^{**}) in order to better reflect the purchasing power of those outside the welfare system. Since the CNI does not include medical costs and mortgage payments, it better reflects the purchasing power of those inside the welfare system, and it is used to deflate welfare benefits.

APPENDIX C

.Calculation Procedures and Sources for Recipient Characteristics and Demographics

The calculation procedures used to construct recipient and demographic characteristics incorporated into the time series analyses are presented in this appendix. Sources of this information and the assumptions employed in carrying out the computations also are summarized.

RECIPIENT CHARACTERISTICS

Data used to construct recipient characteristics are from California Health and Welfare Agency, Department of Benefit Payments, *Aid to Families with Dependent Children: Social and Economic Characteristics of Families Receiving Aid*. The dates of the reports are as follows: 12/1970, 1/1973, 5/1975, 4/1976, 7/1976, 10/1976, 1/1977, 3/1977, 10/1977, 4/1978, 10/1978, 7/1979, 10/1979, 7/1980, 1/1981, 7/1981, 10/1981, 10/1982, 7/1983, 7/1984, 10/1984. The reports of 1/1973, 5/1975, and 3/1977 did not provide separate information on the characteristics of AFDC-Basic and AFDC-UP mothers or children.

In order to estimate the three independent variables used in the closure equation, namely, the number of mothers under age 21 (M_{20}), the number of mothers over age 29 (M_{30}), and the number of children under age six (C_5), the characteristics reports cited above were used. The numbers of mothers in several age ranges were usually reported separately for AFDC-Basic and AFDC-UP, except in several instances as listed above; that is, the number of AFDC-Basic mothers under age 18, those between 18 and 20, and so forth were furnished in the reports. Each of the reports covered a single survey month. There were 21 reports, starting in December 1970 and ending in October 1984. The reports were compiled on an intermittent, non-periodic basis.

For every given datum point, it was necessary to estimate the number of individuals in a certain age category, as, for example, the number of mothers under age 21 (M_{20}). In every report there was a large number of individuals of unknown age. Thus, if one simply took the number of individuals in each selected age range, a large underestimation of the actual number of individuals in that range would be obtained. This necessitated developing a procedure for distributing the number of individuals of unknown age into each age range. The simplest procedure is to increase the number of individuals in each age range by a particular percentage of the number of individuals of unknown age. The percentage taken was the number of people of the particular known age range out of the total number of individuals whose age was known.

Unfortunately, some of the reports compiled data on both the Basic and UP programs together, not separating the data by program. Since it was necessary to have the number of individuals of a certain age range in just the AFDC-Basic program and the numbers provided in the reports overestimated this, each age group including AFDC-Basic and AFDC-UP was reduced by the portion of the total number of AFDC-Basic cases open during the month in question out of the total number of AFDC-Basic and AFDC-UP cases opened that month. The number of cases open during each given datum month was taken from the Caseload Movement and Expenditures Reports (see Appendix G for an example).

After estimating the number of individuals in a selected age group for a particular given datum month, it was necessary to estimate the number of individuals in the selected age group on a monthly basis. This was done by linear interpolation.

DEMOGRAPHICS

Population at Risk

In order to calculate the number of females of child-bearing age who are not on AFDC, several steps were taken. First, the number of females age 15 to 44 in California, including those on welfare, was obtained from the yearly data provided by California Department of Finance, Population Research Unit. Each given datum was in July of each year. These given data were linearly interpolated to monthly counts.

Second, the number of females, age 15 to 44, on AFDC-Basic and AFDC-UP in California during each month was estimated. The case characteristic reports, cited above, were used in order to compute the portion of the AFDC-Basic mothers of known age and the portion of the AFDC-Basic caseload less than 45 years old for each reported datum month. The same portions were computed for the AFDC-UP mothers. Intermediate monthly values of each of these four portions were estimated using linear interpolation.

Third, an estimate of the number of females age 15 to 44 on the AFDC-Basic caseload during each month was estimated to be the product of the total AFDC-Basic caseload, the portion of AFDC-Basic caseload less than 45 years old, and the portion of the AFDC-Basic mothers of known age. An identical estimate was compiled for number of females age 15 to 44 on the AFDC-UP caseload during each month.

Finally, the population at risk (P) was found monthly to be the estimate of the number of females age 15 to 44 in California minus the estimate of the number of females age 15 to 44 on the AFDC-Basic caseload minus the estimate of the number of females age 15 to 44 on the AFDC-UP caseload.

Children Not on Welfare

The number of children not on welfare was estimated in several steps. First, the number of persons in California under age 18, including those on AFDC-Basic and and AFDC-UP, was taken from the yearly counts provided by the California Department of Finance, Population Research Unit. Each given datum was in July of each year. These given data were linearly interpolated to monthly counts.

Second, the number of children provided in the monthly Caseload Movement and Expenditures Reports both on AFDC-Basic and AFDC-UP was subtracted from the total number of children in California. For an example of the caseload movement reports, see Appendix G.

APPENDIX D

Calculation Procedures and Sources for Economic Variables

The calculation procedures used to construct the wage of receptionists (*WI*) for the time series analyses are described below. Since the Consumer Price Index (CPI) and the California Necessities Index (CNI) are used as deflators for any variables valued in dollars, their construction is also discussed here. Sources of this information and assumptions employed in carrying out the computations are summarized.

WAGE OF RECEPTIONISTS

For most of the years considered in the analyses, yearly data on average weekly earnings of office, professional, and technical workers, broken down by gender, in various metropolitan statistical areas were used to calculate the wage index. These are from U.S. Labor Department, Bureau of Labor Statistics, *Area Wage Survey*, for San Francisco-Oakland, Los Angeles-Long Beach, Anaheim-Santa Ana-Garden Grove, and San Diego.

The bulletin numbers used for the San Francisco-Oakland metropolitan area were as follows: 1725-33, 1775-81, 1775-81 (Supplement), 1850-35, 1900-9, 1950-29, 2025-10, 2050-14, 3000-9, 3010-13, 3015-12, 3020-19, 3025-16, 3030-9. In almost all years they were provided in March.

The bulletin numbers used for the Los Angeles-Long Beach and Anaheim-Santa Ana-Garden Grove metropolitan areas were as follows: 1660-64, 1775-38, 1775-38 (Supplement), 1850-86, 1900-77, 1950-61, 2025-61, 2050-59, 3000-63, 3010-66, 3015-62, 3020-55, 3025-65. In almost all years they were provided in October.

The bulletin numbers used for the San Diego metropolitan area were as follows: 1685-20, 1725-32, 1775-40, 1775-40 (Supplement), 1850-13, 1850-77, 1900-79, 1950-73, 2025-73, 2050-70, 3000-71, 3010-68, 3015-67, 3020-70. In almost all years they were provided in November.

The yearly data were linearly interpolated to monthly data by the following procedure. First, reported weekly earnings were brought to monthly counts by multiplying them by 4.33. Since earnings were reported in different months for each of the major metropolitan areas, to develop an estimate for all three areas in the same month the data for San Francisco-Oakland and San Diego areas were linearly interpolated to October, the reported month provided for Los Angeles and its nearby surrounding areas. The populations of three major metropolitan areas are quite different. Consequently, the composite measure of the wage index for Octrober of each year was taken to be a weighted average of the values for each area. The weights were taken to be the ones used by the State of California in compiling California's Necessities Index (see the CNI section below). Next, the monthly values of the index were linearly interpolated between the October values.

The data provided by the Bureau of Labor Statistics for California's wages were very spotty for most low-wage occupations other than the wage of receptionists. The definitions of many other low-wage occupations changed over the years, or in several instances a single occupation was divided into several different ones. The wage of receptionists held a stable definition over the estimation period. For this reason, coupled with other reasons indicated in Chapter 4, the wage of receptionists was found to be a suitable wage index.

DEFLATION

As indicated in Appendix B, all variables valued in dollars in this investigation were deflated by either the CPI or the CNI. The wage index described above and the minimum wage were deflated by the CPI to reflect the purchasing power of those outside the welfare system. The following is a description of how the CPI and CNI monthly values were obtained over the entire historical simulation period.

California Consumer Price Index

The Consumer Price Index-All Urban Consumers was provided by California Agriculture and Services Agency, Department of Industrial Relations, Division of Labor Statistics and Research, San Francisco.

The CPI is a measure of the average change in prices of a fixed market basket of goods. It is based on the costs of food, clothing, shelter, transportation, doctors' fees, and other goods and services that people purchase for day-to-day living. Surveys of prices of the selected goods and services are periodically conducted in three statistical areas in California. These areas are Los Angeles and nearby surrounding areas, San Francisco-Oakland, and San Diego. A price index in each area was formed and then a weighted average of the three indexes was computed to account for variations in the populations of the regions. The weighting factors are 0.65 for Los Angeles and nearby areas, 0.25 for San Francisco-Oakland, and 0.10 for San Diego.

Prior to 1978 there was only one version of the CPI. Thereafter, index numbers were constructed separately for all urban consumers and for urban wage earners and clerical workers. The index numbers used in this investigation are for all urban consumers.

The data for the CPI were given trimonthly from December 1971 to December 1979 as monthly index values. From January 1978 to December 1985 the reporting period was increased to bimonthly. The intermediate monthly estimates of the CPI were obtained by geometric interpolation with the constant monthly percentage increase being the one that allows for geometric interpolation from one given datum month to the next. July 1985 was taken to be the base month of this monthly index, its value equaling 100.

California Necessities Index

The California Necessities Index was provided by California Department of Finance, Financial Research Unit, Sacramento. The CNI is a measure of price changes for selected components of the Consumer Price Index–All Urban Consumers. Like the CPI it follows changes in the prices of a selected market basket of goods. Clothing, food, fuel and utilities, and transportation are the components considered in the index. However, unlike the CPI, the CNI does not include the costs of medical care or mortgage interest rates. Surveys of price changes of the selected goods and services are periodically conducted in the same statistical areas used for the CPI. To account for differences in population in these areas, the CNI uses the same population weighting factors used for the CPI.

The data for the CNI were given as percentage increases for each 12-month period from December 1970 to December 1985. The intermediate monthly estimates of the CNI were obtained by geometric interpolation with the constant monthly percentage increase being the one that would yield each yearly given datum. July 1985 was taken to be the base month of this monthly index, its value equaling 100. This technique tends to concentrate increases during each year toward the end of the year; furthermore, it misses any deflationary effects that, incidentally, occurred in several months during the time interval under consideration.

The main difference between the CNI and the CPI is that the former does not include price variations due to home ownership and medical expenses. It is meant to reflect price changes in goods and services typically purchased by low-income groups, whereas the CPI reflects price changes in goods purchased by a broader sub-population of Californians.

For a detailed description of the constructions of the CNI and CPI see H. I. Halsey, and P. E. Vincent, *Analysis of Alternative Cost-of-Living Indices for Adjusting California AFDC and SSI/SSP Benefit Standards* (Sacramento: California Commission on State Finance, 1981).

APPENDIX E

Simulation Process and Sources

This appendix describes the simulation process used throughout this book. The simulation process is independent of the particular estimation period; the reference estimation period is 1972 to 1984. Several statistics used in Chapter 9 to evaluate the validity of the model also are briefly explained here.

THE SIMULATION METHODOLOGY

Recall from Chapter 9 that the endogenous variables in the model are the AFDC-Basic caseload (C), the total number of accessions (CA), the total number of terminations (CT), the number of cases added (AD), and the number of cases closed (CL). As seen in Chapter 6, both regression equations have lagged independent variables with the largest lag being four months. The beginning data values start in January 1972, with no data existing prior to this date. This implies that for the entire model the first month available for simulation is May 1972. For example, let us suppose that this is the first month to be simulated by the model and this month is taken to be month t for the first step in the simulation process. However, the initial month in the simulation process clearly can be any month after May 1972. Because the largest lag in any equation is four months, all of the endogenous variables four months prior to the beginning of the simulation month, in this case May 1972, take on their actual rather than predicted values.

For the purpose of discussion, initial conditions for the simulation are defined to be all values of each predicted endogenous variable that need to be known in order to start the simulation process. The lag structure in Identity 6.1 implies that the actual values of the caseload (C), total number of accessions (CA), and total number of terminations (CT) are the initial conditions for April 1972. It should be emphasized that accounting errors (ER) discovered during the month is a variable whose values are taken to be known; that is, it is exogenous and therefore any of its needed values are not considered as initial conditions.

Since Identities 6.2 and 6.3 do not contain a lag structure, additional initial conditions are not needed for any of the variables in these identities in order to begin the simulation. Both Equations 6.4 and 6.5 contain lagged variables. Considering both of these equations, it is seen that initial conditions for the cases closed variable (CL) and the total additions variable (CA) need to be known for January 1972 to April 1972.

After obtaining the values of the necessary initial conditions, the simulation is ready to proceed. Finding the values of all the endogenous variables of this system is relatively easy since it is a hierarchical system. A hierarchical system is one in which, after substituting values for all exogenous and lagged endogenous variables, the equations for the remaining endogenous variables can be rearranged in triangular form. This enables all the endogenous variables to be found by substitution. Furthermore, a system of hierarchical equations with independent error terms between them is particularly easy to estimate since it is appropriate to use ordinary least squares. The model in this investigation is hierarchical, and it is assumed that the error terms between equations are independent.

Simulation of the first month involves direct substitution of the necessary three initial conditions and the known value of the accounting errors in Identity 6.1. The result of this step is the simulated caseload (C) for May 1972.

Now the simulated values for the remaining four endogenous variables need to be calculated. The equations in Chapter 6 are followed in the reverse order of their listing. Each equation yields a simulated value of its endogenous variable. First, the predicted value for the number of cases closed variable (CL) for May 1972 is found by substituting into Equation 6.5 four months of initial conditions for the total additions variable (CA) and actual values for the exogenous variables. Similarly, upon substitution Equation 6.4 yields the number of cases added (AD) for May 1972.

Thus far we have obtained the simulated values of the number of cases closed (CL) and the number of cases added (AD) for May 1972. Next, from Identity 6.3, the predicted value of cases closed (CL) and the actual value of transfers to AFDC-UP (TU) yield the total number of terminations (CT) for May 1972. Finally, using Identity 6.2 to find total accessions (CA) for May 1972, the previously found values for cases added (AD) and known values for the exogenous variables, namely, transfers to AFDC-Basic (TB) and other additions (OA) in May 1972, are substituted. One step in this iterative simulation process is now complete with all simulated values of the AFDC-Basic model having been predicted for May 1972.

To proceed to the next month, the five endogenous variables, one from each of the five equations in Chapter 6, are calculated. Month by month this process iterates until the end of the estimation period. At no time are any actual values of the five endogenous variables used except as set forth in the initial conditions.

STATISTICS USED TO EVALUATE MODEL

The statistucs used to evaluate the model are briefly explained here. Perhaps the most widely used measure is the root mean square (rms) simulation error, which is somewhat analogous to the standard deviation of a random variable. The only difference between the standard deviation and the rms error is that instead of subtracting the mean of the variable from each value of the variable as in the standard deviation, the actual historical value of the series is subtracted from its simulated value. Another similar measure is the root mean square percentage simulation error, which is the same idea except measured in terms of the percentage of the same deviation relative to the actual historical series value. There are also two measures of the average deviation of the simulated series from the historical series. One is mean percentage error and the other is the mean simulation error. Ideally the mean errors should be much smaller in magnitude than the rms errors. If the magnitudes are approximately equal, the simulated series consistently either overestimates or under-estimates the historical series. This indicates a biased statistical fit.

Another set of measures developed by Theil, allow one to dissect the root mean square simulation error into various parts in order to see what kind of deviations are contributing to this. Theil's inequality coefficient (U) is the rms simulation error scaled by the sum of the root mean square of the simulated series and the root mean square of the historical series. This implies $0 \leq U \leq 1$ with $U = 0$ indicating perfect fit and $U = 1$ indicating the worst possible fit. Theil's inequality coefficient can be decomposed in a useful way. One term, known as the bias proportion (U^M), measures the extent to which the average values of the simulated and historical series deviate from one another. Another term, known as the variance proportion (U^S) measures how well the simulated series reproduces the variability of the historical series. The third term, the covariance proportion (U^C), measures how well the historical and simulated series covary from each of their means. Both U^M and U^S should be smaller than 0.2 and (U^C) close to 1; otherwise the simulated endogenous variable does not fit well and its model should be revised.

For further discussion of these statistics, see R. Pindyck and D. L. Rubinfeld, *Econometric Models and Economic Forecasts*, 3d ed. (New York: McGraw-Hill, 1981).

APPENDIX F

Variable Definitions and Sources

The following variables are included in the model of AFDC-Basic dynamics. The definition, deflation, and source of each variable is described in this appendix.

$C(t)$ = AFDC-Basic caseload at the beginning of month t.

$CA(t)$ = total number of accessions to the AFDC-Basic caseload during month t.

$CT(t)$ = total number of terminations from the AFDC-Basic caseload during month t.

$ER(t)$ = total number of accounting errors committed in previous months but discovered in month t.

$AD(t)$ = number of new applications and restorations approved during month t [cases added (t)].

$TB(t)$ = number of transfers from AFDC-UP to AFDC-Basic during month t.

$OA(t)$ = number of all other approvals during month t.

$CL(t)$ = number of cases closed during month t, excluding those transferring to AFDC-UP [cases closed (t)].

$TU(t)$ = number of cases transferring from AFDC-Basic to AFDC-UP during month t.

$FBU(t)$ = average size of an AFDC-Basic family budget unit during month t.
[*Source: C, CA, CT, ER, AD, TB, OA, CL, TU, FBU* are from California Health and Welfare Agency, Department of Social Services, Statistical Services Branch, *Aid to Families with Dependent Children— Cash Grant Caseload Movement and Expenditures Report*. Sacramento: 1/1972–12/1984. An example of these reports is furnished in Appendix G.]

$SN(t)$ = AFDC standard of need or minimum basic standard of adequate care (MBSAC) for a family of three (t).
[*Source:* California Health and Welfare Agency, Department of Social Services, *Manual of Policies and Procedures: Eligibility and Assistance Standards*, Section 44-207.212. (Figures from 1/1972 to 12/1984). Deflated by CPI for simulations and CNI for graphs in Chapter 2.]

$TP(t)$ = total payments, or AFDC plus food stamp benefits for a family of three (t).
[*Source:* See Appendix B. Deflated by the CNI(t).]

$E_r^{**}(t)$ = AFDC breakeven for a family of three with the actual welfare benefit formula present in any month t [deflated by CPI(t)].

$E_o^{**}(t)$ = AFDC breakeven for a family of three with the pre-OBRA welfare benefit formula present in any month t.
[*Source:* For $E_r^{**}(t)$ and $E_o^{**}(t)$ see Appendix B. Deflated by CPI(t).]

$DS(t)$ = OBRA shock dummy for November and December 1981 (t).

$DO(t)$ = dummy variable identifying the presence of OBRA's provisions beginning in November 1981 in the accessions equation and beginning in January 1982 in the closures equation (t).

$DB(t)$ = an interaction of the breakeven [$E_r^{**}(t)$] and dummy OBRA [$DO(t)$].

$U(t)$ = seasonally unadjusted number of unemployed (t).
[*Source:* California Health and Welfare Agency, Employment Development Department, Report LF101, Employment Data and Research Division Estimates, Economic Research Group.]

$F(t)$ = number of workers in food and kindred products industries in California (t).

$A(t)$ = number of workers in apparel and other textile industries in California (t).

$NA(t)$ = number of workers in non-agricultural industries in California during month t except for food and apparel industries (t).
[*Source:* For F, A, and NA: Data Resources, Inc., *Employment, Interim Wage and Salary, by Industry*, San Francisco.]

$MW(t)$ = minimum wage (t).
[*Source:* State of California, Department of Industrial Relations, Industrial Welfare Commission, San Francisco. Deflated by CPI(t).]

$WI(t)$ = wage index for switchboard receptionist (t).
[*Source:* See Appendix D. Deflated by CPI(t).]

$CNI(t)$ = California Necessities Index (t).
[*Source:* See Appendix D.]

$CPI(t)$ = California Consumer Price Index (t).
[*Source:* See Appendix D.]

$P(t)$ = population at risk (t).
[*Source:* See Appendix C.]

$K(t)$ = number of children under age 18 not on welfare (t).
       [*Source:* See Appendix C.]

$B(t)$ = births (t).
       [*Source:* California, Health Department, Birth Records Division, Sacramento.]

$C_5(t)$ = number of children on AFDC-Basic under age six (t).

$M_{20}(t)$ = number of mothers on AFDC-Basic under age 21 (t).

$M_{30}(t)$ = number of mothers on AFDC-Basic over age 29 (t).
       [*Source:* See Appendix C, caseload characteristics section.]

SEASONALS

$JA(t)$	=	January (t)		
$FB(t)$	=	February (t)		
$MR(t)$	=	March (t)		
$AP(t)$	=	April (t)		
$MY(t)$	=	May (t)		
$JU(t)$	=	June (t)		

$JL(t)$ = July (t)

$AG(t)$ = August (t)

$SP(t)$ = September (t)

$OC(t)$ = October (t)

$NV(t)$ = November (t)

$e(t)$ = a random error term (t)

Aid to Families with Dependent Children Cash Grant Caseload Movement and Expenditures Report

STATE OF CALIFORNIA — HEALTH AND WELFARE AGENCY
DEPARTMENT OF SOCIAL SERVICES

Send One Copy To:
DEPARTMENT OF SOCIAL SERVICES
STATISTICAL SERVICES BRANCH
744 P STREET, MAIL STATION 12-81
SACRAMENTO, CALIFORNIA 95814

AID TO FAMILIES WITH DEPENDENT CHILDREN — CASH GRANT CASELOAD MOVEMENT AND EXPENDITURES REPORT

STATE USE	COUNTY
1	Final Statewide

FOR MONTH ENDING	MONTH	DAY	YEAR
July	0 / 7	3 / 1	8 / 5

PART A. APPLICATIONS FOR AID AND REQUESTS FOR RESTORATION

1. Pending from last month (Item 5 last month, or explain)	19,689
2. Received during the month (Sum of a and b, below)	44,623
a. Applications (Sum of (1) and (2)) 34,870	
(1) For AFDC-FG.. 28,008	
(2) For AFDC-U.. 6,862	
b. Requests for restoration.. 9,753	
3. Total during the month (Sum of 1 and 2)	64,312
4. Disposed of during month (Sum of a, b, and c, below)	41,100
a. Approved (Sum of (1) and (2)) 21,812	
(1) For AFDC-FG or U (Same as sum of 7a and 7b)................... 21,335	
(2) For Emergency Assistance-Unemployed Parent (Do not include in 7a or 7b) 477	
b. Denied.. 12,243	
c. Other dispositions (Cancellations and withdrawals)...................... 7,045	
5. Investigation proceeding at end of month (3 minus 4)............................	23,212

PART B. CASELOAD

	AFDC—FG (1)	AFDC—U (2)
6. Cases brought forward from last month (Item 10 last month or explain)...........	460,734	75,338
7. Cases added during month (Sum of a through e below)	30,571	6,611
a. Applications approved...................................	13,044	2,416
b. Restorations..	4,957	918
c. Transfers from other counties...........................	2,011	345
d. Intraprogram status change (1) from FG or U segment..................	962	760
(2) from medically needy...................	376	125
(3) from Emergency Assistance	7	328
e. Other approvals	9,214	1,719
8. Total cases open during month (Sum of 6 and 7, above; also a plus b, below)	491,305	81,949
a. Cases receiving cash grant	475,492	77,470
(1) Children in Item 8a cases.................................	(859,939)	(212,117)
(2) Adults in Item 8a cases	(404,808)	(141,413)
(3) Essential persons in Item 8a cases........................	( )	( )
(4) Total persons (Sum of (1), (2), and (3), above)	(1,264,747)	(353,530)
b. Other cases	15,813	4,479
9. Terminated or changed in status during month...............................	26,840	6,996
10. Cases carried forward to next month (8 minus 9)...............................	464,465	74,953

PART C. NET EXPENDITURES

	TOTAL (ROUND TO NEAREST DOLLAR)	
11. Total net expenditures (Sum of a and b, below)	$ 223,422,155	$ 52,268,177
a. Total AFDC with Federal-State-County participation	$	$
b. County supplemental: (1) in cash $_____ (2) in kind $_____	$	$
c. Child support collections: (1) FG $ 16,916,967 (2) U $ 712,221		

CA 237 FG/U (6/84)   REF 26-212

Bibliography

Bane, M. J. "Household Composition and Poverty." In Danziger, Sheldon H., and Weinberg, Daniel H., eds. *Fighting Poverty: What Works and What Doesn't*. Cambridge, Mass.: Harvard University Press, 1986, pp. 209-239.

Bane, M. J., and Ellwood, D. T. *The Dynamics of Dependence: The Routes to Self-sufficiency*. Contract No. HHS-100-82-0038. Washington, D.C.: U.S. Department of Health and Human Services, 1983.

Bassi, J. Laurie, and Ashenfelter, Orley. "The Effect of Direct Job Creation and Training Programs on Low Skilled Workers." In Danziger, Sheldon H., and Weinberg, Daniel H., eds. *Fighting Poverty: What Works and What Doesn't*. Cambridge, Mass.: Harvard University Press, 1986, pp. 133-172.

Blank, Rebecca M., and Blinder, Alan S. "Macroeconomics, Income Distribution, and Poverty." In Danziger, Sheldon H., and Weinberg, Daniel H., eds. *Fighting Poverty: What Works and What Doesn't*. Cambridge, Mass.: Harvard University Press, 1986, pp. 180-208.

Boland, B. *Participation in Aid to Families with Dependent Children Program (AFDC)*. Studies in Public Welfare Paper No. 21, Part 1, Subcommittee on Fiscal Policy, Joint Economic Committee, U.S. Congress. Washington, D.C.: U.S. Government Printing Office, 1973.

Boskin, M., and Nold, F. "A Markov Model of Turnover in Aid to Families with Dependent Children." *Journal of Human Resources* 10 (1975): 467-481.

Burgess, E., and Price, D. *An American Dependence Challenge*. Chicago: American Public Welfare Association, 1963.

California Health and Welfare Agency, Department of Social Services. *Refugees Receiving Cash Assistance Characteristics Survey*. Sacramento, 1985.

California Health and Welfare Agency, Employment Development Department. *Projections of Employment, 1980-1990, by Industry and Occupation*. Sacramento, 1985.

Coe, R. D. "Dependency and Poverty in the Short Run and Long Run." In Duncan,

G. J., and Morgan, J. N., eds. *Five Thousand American Families: Patterns of Economic Progress*, vol. 6. Ann Arbor: University of Michigan, Institute for Social Research, 1978, pp. 273-296.

Coe, R. D. "A Preliminary Empirical Examination of the Dynamics of Welfare Use." In Hill, M., Hill, D., and Morgan, J. N., eds. *Five Thousand American Families: Patterns of Economic Progress*, vol. 9. Ann Arbor: University of Michigan, Institute for Social Research, 1981, pp. 121-168.

Coe, R. D. "Welfare Dependency: Fact or Myth?" *Challenge* 25 (1982): 43-49.

Darity, W., and Myers, S. "Exploring Black Welfare Dependency: Changes in Black Family Structure—Implications for Welfare Dependency." *American Economic Review* 37 (1983): 59-64.

Duncan, G. J., and Coe, R. D. "The Dynamics of Welfare Use." In Duncan, G. J., et al., eds. *Years of Poverty, Years of Plenty: The Changing Economic Fortunes of American Workers and Families*. Ann Arbor: University of Michigan, Institute for Social Research, 1984, pp. 17-24.

Ellwood, David T., and Summers, Lawrence H. "Poverty in America: Is Welfare the Answer or Problem?" In Danziger, Sheldon H., and Weinberg, Daniel H., eds. *Fighting Poverty: What Works and What Doesn't*. Cambridge, Mass.: Harvard University Press, 1986, pp. 78-105.

Evanson, E. "The Dynamics of Poverty." *Focus* 5 (1981): 9-12.

Garfinkel, I. *Income Transfer Programs and Work Effort: A Review*. Studies in Public Welfare Paper No. 13, Subcommittee on Fiscal Policy, Joint Economic Committee, U.S. Congress. Washington, D.C.: U.S. Government Printing Office, 1974.

Garfinkel, I., and Orr, L. L. "Welfare Policy and the Employment Rate of AFDC Mothers." *National Tax Journal* 27 (1974): 275-284.

Gramlich, Edward M. "The Main Themes." In Danziger, Sheldon H., and Weinberg, Daniel H., eds. *Fighting Poverty: What Works and What Doesn't*. Cambridge, Mass.: Harvard University Press, 1986, pp. 341-347.

Gramlich, E. M., and Laren, D. S. "Migration and Income Redistribution Responsibilities." *Journal of Human Resources* 4 (1984): 489-511.

Griffith, J. D., and Usher, C. L. "A Quasi-experimental Assessment of the National Impact of the 1981 Omnibus Budget Reconciliation Act (OBRA) on the Aid to Families with Dependent Children (AFDC) Program." *Evaluation Review* 10 (1986): 313-333.

Halsey, H. I., and Vincent, P. E. *Analysis of Alternative Cost-of-Living Indices for Adjusting California AFDC and SSI/SSP Benefit Standards*. Sacramento: California Commission on State Finance, 1981.

Hausman, L. J., and Kasper, H. "The Work Effort Response of Women to Income Maintenance." In Orr, L. L., Hoolister, R. G., and Lefcowitz, M., eds. *Income Maintenance*. Chicago: Marakham Publishing Co., 1971.

Hill, M. S. "Some Dynamic Aspects of Poverty." In Hill, M., Hill, D., and Morgan, J., eds. *Five Thousand American Families: Patterns of Economic Progress*, vol. 9. Ann Arbor: University of Michigan, Institute for Social Research, 1981.

Hoing, M. "AFDC Income, Recipient Rates and Family Dissolution." *Journal of Human Resources* 9 (1974): 303-322.

Hoing, M. *The Impact of Welfare Payment Levels on Family Stability*. Studies in Public Welfare Paper No. 12, Subcommittee on Fiscal Policy, Joint Economic Committee, U.S. Congress. Washington, D.C.: U.S. Government Printing Office, 1973.

Hutchens, R. M. "Entry and Exit Transitions in Government Transfer Programs: The Case of Aid to Families with Dependent Children." *Journal of Human Resources* 16 (1981): 217-237.

Hutchens, R. M. *Recipients' Movement from Welfare toward Economic Independence: A Literature Review*. Grant 90A-82, 1982. Washington, D.C.: U.S. Health and Human Services Department, 1982.

Jordan, P., Matthews, A., Bluestone, B., Fortuna, M., and Megna, P. *Corrective Action and AFDC Dynamics: An Empirical Study in Six Jurisdictions*. Grant No. 5-21474. Boston: Boston College, Social Welfare Institute, Public Assistance Data Analysis Laboratory, 1981.

Levy, F. "The Labor Supply of Female Household Heads, or AFDC Work Incentives Don't Work Too Well." *Journal of Human Resources* 4 (1979): 76-97.

Masters, S. and Garfinkel, I. *Estimating the Labor Supply Effects of Income Maintenance Alternatives*. Institute for Research on Poverty Monograph Series. New York: Academic Press, 1977.

McCarthy, Kevin F., and Valdez, Burciaga R. "California's Demographic Future." In Kirlin, J. J., and Winkler, D. R., eds. *California Policy Choices*, vol. 2. Sacramento: Sacramento Public Affairs Center, 1985, pp. 37-62.

McDonald, M. *Food Stamps and Income Maintenance*. Institute for Research on Poverty Monograph Series. New York: Academic Press, 1977.

Moffit, R., and Wolf, D. A. "The Effect of the 1981 Omnibus Budget Reconciliation Act on Welfare Recipients and Work Incentives." *Social Service Review* (June 1987): 247-260.

Moscovice, I., and Craig, W. "The Omnibus Budget Reconciliation Act and the Working Poor." *Social Service Review* (March 1984): 49-61.

Murray, Charles A. Losing Ground: American Social Policy, 1950-1980. New York: Basic Books, 1984.

Orr, L. L. "Income Transfers as a Public Good: An Application to AFDC." *American Economic Review* 5 (1976): 359-371.

Pindyck, R., and Rubinfeld, D. L. *Econometric Models and Economic Forecasts*. 3d ed. New York: McGraw-Hill, 1981.

Plotnick, R. "Turnover in the AFDC Population: An Event History Analysis." *Journal of Human Resources* 18 (1983): 65-81.

Plotnick, R., and Lidman, R. M. "Forecasting Welfare Caseloads: A Tool to Improve Budgeting." Unpublished manuscript. Contracts 2000-46181 and 6500-52438. Seattle: Washington State Social and Health Services Department, 1986.

Rein, M., and Rainwater, L. "How Large Is the Welfare Class?" *Challenge* 20 (1977): 20-23.

Rein, M., and Rainwater, L. "Patterns of Welfare Use." *Social Service Review* 52 (1978): 511-534.

Rence, C., and Wiseman, M. "The California Welfare Reform Act and Participation in AFDC." *Journal of Human Resources* 13 (1978): 37-57.

Ross, H., and Sawhill, I. *Time of Transition: The Growth of Families Headed by Women*. Washington, D.C.: Urban Institute, 1975.

Rydell, C., Palmerio, T., Blais, G., and Brown, D. *Welfare Caseload Dynamics in New York City*. Report No. R-1441-NYC. New York: Rand Institute, 1974.

Sanger, M. B. "Generating Employment for AFDC Mothers." *Social Service Review* (March 1984): 28-46.

Sanger, M. B. *Welfare of the Poor.* New York: Academic Press, 1979.

Sawhill, I., et al. *Income Transfers and Family Structure.* Washington, D.C.: Urban Institute, 1975.

Schram, Sanford F. "State Discretion in AFDC Eligibility: Response to Reagan Welfare Revisions." Unpublished manuscript. Madison: University of Wisconsin, 1987.

Sun, B. "An Investigation into the Effects of Welfare Program on Welfare Patterns." Ph.D. dissertation, Brandeis University, 1976. In *Dissertation Abstracts International.* University Microfilms No. 76-16, 258.

U.S. Commerce Department, Bureau of the Census. *Current Population and Household Estimates to 1985, with Age and Components of Change.* Current Population Reports, series P-25, no. 998. Washington, D.C.: U.S. Government Printing Office, 1986.

U.S. Commerce Department, Bureau of the Census. *Statistical Abstract of the United States, 1987.* 107th ed. Washington, D.C.: U.S. Government Printing Office, 1986.

U.S. Commerce Department, Bureau of the Census. *United States Population Estimates and Components of Change: 1970-1986.* Current Population Reports, series P-25, no. 1006. Washington, D.C.: U.S. Government Printing Office, 1986.

U.S. Commerce Department, Bureau of Economic Analysis. *Business Conditions Digest.* Washington, D.C.: U.S. Government Printing Office, 1982.

U.S. General Accounting Office. *An Evaluation of the 1981 AFDC Changes: Final Report.* Washington, D.C.: U.S. Government Printing Office, 1985.

U.S. Health, Education and Welfare Department, National Center for Health Statistics. *Summary Report: Final Natality Statistics, 1970.* Monthly Vital Statistics Report, vol. 22, no. 12, Supplement. Rockville, Md.: Public Health Service Publication No. HRA-74-1120, 1974.

U.S. Health and Human Services Department, Family Support Administration, Office of Refugee Resettlement. *Summary of Refugee Cash Assistance Caseload and Number of Recipient Assistants as of 9/30/1986.* Washington, D.C.: 4th QPRs, 1986.

U.S. Health and Human Services Department, National Center for Health Statistics. *Advance Report of Final Natality Statistics, 1985.* Monthly Vital Statistics Report, vol. 36, no. 4, Supplement. Hyattsville, Md.: Public Health Service, DHHS Publication No. PHS-87-1120, 1987.

U.S. Health and Human Services Department, National Center for Health Statistics. *Birth and Fertility Rates for States: United States, 1980.* National Vital Statistics System, series 21, no. 42. Hyattsville, Md.: Public Health Service, DHHS Publication No. PHS-84-1920, 1984.

U.S. Health and Human Services Department, Social Security Administration, Office of Family Assistance. *Characteristics of State Plans for AFDC under the Social Security Act Title IV-A: Administrative Eligibility Assistance Payments.* Washington, D.C.: U.S. Government Printing Office, 1986.

U.S. Health and Human Services Department Social Security Administration, Office of Family Assistance. *Research Tables Based on Characteristics of State Plans for AFDC: Administration Eligibility Assistance Payments, in Effect October 1, 1985.* Washington, D.C.: U.S. Government Printing Office, 1986.

U.S. Health and Human Services Department, Social Security Administration, Office of Family Assistance, Office of Policy and Evaluation. *Findings of the May 1981-May 1982 Aid to Families with Dependent Children Study: Recipient Characteristics, Financial Circumstances—The Effects of the Omnibus Budget Reconciliation*

Act of 1981. Washington, D.C.: Social Security Administration Publication No. 13-11731, 1985.

U.S. Health and Human Services Department, Social Security Administration, Office of Family Assistance, Office of Policy and Evaluation. *Recipient Characteristics and Financial Circumstances of AFDC Recipients.* Washington, D.C.: U.S. Government Printing Office, 1986.

U.S. House of Representatives, Committee on Agriculture. *Food Stamp Act of 1977.* Report no. 95-464, 95th Congress. Washington, D.C.: U.S. Government Printing Office, 1977.

U.S. House of Representatives, Committee on Ways and Means. *Background Material and Data on Programs within the Jurisdiction of the Committee on Ways and Means.* Washington, D.C.: U.S. Government Printing Office, 1986.

U.S. House of Representatives, Committee on Ways and Means, Subcommittee on Oversight and Subcommittee on Public Assistance and Employment Compensation. *Effects of the Omnibus Budget Reconciliation Act of 1981 (OBRA) Welfare Changes and the Recession on Poverty.* Prepared by Mathematica Policy Research, Inc., under contract to the Congressional Research Service. Washington, D.C.: U.S. Government Printing Office, 1984.

Urban Systems Research and Engineering. *AFDC Standards of Need: An Evaluation of Current Practices, Alternative Approaches and Policy Options.* Contract No. SSA 600-79-0029. Washington, D.C.: U.S. Social Security Administration, Office of Research and Statistics, 1981.

Usher, C. L., and Griffith, J. D. *The 1981 AFDC Amendments and Caseload Dynamics.* Research Triangle Park, N.C.: Research Triangle Institute, 1983.

Wilson, William Julius, and Neckerman, Kathryn M. "Poverty and Family Structure: The Widening Gap between Evidence and Public Policy Issues." In Danziger, Sheldon H., and Weinberg, Daniel H., eds. *Fighting Poverty: What Works and What Doesn't.* Cambridge, Mass.: Harvard University Press, 1986, pp. 232-259.

Wiseman, Michael. *Change and Turnover in a Welfare Population.* Working Paper No.70. Berkeley: University of California, Department of Economics, Income Dynamics Project, 1976.

Wiseman, Michael. "The Welfare System." In Kirlin, J. J., and Winkler, D. R., eds. *California Policy Choices*, vol. 2. Sacramento: Sacramento Public Affairs Center, 1985, pp. 133-202.

Wiseman, Michael. *Work Incentives and Welfare Turnover.* Working Paper 84-01. Berkeley: University of California, Department of Economics Welfare and Employment Studies Project, 1984.

Index

About the Author

VICKI N. ALBERT has been an Assistant Professor of Social Work at the Ohio State University. She has contributed papers to the University of Wisconsin, Madison, Institute for Research on Poverty Discussion Papers and to the University of California, Berkeley, Institute of Business and Economics Research, Research Papers in Economics.